STRUGGLE FOR THE CITY

RDD
RHETORICAND**DEMOCRATIC**DELIBERATION
VOLUME 33

Rhetoric and Democratic Deliberation focuses on the
interplay of public discourse, politics, and democratic action.
Engaging with diverse theoretical, cultural, and critical
perspectives, books published in this series offer fresh
perspectives on rhetoric as it relates to education, social
movements, and governments throughout the world.

A complete list of books in this series is located at the back
of this volume.

STRUGGLE FOR THE CITY

CITIZENSHIP AND RESISTANCE IN
THE BLACK FREEDOM MOVEMENT

DEREK G. HANDLEY

The Pennsylvania State University Press | University Park, Pennsylvania

This volume is published with the generous support
of the Center for Democratic Deliberation at the
Pennsylvania State University.

Library of Congress Cataloging-in-Publication Data
Names: Handley, Derek G., author.
Title: Struggle for the city : citizenship and resistance
    in the Black freedom movement / Derek G. Handley.
Other titles: Rhetoric and democratic deliberation ;
    v. 33.
Description: University Park, Pennsylvania : The
    Pennsylvania State University Press, [2024] | Series:
    Rhetoric and democratic deliberation ; volume 33 |
    Includes bibliographical references and index.
Summary: "Explores the rhetorical strategies used
    by African American residents of Pittsburgh,
    Milwaukee, and St. Paul in the 1950s and 1960s as
    they attempted to protect their communities against
    federal, state, and local urban planning"—Provided
    by publisher.
Identifiers: LCCN 2024026557 | ISBN 9780271097756
    (hardback) | ISBN 9780271097763 (paperback)
Subjects: LCSH: Urban renewal—Pennsylvania—
    Pittsburgh—History—20th century. | Urban
    renewal—Minnesota—Saint Paul—History—20th
    century. | Urban renewal—Wisconsin—Milwaukee—
    History—20th century. | African Americans—Civil
    rights—History—20th century. | Civil rights
    movements—United States—History—20th century.
    | Rhetoric—Political aspects—United States—
    History—20th century. | Hill District (Pittsburgh,
    Pa.)—History—20th century. | Rondo (Saint Paul,
    Minn.)—History—20th century. | Bronzeville
    (Milwaukee, Wis.)—History—20th century.
Classification: LCC HT177.P5 H36 2024 | DDC
    307.3/41608996073—dc23/eng/20240625
LC record available at https://lccn.loc.gov/2024026557

The Pennsylvania State University Press is a member
of the Association of University Presses.

It is the policy of The Pennsylvania State University
Press to use acid-free paper. Publications on uncoated
stock satisfy the minimum requirements of American
National Standard for Information Sciences—
Permanence of Paper for Printed Library Material,
ANSI Z39.48–1992.

For my mother, Lessie Mae Handley, who instilled the love for education and social justice.

CONTENTS

ILLUSTRATIONS

ACKNOWLEDGMENTS

Numerous individuals and institutions made the completion of this project possible. Jessica Enoch introduced me to rhetoric studies as an academic discipline and encouraged me to pursue a PhD. Linda Flower cemented my desire to do community work and showed me how to write at the graduate level. Barbara Johnstone helped me develop the seeds of this book in a graduate seminar. My friend, mentor, and adviser Andreea Ritivoi saw this project in its infant stages as a dissertation and guided me along to its completion. David Kaufer helped me to think theoretically about the relationship between rhetoric and leadership. Joe Trotter expanded my knowledge of African American urban history, and I will always be thankful that he convinced me to stay in graduate school when I thought about leaving my program.

Many other scholars have offered valuable input, suggestions, and support in the writing of this book. I am deeply indebted to Ralph Proctor, Carlos Peterson, Marvin Anderson, Clayborn Benson III, and Reggie Jackson for sharing their stories and keeping their community histories alive. Christa Olson was generous with her time at a Rhetoric Society of America (RSA) Summer Institute to share her knowledge about doing a rhetorical history project, and later to help me learn about the publishing process. She, along with Adrienne Brown, Cedric Burrows, Sara Vanderhaagen, and Bill Keith, read drafts of this manuscript and provided very useful insights that made this a stronger book. I am indebted to respondents Kirt Wilson, Cheryl Glenn, and Keith Gilyard, who heard parts of this work when I presented at Penn State's Camp Rhetoric. They have served as both friends and mentors in my professional journey.

I am thankful for the readers and workshop leaders at several RSA conferences who provided critical perspectives and feedback during various stages of this project: Jacqueline Jones Royster, Roxanne Mountford, Jack Selzer, Kyle Jensen, David Fleming, Amy Wan, Christian Lundberg, Joona Trapp, Krista Ratcliffe, Karma Chavez, Victoria Gallagher, Andre Johnson, Michael Burns, and Gregory Clark. I am also grateful for the support from colleagues past and present at the Community College of Allegheny County, United States Naval Academy, Lehigh University, Amherst College, and University of Wisconsin–Milwaukee (UWM), including Jean Aston, Lee Nott, Sharika Crawford, Noah Comet, Marlon Moore, Joan Shifflet, Brooke Rollins, Lyndon Domnique, Seth Moglen, Barry Kroll, Rhonda Cobham-Sander, Shevaun Watson, Rachel Bloom-Pojar, and Maria Novotny. Also very helpful to me in thinking through parts of the project in our Rhetoric and Place graduate course were UWM graduate students Kristin Gates, Alexandra Balaram, and Madison Williams.

Several institutions and organizations provided resources for which I am thankful. I am grateful for the help and support from the staff at the Library of Congress, Carnegie Museum of Art, Heinz History Center, University of Wisconsin–Milwaukee Libraries Archives Department, Marquette University Special Collections and University Archives, Wisconsin Historical Society, and the University of Minnesota Libraries. Carnegie Mellon University's Center for Africanamerican Urban Studies and the Economy (CAUSE) provided funding to support research in Milwaukee and supplied recordings from the Remembering Africanamerican Pittsburgh Oral History Project (RAP). The Chamberlain Project Fellowship at Amherst College provided funding to conduct research in Pittsburgh, and their Center for Humanistic Inquiry provided a weekly quiet space in which to write. Lehigh University's Faculty Research Grant provided funding to conduct research in Minneapolis and St. Paul. Lehigh University also sponsored a book proposal writing group, which was led by Kate Bullard. The James Weldon Johnson Institute (JWJI) for the Study of Race and Difference at Emory University provided time, space, and funding so that I could live inside my head for a year in order to complete the dissertation. My fellow fellows at JWJI provided unmeasurable support, feedback, and professional insight. A UWM Center for 21st Century Studies fellowship helped fund a manuscript workshop and provided resources so that I could transform the dissertation into a monograph.

The reviewers of this manuscript deserve very special praise. Shirley Logan and Robert Asen offered incredibly constructive feedback to strengthen my argument and improve the prose. I'm grateful for their efforts. Portions of chapters 1 and 4 first appeared in "'The Line Drawn': Freedom Corner and Rhetorics of Place in Pittsburgh, 1960s–2000s," *Rhetoric Review* 38, no. 2 (2019), published by Taylor and Francis. These excerpts were reprinted by permission of the Informa UK Limited, trading as Taylor & Francis Ltd., http://www.tandfonline.com.

I am also thankful for my "brain trust," headed by Mary Glavan, who served as an editor and was instrumental in helping me get this book over the finish the line. This group also includes Jack Morales, Justin Mando, and

Carolyn Comer, who pushed, stretched, and expanded my brain for how this project can work. My good friends Cornella Ellis, Randy Bostick, and Patrick Rucker kept me grounded and provided escapes from academia.

I wish that my parents, Joe and Lessie; my sisters Glenda and JoAnn; and my brother, Joe, were still here to share in this milestone, but I know they would be proud. I am grateful for the love and support of my sisters Delores, Margaret, and Mickey, as well as extended family and friends who supported me during this arduous journey. I thank my sons, Marcus and Kwei, for sharing their father with the writing of this book. There are many more in my village of family and friends that I did not name, but I do thank them for their support and encouragement in writing this book.

Finally, but most importantly, I would like to thank my partner, Rebecca, without whom the writing of this book would not have been possible. She sets the standard of excellence, and I strive to be the half the scholar that she is.

A few years ago, several of my students from the Community College of Allegheny County and I were standing at the corner of Centre Avenue and Crawford Street waiting for our guide to arrive to give us a walking tour of Pittsburgh's historic Hill District, the home of August Wilson and the setting for nearly all his Century Cycle plays. During our wait, an elderly woman in the passenger seat of a car driving by rolled down her window and said loudly in our direction, "We are still slaves." Perhaps if we were standing at a different location in Pittsburgh, her comments would sound strange, but we were standing at the Freedom Corner Memorial, a historic site of protest, struggle, and civic engagement during African American residents' fight against urban renewal in the 1950s and 1960s.

Pittsburgh, like many other Northern cities, was a destination for many African Americans migrating from the Deep South, including my parents. My mother came to Pittsburgh from rural North Carolina soon after World War II. My father came to Pittsburgh in the early 1940s from rural Alabama. The Southern immigrants sought better jobs, better opportunities, and better treatment as human beings than they had in the Jim Crow South, but the North had its own racial problems.[1] The first stop for my parents, as well as many other migratory African Americans to Pittsburgh, was the Hill District. I would often hear stories from family members about the Hill District's heyday in the '40s and '50s as a "jumping town" with an exciting night life, about how you could run into celebrities and see Negro League baseball players eating in the fancy restaurants, how you could buy anything you needed from the markets. Similar stories were told of the Bronzeville neighborhood in Milwaukee and the Rondo neighborhood in St. Paul.

Many of these Black spaces were lost due to "urban renewal"—the now notorious term for the redevelopment of city neighborhoods considered "blighted" by federal and local governments. All who lived in the Hill District, including many in my family, were directly affected by urban renewal, whether they were forced to move or saw their surrounding neighborhood get more crowded by those who were forced to move in. Everyone lamented the destruction of the Lower Hill and how the neighborhood was not the same. Although in recent years parts of the Hill District have been sites of crime, drugs, and gun violence, it is still a place of tremendous pride for those who lived and grew up there. It is this historical story of urban renewal and resistance in the 1950s and 1960s that this book explores.

Pittsburgh, Milwaukee, and St. Paul, like many other Northern cities, were destinations for many African Americans, like my parents, migrating from the Deep South in the 1940s. The same types of stories were told by residents from Milwaukee and St. Paul.[2] I imagine that many things seemed better at first in these "Promised Lands," but migrating African Americans soon learned that the North's systemic racial problems would create their own set of barriers and setbacks. But because of these barriers, Black people in these Northern communities organized and became activists in the fight for "full citizenship"—people like my mother, with only her high school education, who served in various organizations, including the local chapter of the NAACP (National Association for the Advancement of Colored People).

This book is not only about the African American rhetorical history of urban renewal, but it is also my own attempt to make sense of the problems, barriers, and setbacks to Black Freedom in the United States. I believe in doing so, I will better understand the lived experiences of my family members who struggled to provide a better life for me.

INTRODUCTION

It comes as a great shock to discover that the country which is your
birthplace and to which you owe your life and identity has not, in its
whole system of reality, evolved any place for you.
—James Baldwin, "The American Dream and the American Negro"

The bulldozers arrived early the morning of May 31, 1956, at 1206 Epiphany
Street in the Lower Hill neighborhood of Pittsburgh, Pennsylvania. Nearby
residents watched the demolition of the building with the understanding
that their homes, businesses, and churches would soon be next to face the
wrecking ball. However, some took comfort in the fact that they had been
promised new, clean public housing in other parts of the city. Others believed
that this public housing would be built on the very acres that were being
razed by the bulldozers and wrecking balls.

A few months later, on September 20, the housing chairman of the
branch chapter of the Milwaukee NAACP, Bernard Toliver, wrote to national
headquarters asking for "any advice and free literature" on how to open
the housing market for "Negroes" in response to the fast-moving developments of the local urban renewal program. These developments would later
include targeting and demolishing the Bronzeville neighborhood, the heart
of Milwaukee's African American business community, in order to build the
I-94/I-43 freeway.

In St. Paul, Minnesota, six days after Toliver's letter requesting help, the
local police arrived on an unseasonably warm day at 449 Rondo Avenue
wielding axes and sledgehammers. Inside the house lived Reverend George
Davis and his wife, Bertha Miller Davis, who was blind and rarely left their

home. The Davises' home was one of many slated to be demolished for the construction of I-94. But the eighty-year-old Davis, who years prior had fled from the Jim Crow South to live in Minnesota, stood in the doorway with a shotgun, refusing to leave his home. The Davis family was one of the last of the 650 families in the Rondo Avenue neighborhood displaced by the construction of I-94, which "split the heart" of the city's Black community.[1] These neighborhoods, three proud Black communities, were never the same again.[2]

These events suggest much about the widespread but local threat of urban renewal policies to African American communities in Northern cities, communities that were already restricted as to where they could live. The Housing Acts of 1949 and 1954, as well as the Highway Act of 1956, disproportionately affected African Americans through urban renewal, which many dubbed "Negro Removal." In the mid-twentieth century, mostly white city governments were not interested in improving Black neighborhoods but rather in tearing them down to build sports arenas, highways, and high-end apartment buildings. Many of these urban renewal projects were designed to either keep white families from moving to the suburbs or to encourage white families to return to the city for sporting events and entertainment.

During the height of urban renewal programs, spaces became even more racialized through federal policy, social customs, local laws, and violence. Because urban renewal policies increased the formation of racialized spaces and intensified segregation, the democratic ideals of citizenship, such as freedom, inclusivity, equality, and liberty, were hindered. Uncovering communities' rhetorical responses to urban renewal helps us better understand these ideals of citizenship as well as urban history. Spaces designated as "blighted" or "slum" by city governments were most often inhabited by Black residents.[3] This labeling of "Black spaces" as blighted made it easier for city governments to reclaim this space to create "white spaces," such as highways to connect the suburbs with white spaces downtown.

Restrictions on housing based on race predetermined where African Americans could live after being displaced from their homes. This overt form of racism is one way in which spaces in the city become racialized as either Black-only or white-only places. As Mary Triece notes, racialized spaces create "unjust geographies."[4] One way that spaces became racialized, unjust geographies is through the language and narratives circulated to describe them. When we better account for how language functioned to create and perpetuate racialized spaces in Northern cities, we better understand the interconnectedness of rhetorical strategies (language-in-action), space and place, and forms of citizenship. A rhetorical history of urban renewal thus reveals how racialized spaces (1) limited the organizing and rhetorical agency that took place in African American communities, (2) drew from African American cultural history to inform the materiality of these spaces, and (3) influenced the types of rhetorical actions and forms of citizenship that could take place in response to urban renewal. The policies of urban renewal were an attempt by cities to take historically and segregated Black spaces and make them white. Resistance to these attempts was conducted in creative and innovative ways by the Black community.

Because of segregation, African Americans had limited or no representative power in Northern city governments in the mid-twentieth century and lacked traditional civic means to prevent being uprooted from their homes, businesses, and churches. Compounding the trauma of forced removal, African Americans were not free to move anywhere else in their cities due to redlining by financial institutions (preventing African Americans from getting mortgages in certain areas), racist housing covenants that restricted African Americans from certain rental properties, and outright physical and verbal hostility from white residents when African American families tried to move into exclusively white neighborhoods.[5] In other words, white residents enforced a strict segregation of space in many urban neighborhoods. This violence, along with racist housing laws, restricted African Americans to living in "blighted" neighborhoods. These tensions are often what get highlighted in urban renewal histories—a focus on the racist policies/practices that victimized African American communities. But what they hide, as I discuss later in this introduction, is how the communities responded. We need to look at these responses as creative and strategic acts of citizenship.

Despite the wrecking balls destroying numerous African American homes, churches, and businesses nationwide, many residents tried to stop or modify the urban projects; in some instances, they were successful. Because of segregated spaces and limited access to legislative power, how did African Americans enact the modes of citizenship that were available to them—that is, how did they resist, modify, and in some cases stop the destruction of their neighborhoods? Who were these organizers, leaders, and residents at the local level of a social movement that valiantly resisted urban renewal?

This book is their story. It is the story of a people who worked and organized to be treated like all citizens. It is the story of three Black communities in crisis over the fear of losing their homes and businesses, and their rhetorical actions in response to the power of city and federal governments. The Hill District in Pittsburgh, the Bronzeville neighborhood in Milwaukee, and the Rondo Avenue neighborhood in St. Paul all saw the formation of grassroots organizations that worked alongside national organizations, such as the NAACP and the National Urban League, to resist urban renewal. These communities are representative of African Americans living in the urban North where urban renewal destroyed the economic resources of the African American neighborhoods. Bridging recent work in rhetorical, historical, and African American studies, this book aims to strengthen our understanding of the Black Freedom Movement (which includes the Civil Rights Movement and the Black Power Movement)[6] and better account for the places, narratives, and agency that different forms of citizenship produce, especially in resistance to dominant and persuasive narratives of urban renewal.

Primarily a story about the rhetorical strategies and tactics developed in response to urban renewal, this book draws from Black people's own cultural rhetorical traditions in the practice of parrhesia, "speaking truth in the face of danger."[7] Urban renewal was that danger. But urban renewal was also a story of mobility, another example of forced migration of African Americans in the history of the United States. Many of those forced to move were Black people who migrated to the urban North to escape Jim Crow, poverty, and sharecropping. Their dreams of housing independence and "first-class citizenship" were met with Northern disdain, de facto segregation, and outright physical violence. Their responses speak to the resilience of the people. These responses also illuminate the integral role that rhetoric—the strategic use of language and other symbolic means—played in African American communities' resistance to urban renewal during the Black Freedom Movement. In conducting a rhetorical history of urban renewal, this book reveals the resilience of African Americans by examining their rhetorical actions in response to urban renewal during the Black Freedom Movement.

This research and analysis of urban renewal discourse contributes to African American rhetorical history and urban history by demonstrating the important role of urban renewal arguments and Black Rhetorical Citizenship, the framework I develop in this book, within the overall circulation of the discourse of the Black Freedom Movement. The African American struggle against urban renewal policies also provides a useful site for extending discussions of counter publics, rhetorical agency, and rhetorics of place. And finally, this rhetorical history provides a different perspective on current research by rhetorical scholars of place by demonstrating how rhetorics of place are a central part of African American rhetoric.

Black Communities in the "Promised Land"

African Americans who made the journey north from the dangerous, racist, and dehumanizing Jim Crow South sometimes referred to the North as the biblical "promised land" where freedom and prosperity could be obtained. Pittsburgh, St. Paul, and Milwaukee were all cities in the "Midwestern stream" of the Great Migration.[8]

Lower Hill

The Hill District neighborhood was the center of African American life in Pittsburgh. The construction of a sports arena in the late 1950s destroyed the area known as the Lower Hill. It was originally a German and Jewish section of town, but the Great Migration brought numerous African Americans. The threat of urban renewal to the rest of the Hill District led to residents creating the Citizens Committee for Hill District Renewal (CCHDR). Alongside the United Negro Protest Committee (UNPC, another local group), as well as the Pittsburgh chapters of the Urban League and the NAACP, the CCHDR would be instrumental in organizing the response to urban renewal in the city.

Rondo

The African American population in St. Paul was smaller than in both Milwaukee and Pittsburgh. African Americans were located in the Rondo neighborhood. In response to the planned highway construction through the central business section of Rondo, residents created the Rondo–St. Anthony Improvement Association, which was led by a preacher and a barber. However, the neighborhood was essentially destroyed when the I-94 construction took place in 1956.

Bronzeville

The Bronzeville neighborhood in Milwaukee was first inhabited by German and Jewish immigrants. African Americans began arriving in larger numbers by the mid-twentieth century, but strict segregation practices restricted them to the north side of the city. Traditional Black organizations, including the Milwaukee chapters of the NAACP and the Urban League, were the primary groups to respond to urban renewal; still, at least one grassroots group, the Walnut Area Improvement Committee (WAICO), formed in response to urban renewal. While some scholars have argued that the small size of the Black population in Milwaukee may have contributed to less resistance to the highway projects, Milwaukee residents used urban renewal policies as an opportunity to focus on open housing laws (as did the residents of Rondo) to better accommodate the rapidly growing African American population and alleviate poor housing conditions.

Activism and African American Rhetorical History

The history of US governmental power and African American rhetorics of resistance to it have returned to the forefront of our consciousness with the emergence of Black Lives Matter (BLM) activism, revitalizing our need to understand the rhetorical strategies of resistance at work in the Black Freedom Movement.[9] Rhetorical history and analysis of the Black Freedom Movement in the North, which includes milestone events that coincide with the Montgomery Bus Boycott, Selma Marches, and March on Washington, reveal the impact African American residents in Northern cities had on the movement, including rhetorical strategies of resistance. These strategies continue to influence the actions of the Black Freedom Movement nationwide, including Black Lives Matter.

Because this book explores urban renewal as a rhetorical situation, it uncovers rhetorical strategies of resistance at work in the Black Freedom Movement—in particular, rhetorics of place (counternarratives, placemaking, and critical memory) and rhetorical leadership (community organizing, distributed agency, and critical memory) enacted by African Americans in response to urban renewal in the North. Predominant scholarly analyses of African American rhetorical history have focused on the actions of Southern leaders to better understand grassroots organizing among African Americans.[10] Although these histories provide much-needed insight on the Black Freedom Movement, the existing narrative in rhetorical scholarship tends to overemphasize the South and neglect the key role Northern cities played in the rhetorical history of the Civil Rights Movement. This book therefore addresses the central question of what rhetorical resistance to urban renewal and housing policies looked like in smaller Northern cities during the overlap of the Civil Rights and Black Power Movements, where smaller, underrepresented communities had to find alternative ways to enact citizenship and resist harmful policies. African Americans faced different challenges, such as housing restrictions and urban renewal projects, despite having the ability to vote, unlike many of those living in the South during this same time. These Northern sites have not been examined nearly enough but contribute significantly to the history of the Black Freedom Movement. Thomas Sugrue's *Sweet Land of Liberty: The Forgotten Struggle for Civil Rights in the North* maintains that civil rights in the North was just as important as the movement in the South and cites the works of many forgotten and unknown individuals in the civil rights struggle in Detroit, Chicago, and Philadelphia. His work has been extended by other urban historians on the struggle of African Americans in the North as well.[11]

However, these important historical studies of Northern urban African American communities do not fully address how rhetorical acts of civic engagement—discursive and material—by African Americans on the ground level served as strategies of resistance and forms of citizenship during the Black Freedom Movement in Northern cities. *Struggle for the City* focuses on the organizing, mobilizing, and protesting by Black people as they responded to urban renewal and housing discrimination. Doing so centers the rhetorical agency of the people and makes visible the cultural rhetorical traditions of the people/communities involved. Because stories of urban renewal are often told from the perspective of city and federal government or highlight only the devastation and victimization of Black people, these narratives exclude too many of the agentive actions of African Americans: the organizing, educating, and civic engagement that took place in these neighborhoods, actions that are part of the long Black Freedom Movement in the United States.

The Racial Master Narrative of Urban Renewal / "Negro Removal"

What the residents of Rondo, Lower Hill, and Bronzeville didn't know, and perhaps had no way of knowing, was that the process of acquiring their homes had begun years prior and was rooted in the language of urban renewal. Only weeks after the US Supreme Court passed down its verdict in *Brown v. Board of Education*, President Eisenhower signed into law the Housing Act of 1954.[12] Although both legal milestones would have significant consequences for African Americans in Cold War America, it was the Housing Act of 1954 that drastically altered the living conditions for vast numbers of African Americans across the United States. The Housing Act of 1954 gave American cities unprecedented power to build sports arenas, highways, apartment buildings, and shopping areas, which transformed the material layout and appearance of their cities.

Eisenhower saw the signing of the Housing Act of 1954 as a significant accomplishment during his administration. On the signing of the act, he wrote in a public relations statement:

> The country will be benefited by the Housing Act of 1954 which has now become law. It has been one of our major legislative goals. It will raise the housing standards of our people, help our communities get rid of slums and improve their older neighborhoods, and strengthen our mortgage credit system. . . . Millions of our families with modest incomes will be able, for the first time, to buy new or used homes. Families will be helped to enlarge or modernize their present homes. Another feature of the law is especially important. Many families have to move from their homes because of slum clearance and other public improvements. This law provides especially easy terms for these deserving people. The new law makes available, for the first time, a practical way for our citizens, in the towns and cities of America, to get rid of their slums and blight.[13]

Eisenhower's statement reveals the law's difficult and at times conflicting goals. What is the difference between a "slum" to get rid of and an "older neighborhood" to improve? The application of the law resulted in over-crowding in many Black neighborhoods because local governments did not follow through on the promise of new homes for all of those "deserving" displaced people.

As I will show, Eisenhower and others in the federal government made it possible for local governments—which implemented the law—to privilege language that supported their preferred interpretations of the Housing Act of 1954. The language of the law empowered city governments to increase their usage of eminent domain to seize property "to redevelop blighted areas, and drastically reduced the funds to build public housing."[14] City governments spent federal dollars to demolish neighborhoods labeled "blighted" and rebuild them for private development. This approach in combating "blight" suited the needs of private construction and real estate companies because "urban revitalization required the condemnation of blighted properties and the transfer of this real estate to developers who would use it more productively."[15] This differential treatment was justified because city planners believed that certain areas of the city could better serve the larger public, meaning more white people. City officials needed a new "language of urban decline" to argue for clearing certain neighborhoods and leaving others unaffected.[16] As a result, the urban landscapes of numerous American cities were altered dramatically.

The language of the Housing Acts of 1949 and 1954, as well as the Highway Act of 1956, provided the roots for an urban renewal "master narrative" that could be used by federal officials and city governments to justify their plans to obliterate Black neighborhoods. Master narratives, according to Hilde Lindemann-Nelson, are "stories found lying about in our culture that serve as summaries of socially shared understandings," which we also use to "justify what we do."[17] The master narrative of urban decay and renewal was centered on African Americans and shaped the way other city residents sought solutions to the city's problems. The primary urban renewal narrative dictated that the "good" (buildings, neighborhoods, citizens) must overcome, defeat, or eliminate the "bad" (blight, crime, sickness) in order for all of the city to prosper. Taking Lindeman-Nelson's claim further, I suggest that "socially shared understandings" are created when specific narratives of past or future events are repeated over time. In particular, racial narratives "garner an accepting audience in part because of their familiarity and in part because of the perception that they allow us to make sense of the world, and they are therefore replicated and repeated."[18] In other words, the repetition and circulation of the racial narratives of urban renewal helped create the environment in which there was only one solution—bulldozing neighborhoods.

Through the master narrative of urban renewal, federal and local government officials created a myth that their city would transform into a "city of tomorrow," a "modern acropolis," "a city upon a hill."[19] This narrative of replacing blight with beautiful buildings was repeated continuously in newspaper editorials and political speeches throughout the early period in which urban renewal projects were taking place. The narrative was simple. For American cities to become "modern" or even to survive, the "blighted" and mostly African American spaces had to be demolished and remade into spaces used by majority white people. While not the only way in which city governments argued for urban renewal, this master narrative was at work in much of the news media and government publications at the time, suggesting its effectiveness.

This urban renewal master narrative contains several discursive features that make it effective: (1) metaphors of sickness or disease, (2) euphemisms of progress toward idealized futures, and (3) absence of either racial division or inclusion. Although these features do not have clear delineation points, their overlapping repetition across urban renewal narratives conveys that only the complete razing of neighborhoods can be recognized as urban renewal.

Metaphors of Disease and Sickness in the Master Narrative

Ancient rhetoricians have long remarked on the persuasive power of meta-phor in language. Aristotle, for instance, called metaphors a "bringing before the eyes" that has "clarity and sweetness and strangeness."[20] Recognizing the effect of metaphor on audiences and the usefulness of metaphors in creating knowledge, Aristotle believed that "to learn easily is naturally pleasant to all people, and words signify something, so whatever words create knowledge in us are pleasurable."[21] Quintilian viewed metaphor as a trope that is "the artistic alteration of a word or phrase from its proper meaning to another."[22] The persuasive power of the master narrative of urban renewal was under-girded and amplified by metaphors.

More recent accounts of metaphor demonstrate how metaphors shape understanding because they are pervasive in everyday life, not just in lan-guage but also in thought and action, making it easier for an audience to understand a complex idea. George Lakoff and Mark Johnson, for example, assert that "the essence of metaphor is understanding and experiencing one kind of thing in terms of another."[23] In this way, metaphors structure the way we think and the way we act, "and our systems of knowledge and belief, in a pervasive and fundamental way."[24] In other words, metaphor adds a structuring principle to our thinking, focusing attention on aspects of what-ever phenomenon is under scrutiny; at the same time, metaphor can hide other aspects of that same phenomenon.[25] Metaphors are particularly apt at (re)structuring people's thoughts about political subjects.[26]

These theories of metaphor help us understand how narrative and meta-phor are closely linked. Metaphors provide background and foundation for narratives, and narratives do the same for metaphors. Because metaphors emerge from and support stories, narratives can also become metaphors whereby concepts may be "formed by and understood as both [metaphors and narratives], separately and in combination."[27] For example, Linda Berger explains that narrative "leads to the shorthand use of metaphors: once a story is embedded in tradition and culture, the die is cast and you no longer have to tell the tale, you can simply use the name of the character or the title of the story as a metaphor, and the plot, characters, and moral will follow, appear-ing to be logical entailments."[28]

This shorthand use of metaphors highlights the rhetorical potential of "blight" in the metaphors surrounding urban planning, which were instru-mental in both the construction and the effectiveness of the urban renewal master narrative. This language of blight and its historical reference to mysterious infestations served racially a motivated political purpose: to clear and rebuild the parts of the city that were occupied by African American communities.[29] Although blight appears to be a "race-neutral" term, it was primarily deployed to reference certain neighborhoods, becoming a stand-in or name for Black communities and even being seen as an "effect" of these communities.

In traditional usage, blight is defined as "a disease or injury of plants marked by the formation of lesions, withering, and death of parts."[30] Blight sometimes grows to the point that it will destroy the plant, so the diseased part of the plant must be removed for the plant to survive. Because it leverages this metaphor and narrative of disease, "blight" becomes a threat to the health of the city and helps to justify government officials' seizure of private property. Blight also evolved into a warlike metaphor: from something that requires treatment, removal, and perhaps healing into something that must be struggled against and defeated. In other words, the spread of "blight" is the city's antagonist; it provides the central conflict in the narrative that government officials—the city's heroes—must defeat. In this narrative, victory in the struggle against "blight" results in the city's prosperity and growth, a place where new, modern buildings and different people replace the diseased parts.

As illustrated in the following examples, it was primarily African American neighborhoods that were referred to as "blight" or as being "blighted." Applying this metaphor continuously to poor areas created an imagined reality in which strong measures had to be taken immediately to stop the "disease" of blight. By referring to poverty and poor housing as blight, its removal (or relocation) would mean that the community would thrive again. Furthermore, city governments were required to label a place as "blighted" in order to receive federal funds for redevelopment, creating an urban policy of demolishing and rebuilding a city to rid it of "blight." Using blight metaphorically to refer to certain neighborhoods also limited how citizens might imagine other approaches to improving the neighborhood's conditions.

Blight metaphors, along with specific notions of "curing" blight, were prevalent in the congressional deliberations of the Housing Act of 1954. In fact, much of the language of urban renewal can be traced to the Hearings Before the Committee on Banking and Currency, which, in large part, debated the concerns of private building and banking industries. For example, in a statement read during the hearing, Norman P. Mason from the US Chamber of Commerce noted:

The chamber has worked for many years to encourage the *elimination of slums* and the restoration of *blighted urban* areas to economic and social usefulness. While we had reservations about the urban rehabilitation plans established in the housing acts of 1949, believing it to be too limited and too costly, the pending legislation promises to *remove these defects.* This legislation places a definite responsibility on the locality to put its own house in order with ordinances and enforcement of these ordinances to assure the proper maintenance of housing and to prevent its overcrowding, before that community can go to the Federal Government for assistance. It lets the Federal Government help in such a way as to encourage the conservation of sound structure. It helps to retard the *decline* of existing neighborhoods and to *eliminate the causes of blight* before it becomes necessary to do a *wholesale clearance* operation. Because of these desirable features, the provisions of title IV of the bill are strongly supported by the chamber and we urge their enactment.[31]

Using the metaphor of blight in this context limits other possible approaches to improving neighborhood conditions once the neighborhood receives the "blight" designation. First, the repetition of blight paired with words like "clearance" and "elimination" suggests that the only way for neighborhoods to achieve "usefulness" is to excise all or portions of the neighborhood—like a cancer that must be cut out. Second, the usage of blight also does racial work, suggesting that the causes of blight are within the neighborhoods themselves without explicitly naming the causes. This allows the audience to infer causal relationships, particularly those related to race. Blight is deployed in several ways in the nine-hundred-page transcript of the hearing: "blight" is mentioned more than 140 times, "modern or modernization" 139 times, and the phrase "slum clearance" nearly 200 times. This language of urban renewal, especially metaphors of disease and sickness that leveraged "blight" as the disease, was also used locally in cities like Pittsburgh, Milwaukee, and St. Paul, and in each locale this language was used to create a narrative to fit the desired projects.

Progress Toward an Idealized Future in the Master Narrative

Urban renewal policies began to take root during the euphoria of post–World War II America. The phrase "urban renewal" offers a sense of hopefulness for a better future, a desire for newness that was shared by many Americans after winning the war. A more literal definition of renewal is "to make like new: restore to freshness, vigor, or perfection, and to make new spiritually."[32] Synonyms for the word include regenerate, revive, and rebuild. With this sentiment in mind, the goal of many American cities was to become "modernized," and this desired modernization was implied in euphemisms such as "Renaissance." A euphemism is the use of a supposedly less objectionable variant for a word that has negative connotations.[33] The choice of these words may suggest its significance. Carol Cohn, for example, describes how euphemisms used by military intellectuals "were so bland that they never forced the speaker or enabled the listener to touch the realities of nuclear holocaust that lay behind the words."[34] In a similar way, euphemisms and metaphors used within the urban renewal master narrative hid the realities faced by African Americans most affected by urban renewal.

The urban renewal master narrative dictates that the defeat of the antagonist (i.e., blight) will result in an idealized future for all citizens, a sentiment that leveraged the hope and optimism of the time. This utopian vision for urban redevelopment in Northern cities was created, in part, by the euphemisms for demolition deployed consistently by city politicians and newspaper editorials. The overwhelming use of the words "modern," "renewal," and "Renaissance" as euphemisms for the destruction required by many urban renewal policies encapsulates what Kenneth Burke calls a "body of identifications" in *A Rhetoric of Motives*. As Burke states, "Often we must think of rhetoric not in terms of some one particular address, but as a general body of identifications that owe their convincingness much more to trivial repetition and dull daily reinforcement than to exceptional rhetorical skill."[35] In other words, the body of identifications (e.g., metaphors and euphemisms) at work within the urban renewal master narrative was effective in large part because of how frequently it was repeated in speeches and in print.

Working alongside euphemisms of demolition is the notion of progress toward an idealized future, which can be traced to the 1949 Housing Act. A portion of that law says that through the clearance of slums and blight, American families will have more suitable housing and thus contribute "to the development and redevelopment of communities and to the advancement of the growth, wealth, and security of the nation."[36] This language gives the law a sense of hope for a better city.

Accompanying notions of progress are ideas of safety and security, which were echoed in a congressional hearing for the 1954 Housing Act. In a written statement in support of amending the 1949 Housing Act, William L. Rafsky—housing coordinator for the City of Philadelphia—argued that a decrease in crime would result from passing and implementing the revised Housing Act. He writes:

> Indicative of the high price of inferior housing is the fact that in 1953, 65.3 percent of all police arrests were of individuals who resided in Philadelphia's officially certified blighted areas, which contain only 23.5 percent of the city's population. Similar statistics on juvenile arrests reveal that unless our slums are removed, significant numbers of our future juveniles from these areas are doomed to a life of crime. Despite the fact that the cause of crime is usually far more complex than physical environment, it would be ostrich like to ignore the fact that in the third largest city in the country, arrests of juveniles residing in deteriorated neighborhoods were 46.4 percent of the total, as compared to the area's juvenile population of 25.2 percent of the entire city. Similarly, our losses of life and property by fire, our health, and our welfare problems are concentrated in districts where sub-standard housing predominates. From the longer-range point of view, Philadelphia's survival depends upon the solution to this problem.[37]

Despite the attempt to modify the strength of his claim, Rafsky establishes the blighted neighborhoods as the primary source of many of the ills of the city and a significant threat to the city's well-being. Naming this causal relationship (i.e., blight causes juvenile crime) not only raises the stakes of passing the act; it also does racial rhetorical work. If blighted neighborhoods cause crime, what might cause the blight? While race is not explicitly named, audiences of the time may be inclined to connect the neighborhood's primarily Black residents to the sources of the blight. This inference not only suggests that removal of the residents is the only way for the city to "survive," but it also does the rhetorical work in a way that appears "race neutral." In terms of the master narrative, Rafsky seems to be suggesting that blight is antagonistic to the safety and security required for modernization and progress.

Repetition of Wishes and Fears and the Absence of Racial Division

At the onset of the urban renewal policy, many African Americans did not strongly resist urban renewal. Organized civic resistance and mass protests to urban renewal often developed *after* initial urban renewal projects had been completed. Why didn't African Americans resist the implementation of a policy that would be detrimental to them? Why didn't most African American organizations and residents resist when city governments invoked the policy of eminent domain, which left many residents without homes? One reason, I argue, is that the urban renewal master narrative did not overtly use race in its language. In other words, racial division and everyday practices of segregation were absent from the language of urban Renaissance, renewal, and progress. For instance, in the previous quote, Rafsky explains crime in terms of blight rather than in relation to older narratives more recognizably connected to anti-Black racism, which might have, initially, seemed like a step forward. Thus, somewhat ironically, the absence of racial division from the master narrative of urban renewal and the promises made of better housing allowed many African Americans to hope that they, too, would be potential beneficiaries of urban renewal policies and programs.

The mythical image of the ideal city set in a future that has seemingly overcome racial division is perhaps rooted in the idealism of a postwar America. At least this was the thinking of many African Africans who waged the Double V campaign: victory against the Axis overseas, and victory against racists at home. Kenneth Burke explains that a myth is not an idea but an image, a term that takes us "from the order of reason to the order of imagination."[38] Since the myth of the ideal city omitted any discussion of the racial divide and there were no images of people in many depictions of "modern buildings" and new housing or highways, everyone could imagine whom they wanted to see inhabiting those spaces. Many African Americans envisioned improved housing and more economic opportunity. They saw themselves living in and enjoying pristine buildings on flawless landscaped grounds. For some African Americans, this hope for the city was more inclusive than that of those who held racist beliefs; for African Americans, a modern city would also mean civil relations between the two races and open housing. Initially, many African Americans hoped that they would now equally benefit from the exciting changes proposed to the urban center because they, too, were part of Chicago, St. Paul, Detroit, Milwaukee, and Pittsburgh. However, instead of realizing this initial hope, many African Americans eventually found themselves forced into crowded neighborhoods in other parts of town and restricted from living in white areas of the city. As African Americans realized what was happening, they organized, educated themselves on urban renewal, and engaged in civic action—citizenship as resistance.

Black Rhetorical Citizenship

Because African Americans are endlessly positioned as in opposition to the political and social structures of white America, activism is required for survival for African Americans. Despite often being denied full formal access to civic institutions, African Americans, for their safety and flourishing, have adapted by finding their own forms of civic engagement, which go far beyond legal citizenship and voting. One of the primary contributions of this study is Black Rhetorical Citizenship (BRC), a conceptual framework that situates citizenship as both a site of resistance and "a mode of public engagement"[39] that cannot be divorced from race and the effects of racism. Grounded in theories of African American rhetoric and rhetorical citizenship, BRC envisions citizenship not as specific moments of individual agency, such as voting, but rather as complex discursive processes that emerge across rhetorical situations that include, importantly, the dynamics of racialized place and space. BRC existed before legal citizenship was available to African Americans. In the nineteenth century, Frederick Douglass was the Black rhetorical citizen par excellence, despite his status as an enslaved person for the first part of his life. His contemporary, Frances Harper, lectured against slavery, argued for women's rights, and supported the Underground Railroad.[40] In BRC, such tactics of resistance, which may initially appear unimportant, not only become more visible but also increase in magnitude and "spread across social, cultural, and political sites."[41] Conceptually, BRC is informed by Maulana Karenga's claim that African American rhetoric is a rhetoric of community, resistance, and possibility.[42] Given rhetoric's significance to African Americans, we must consider rhetoric as a tool for liberation and freedom.[43] Rhetorical research focused on African Americans must therefore include the varying ways of knowing, acting, and engaging that are rooted in the African American rhetorical tradition. Rhetoricians can analyze "urban renewal" from the top down, tracking policies of racism, white supremacy, and so on, and the rhetorics that justify them, as they mowed through African American neighborhoods. This approach treats rhetoric primarily as a tool for repression and dominance. But because BRC approaches rhetoric as a tool for liberation and freedom, it puts African American rhetorics at the center and relegates oppressive rhetorics to the margin.

BRC highlights modes of rhetorical engagement of Black communities in response to actions, laws, and policies enacted by the majority. It includes alternate forms of engagement, alternate content, and alternate spaces that

Black people employ to make change. These alternate spaces may include church sanctuaries, bars/taverns, recreation areas, hair and barber salons, or the community center classroom. BRC illuminates a shadow political system that attempts to navigate white institutions of power while maintaining Black autonomy. BRC constitutes, creates, and maintains durable discursive spaces for the Black political community to understand, deliberate, and engage with majority political discourse and institutions. If white America represents the default values, arguments, and issues of the dominant mediated public sphere, BRC is an overlapping set of counter publics. BRC helps us to better understand the goals, formations, and maintenance of community that Black people use to engage with the political institutions of the majority in the hopes of infusing change within them. This view of citizenship situates African Americans' varied responses to urban renewal policies not as a series of individual acts (protests, getting elected to an office, working in a municipal department) but rather as rhetorical agency circulating and being distributed through a social movement. By drawing on African American rhetorical history and theories of space and place, BRC better accounts for the actions of African Americans during the Black Freedom Movement because it examines the coaction of the community rather than focusing primarily on individual rhetors.

Black Rhetorical Citizenship is an umbrella term that embraces scholarship from Black studies, rhetoric studies, discourse analysis, political philosophy, political science, sociology, and other fields in the humanities that offer ways of "conceptualizing the discursive, processual, participatory aspects of civic life."[44] BRC operates within the nuanced story of urban renewal and uncovers acts of rhetorical citizenship. Among scholars of rhetoric, the concept of rhetorical citizenship encompasses all the discursive (i.e., rhetorical) acts of deliberating citizens.[45] These discursive acts should not be viewed simply as preparation for civic action but rather as "constitutive of civic engagement."[46] In other words, rhetorical actions, such as citizens deliberating in public or even within themselves, should be considered just as vital to citizenship as legal entitlements, like voting.[47] Rhetorical citizenship as a conceptual frame thus accentuates "the fact that legal rights, privileges and material conditions are not the only constituents of citizenship; discourse that takes place between citizens is arguably more basic to what it means to be a citizen."[48] The concept of rhetorical citizenship thus highlights the role of rhetorical agency as a community, not just an individual phenomenon, in civic engagement—that is, "citizens' possibilities for gaining access to and influencing civic life through symbolic action."[49]

A rhetorical understanding of citizenship relies heavily on the ideals of a participatory democracy. But rhetorical citizenship as defined by these scholars does not fully contain how African Americans access traditional publics as deliberative participants or create counter publics that resist exclusionary norms. Spatial dynamics and mobility restrictions often hinder members of marginalized communities from accessing publics with the most political power, those where "official" deliberation and decision-making take place; when members of these communities *do* get access, they often cannot be heard. In addition, existing concepts of rhetorical citizenship may not fully account for the ways white supremacist practices require different civic acts by African Americans or the variety of ways to resist these practices. Given that the realities of segregation and other exclusionary dynamics of race affect how African Americans practice civic engagement—that is, rhetorically enact citizenship—theories of African American rhetoric must be incorporated into our understanding of rhetorical citizenship, particularly when African Americans are the subject of the study. When we do so—especially in the case of urban renewal and housing policies—different forms of rhetorical agency become visible.

BRC uncovers forms of democratic participation that incorporate place and cultural traditions that extend the concept of citizenship to previously unrecognized rhetorical strategies. According to William Keith and Paula Cossart, "Rhetorical citizenship is that set of communicative and deliberative practices that in a particular culture and political system allow citizens to enact and embody their citizenship, in contrast to practices that are merely 'talking about' politics."[50] This definition gets closer to the importance of the influence of culture on communicative and deliberative acts of citizenship. African American rhetorical and cultural traditions inform the ways in which communities resisted harmful government policies; for a minority group excluded from the halls of power, "talking" politics assumes huge importance by constituting rhetors as legitimate rhetorical actors. BRC incorporates these ways of knowing and uncovers (or recovers) acts of rhetorical agency by African Americans. Thus, BRC creates conceptual space to analyze an overlapping set of publics in which the merits of urban renewal and resident displacements are discussed, argued, and resisted.

Black Rhetorical Citizenship informs how we deploy our methodological tools as rhetorical critics. It enables *Struggle for the City* to uncover both the Black agency and Black solidarity of residents during urban renewal, ensuring that African Americans remain at the center of the dialogue of their own displacement instead of being overshadowed by those conducting the displacement. In this way, BRC seeks to center average African American citizens in rhetorical histories, highlighting rather than marginalizing their work as complex rhetorical actors playing leading roles in the narratives of their own communities. As a methodology, BRC asks that we look beyond many of the typical representations and artifacts of rhetorical action. This means that we may have to look closer at institutional archives to uncover the Black voice. We must examine local Black newspapers to hear "the word on the street." We have to use oral histories of these traumatic events as a road map to uncover names from the past and to set the scene for important events. We have to be less interested in the machinations and pontificating of white political figures and more interested in the Black voices speaking at public hearings, organizing the community, and writing letters to the editors. We have to be less interested in highlighting the actions of the "white liberal helping the good Black folks" and more interested in how Black people recruited, accepted, and employed non-Black allies to serve the cause of Black Freedom.

BRC also draws attention to the variety of rhetorical acts of resistance that the African American community employs in the fight for full citizenship. When applied to urban renewal and housing policies during the 1950s and 1960s, BRC calls for analysis of multiple case studies, an approach that helps us to recognize and better understand how these rhetorical strategies were, fundamentally, creative acts of civic engagement heavily shaped by the dynamics of segregated spaces in the urban North. As a qualitative approach to research, multiple case studies in context, accessed across a variety of data sources,[51] allows for different analytic methods to be combined to illuminate a case from different perspectives.[52] This approach creates a framework for valuing these different perspectives; thus, this book employs various modes of analysis, including rhetorical analysis, discourse analysis, narrative analysis, and public address. Because rhetoricians draw from "the past to interpret how discourse shaped the meanings of past events,"[53] my primary focus is on how the performance of rhetorical citizenship functions as resistance to local governments and urban renewal projects. Prioritizing "bottom-up" arguments from African American citizens and organizations not only allows me to compare the rhetorical strategies between African American residents in each of the sites; it also allows me to make broader arguments about African American rhetoric, such as how residents in the urban North informed the larger Civil Rights Movement.

Using BRC as a foundational concept that informs a methodological framework, *Struggle for the City* reveals several key ways that African American communities responded to the exigency of urban renewal policies: counternarratives, placemaking, community organizing, and critical memory. These rhetorical strategies fall within the two overlapping categories of rhetorics of place and rhetorical leadership. By examining urban renewal discourse through Black newspapers, documents from Black organizations, and oral histories, we see African American residents resisting urban renewal by building a political community. We learn that citizenship is a form of resistance—indeed, a rhetorical act of survival—used by African American organizations such as the Citizens Committee for Hill District Renewal in Pittsburgh, the Northside Community Inventory Committee in Milwaukee, and the Rondo–St. Anthony Improvement Association in St. Paul.

The Role of Citizenship in African American Rhetorical History

The greatest hope of Reconstruction (and there were many) was the notion that African Americans would become citizens in the fullest sense (not just legally) by simply amending the Constitution. But, in fact, enacting citizenship requires a complex cultural and political infrastructure, which was denied to many African Americans and which white America was in no hurry to supply. Although African Americans became "legal citizens" after the passage of the Fourteenth Amendment in 1868, their ethnic heritage was used to exclude them from many of the benefits of citizenship.[54] Thus, throughout American history, citizenship has been both the practice and the goal of African Americans so as to "deal with their experience of alienation in America."[55] By the twentieth century, the language of "full citizenship"—the cultural capital that white Americans automatically receive—continued to fuel the Black Freedom Movement; it was used in preparation for fighting political battles, demanding legal reforms, and resisting what the majority continued to think was the right way to do things. The federally backed urban renewal program of the 1950s and '60s was one such "right way." African Americans in Northern cities, many of whom had recently migrated from the Jim Crow South, were forced to be more civically engaged because their homes, businesses, and churches were at stake; even if they had nominal access to institutions, they needed to create and participate in their own forms of citizenship.

As it developed meaning for many in the Black Freedom Struggle, citizenship became a goal or destination to achieve. It came to signify action, freedom of movement, and protection of place/space. For Black people, citizenship is "distinct from traditional definitions of legal and political citizenship that entail obeying laws and helping to craft them."[56] In other words, citizenship is a mode of resistance. To be an African American in the United States is to be civically engaged, to enact Black agency. There is no choice: citizenship, defined as discursive engagement with the dominant institutions, is a form of action—an organizing mechanism—and it is survival.

For many African American organizations and institutions, citizenship requires active participation that includes not only voting and deliberation but also organizing communities, providing civic education, and speaking out on issues. In other words, citizenship is a "rhetorical force," as discussed by rhetoric scholar Candice Rai, "so freighted with meaning, simply evoking it summons all of the networked webs of associations, dispositions, identities, affects, practices, and contested beliefs attached to it within our collective, public memories."[57] Citizenship is the work showing that you belong someplace and deserve equal treatment under the law. In response to urban renewal policies, African Americans were defining these beliefs about citizenship while engaging civically in contested issues with government officials.

This book, written at a time when scholars are discussing and critiquing the utility of citizenship as an analytical framework, draws attention to how important the language of citizenship is within the Black Freedom Movement.[58] While some scholars critique citizenship's reliance on oppressive colonial institutions, I maintain that a rhetorical analysis of the actions of African Americans cannot avoid the language or framework of citizenship, insofar as their world-making cannot avoid engaging the political institutions of their oppressors.[59] The language of citizenship for African Americans dates as far back as the Dred Scott decision by the US Supreme Court in 1857, where Chief Justice Roger Taney wrote: "There are two clauses in the Constitution which point directly and specifically to the negro race as a separate class of persons and show clearly that they were not regarded as a portion of the people or citizens of the Government then formed."[60] In fact, the Black Freedom Movement has often been characterized by African American activists as the right for "first-class citizenship" or "full citizenship." Famed historian Rayford Logan, in his introduction to *What the Negro Wants*, defines first-class citizenship in part as the "equal protection of the laws," "abolition of public segregation," and the "equal recognition of the dignity of the human being."[61] What this quote suggests is that citizenship from a Black perspective does not merely signal belonging to a nation-state or legal status. Rather, it is a term for freedom, humanity, liberation, and mobility. For these reasons, the language of citizenship is integral to the history of African Americans and the goals of the Black Freedom Movement.

Furthermore, activism and resistance rhetoric have also been central to notions of "full citizenship" among African Americans. Rhetoric of resistance and the rhetoric of community are staples of African American rhetoric. As Ella Forbes argues, white people prefer to see peaceful, nonviolent images of African Americans as opposed to those of self-empowerment. Giving numerous examples of powerful resistance rhetoric by African Americans in the nineteenth century, she asserts that African American rhetoric "has consistently challenged the notion of African American passivity and civility."[62] The Colored Convention Movement of the nineteenth century was indicative of Black Americans organizing and agitating for change.[63] For African Americans, both resistance rhetoric and African American rhetoric are rooted in "the rhetoric of communal deliberation, discourse, and action, oriented toward that which is good in the world."[64] Importantly, African American rhetoric recognizes the humanity in all persons and does not seek to achieve its goals through verbal or physical violence. Resistance rhetoric for African Americans in general means taking actions that benefit everyone and not just Black people. In short, for African Americans, citizenship is just as much about resisting oppressive institutions through creative forms of civic engagement as it is about negotiating or enjoying the putative benefits of these institutions.

We're perhaps most familiar with how citizenship was wielded in the Montgomery Bus Boycott, the Selma March, and the Birmingham confrontations as instruments to change existing law. The Southern civil rights leaders decided to challenge the Goliath of the nation-state to gain rights for African Americans, using the court system, marches, boycotts, and so forth to get laws passed and/or changed as well as enforced. To be clear, I am not claiming that citizenship was a rallying point for *all* Black Freedom Movements and organizations; for instance, some were challenging and refusing citizenship as a useful concept for struggle in relation to international decolonization movements. Although many of the so-called Black radical groups used a variety of means to accomplish their civic goals, we can see how members of the Black Panther Party invoked the language and actions of citizenship when, proclaiming their Second Amendment rights and citing existing state law, they stood on the California state capitol steps just before marching inside the legislative building wielding shotguns to demonstrate their opposition to an anti-gun bill.[65]

Citizenship as a concept also indicates a sense of belonging to a place and a community. For example, organizations like the Black Panther Party and other Black nationalist groups within the Black Freedom Movement used the language of citizenship in reference to belonging to the Black community: a self-help ethos, "we belong to each other and are citizens of our community." Perhaps more germane to this study, arguments over space and place are often at the center of rhetorical histories of the Black Freedom Movement. African American residents belonged to the city, but they also felt a stronger sense of belonging to their neighborhoods, which were often organized and reinforced legally, economically, and politically by racial identity. Citizenship in this manner, while still linked to notions of the nation-state, plays a vital role in connecting members to a shared sense of community, which extends even to the wider African diaspora.

In urban environments, spaces became racialized through federal policy, social customs, local laws, and housing covenants,[66] and these racialized spaces played an "active role in the construction and organization of social life."[67] Because many urban renewal projects and policies forcefully migrated and/or restricted African Americans to carefully targeted areas, space was contested both materially and culturally. Names of neighborhoods could be invoked to indicate the race of the people who lived there. For instance, some white residents stated that they did not want their neighborhood to become a "Hill District," which was predominately African American.

Because African Americans were concentrated in and restricted to specific areas of cities, they had to build organizations and coalitions with institutions close to them. And these organizations and institutions provided places in the African American community in which members of the community could deliberate and discuss ideas and propose actions without fear of reprisal. For instance, Black churches were instrumental in the Black Freedom Struggle because they, like other Black-controlled institutions, provided safe spaces or "hush harbors" for discussions and organizing without fear of the "hegemonic gaze of whiteness."[68]

Yet this notion of place cannot be separated from movement, both of which are conceptually and materially integral to African American history. Ira Berlin notes that "six million black people—about fifteen times the number of the original African transit—fled the South for the cities of the North making urban wage workers out of the sharecroppers and once again reconstructing black life in the United States."[69] Here, Berlin emphasizes how movement alternates with a sense of place, a tension captured in Black Atlantic scholar Paul Gilroy's phrase "routes and roots."[70] Through the Great Migration, African Americans moved into Black neighborhoods in the North and were either fighting to save these places, resisting forced relocation, or arguing to move freely to anywhere in the city that they could afford. Thus, place and movement are entwined, overlapping, circulating, engaging, and renewing within the African American struggle for "full citizenship" and the language of urban renewal. This tension between space, place, and race within the concept of citizenship reveals why it is necessary for further examination.

Rhetorics of Resistance in the "Promised Land"

Struggle for the City advances a narrative that the community fight against urban renewal was an important feature of the Black Freedom Movement in the urban North. This project shifts between chronological and conceptual development by highlighting when the three communities first became aware of urban renewal and the rhetorical strategies created in response. It identifies key features of urban renewal discourse by tracing the history of urban renewal alongside distinct rhetorical actions, including the actions of resistance taken by African American residents—counternarratives, place-making, distribution of agency, and critical memory. Specific examples of these rhetorical actions are situated in chapters that focus on a single city—Pittsburgh, Milwaukee, or St. Paul. Although these three Black communities faced similar threats, they each handled them in slightly different ways because of the size, resources, and local histories within these places.

Chapter 1 provides the historical background of urban renewal policies and actions in Pittsburgh, Pennsylvania. I explore how citizenship performance creates power through rhetorics of place. First, as the imminent destruction of the Lower Hill became apparent, counternarratives of place that resisted the dominant narrative of blighted neighborhoods began to appear in the African American newspapers. These narratives challenged the existing master narrative of urban renewal history in Pittsburgh. Second, this chapter shows how residents employed a materialist rhetoric of place by producing a map that depicted their vision of a renewed and revitalized neighborhood that ran counter to the city's plans. In the final section, I discuss how Pittsburgh's Freedom Corner spoke symbolically and materially as a "place in protest."[71]

Chapter 2 explores how African American residents in St. Paul, Minnesota, organized in response and resistance to the dominant narrative of blighted neighborhoods and asserted new visions for their communities. This chapter also explores how race is implicated in the contested spaces and places of urban renewal policies. I argue that the Davis home on Rondo Avenue and his subsequent refusal to leave are illustrative of how urban

African American neighborhoods became racialized "rhetorical spaces" that informed the deliberative process and rhetorical actions taken for the survival of the community.

Chapter 3 examines the ways African American residents and organizations in Milwaukee, Wisconsin, built partnerships with nearby academic institutions to increase their rhetorical agency to impact city officials in urban renewal discussions. African American residents of Milwaukee created leadership seminars in part as a rhetorical strategy to resist urban renewal by establishing the conditions for the distribution of agency within the Milwaukee African American community. By building relationships with individuals who had prominent roles in the Catholic Church, University of Wisconsin–Milwaukee, and Marquette University, the African American community created coalitions that provided resources: speakers who assisted the residents to shape discussions of their community, and space to learn about urban renewal policies and thus develop strategies to resist them.

Chapter 4 articulates a theory of critical memory and how the remembrance of urban renewal loss informs the present and shapes the future in Pittsburgh, St. Paul, and Milwaukee. This chapter outlines ways in which African American communities memorialized lost communities through material rhetorics. It concludes with a discussion on how sites of urban renewal resistance inform current social movements such as the Black Lives Matter movement.

The book concludes with thinking about the ways in which future rhetorical scholarship on public policy decisions should consider the ideas of agency within cultural rhetorics. It discusses how African American residents troubled, disrupted, and at times influenced the local government's claims for what was best for their city, which illuminates the powerful role cultural rhetorical traditions serve in social movements, rhetorical theory, and civic engagement.

I

COUNTERNARRATIVES OF HOME IN PITTSBURGH, PENNSYLVANIA

What [urban renewal] was really about was turning black people into white people, without a critique of what is wrong with white people, what was wrong with the world that blacks were being asked to become a part of. That's the whole integration-into-a-burning-building kind of thing. That's why it didn't make any sense, and why it was so devastating. Nobody asked what was important, what was valuable about the black community that shouldn't go, that should resist the bulldozers.

—John Edgar Wideman[1]

In October 1957, the Hill District Home Owners and Tenants Association gave public officials a tour of the Middle Hill in hopes of avoiding the mass demolition that the Lower Hill had suffered in the year prior.[2] The goal of the tour was to refute the claim that their neighborhood was blighted. However, this attempt did not persuade the city officials to stop their planning, and a few months after the tour, the City of Pittsburgh acquired fifty million dollars in federal funds to clear the Middle and Upper Hill, the areas circumscribed by the yellow line on the maps shown in figure 1. This failure to convince city officials not to demolish the rest of the Hill resulted in the formation of the Citizens Committee for Hill District Renewal (CCHDR), led by realtor Robert Lavelle, businesswoman Frankie Pace, and civil rights activist James McCoy Jr.[3] This new organization, along with the United Negro Protest Committee (UNPC), the Urban League, and the NAACP, began a decade-long fight to push the city to rehabilitate individual homes in the Hill District rather than pursue massive redevelopment. In essence, the CCHDR argued

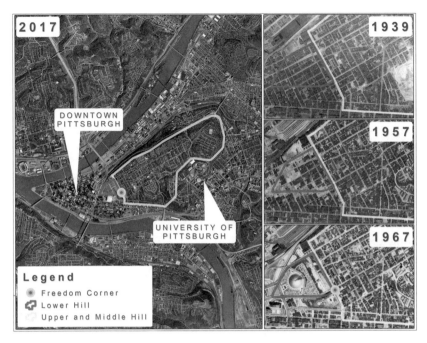

Fig. 1. Historical overhead images of the Hill District in Pittsburgh. Photos: Allegheny County and USDA. PEMA imagery acquired from Pennsylvania Spatial Data Access. https://www.pasda.psu.edu.

against any future development in the Hill that did not include significant input from the community.

This scene in Pittsburgh was playing out in many cities in the United States during the 1950s and 1960s. The threat of upheaval by urban renewal meant rhetorical strategies would have to be developed to affect changes in urban policies. These policies impacted the mobility of residents because of private and government segregation practices (redlining, covenants, etc.). To be clear, the African American community was not a monolithic body where everyone had the same knowledge about the operations of city government or agreed on the best practices to proceed in light of the city's plans.

Although many Pittsburgh residents, including many African Americans, were excited about the city's redevelopment plans, the means of achieving them became a central point of contention.[4] Racial segregation inherent within urban renewal and federal housing policies was the source of this contention. These issues were magnified by urban renewal policies that took away African American housing without creating sufficient replacements. Homeowners, renters, small business owners, and church congregations were often unable to stop the city from "buying" property at prices the city determined and demolishing them for civic projects like sports arenas, highways, and high-end apartment buildings. This conflict led African Americans to organize politically and develop rhetorical strategies to save their neighborhoods and modify public policies. As we will see, African American residents in Pittsburgh responded by organizing within the community, creating alternative maps, and using visual protest to resist the threat of urban renewal.

This chapter seeks to accomplish two goals. Viewed through the lens of Black Rhetorical Citizenship (BRC), it shows how some Hill District residents resisted the master narrative of urban renewal by recalling the history of the Lower Hill and using that history to help organize the community to offer new urban planning solutions. First, this chapter analyzes the Housing Acts of 1949 and 1954 to show how the language of these laws provided the roots for an urban renewal "master narrative." City governments relied on this master narrative to justify eminent domain and remove "blight" and "slums," which often meant African American neighborhoods. The narrative features embedded within both acts contribute to the arguments made by city influencers to construct the urban renewal projects that led to the destruction of the Lower Hill. The arguments made by federal and local city officials reveal that the same narrative of urban renewal discourse was being used by city governments nationwide to similar effect. The master narrative constrained the types of citizenship that could effectively be enacted by residents by placing them as opponents to the healing of the city of blight.

Second, this chapter explores one historical moment in Pittsburgh when Black residents used counternarratives of the Lower Hill as tools for resistance and civic action to save the rest of the Hill District from urban renewal projects. I first explain how rhetorical strategies of place, such as visual and textual counternarratives, operate within the framework of BRC—that is, the civic actions taken by the Black community, which were informed by the community's available culture and its material resources. With this conceptual perspective, we can see how residents creatively resisted the master narrative of their community and what this resistance reveals about the possibilities of resistance rhetoric. Then I show how residents of the Hill rearticulated the meaning of the corner of Crawford Street and Centre Avenue through protest, billboards, and meetings, making it both a symbolic and a material site of civic resistance, civic engagement, and community unification. These rhetorical strategies of resistance constitute, in part, the "active or participatory aspect" of BRC.[5] This rearticulation of "Freedom Corner" created the symbolic importance for the intersection. The memorial placed at the site decades later not only recognizes this rhetorical history but also provides a rhetorical platform for current and future residents of Pittsburgh.

The Master Narrative of Urban Renewal and the End of the Lower Hill

The destruction of the Lower Hill and other African American neighborhoods in the urban North began long before many people realized that their neighborhoods were being targeted. Because the history of the 1954 Housing Act is complex, understanding the role it plays in urban renewal's master narrative requires untangling the debates, declarations, and processes that led to the law's passage. The genesis of the Housing Act of 1954 began in public housing debates during the 1930s and sprouted from the overwhelmingly negative reaction to the Housing Act of 1949 by conservatives in Congress and by the building industry.[6] The 1949 act was unpopular among private housing interests but lauded by those interested in the social conditions of inner cities. The legislation declared that "the general welfare and security of the Nation and the health and living standards of its people require housing through the clearance of slums and blighted areas, and the realization as soon as feasible of the goal of a decent home and a suitable living environment of communities and to the advancement of the growth, wealth, and security of the Nation."[7] The supposed good intention of the law was to help many Black residents by providing housing instead of tackling the source of many of the problems in the city—racism and segregation. As Alexander Von Hoffman argues, the Housing Act of 1949 was contradictory and "relied too heavily on simple solutions—new dwelling units and slum clearance—to solve complex problems of American cities."[8] By focusing on building "wholesome homes" for low-income families through federal spending,[9] the language of the law situates clearance for development in cities as contributing to the security of the nation. This language gives the law a sense of not only urgency but also inevitability. The Housing Act of 1949 authorized more than a billion dollars in loans and grants over a five-year period to local governments to help them acquire the land for redevelopment and to cover the "loss involved in connection with slum-clearance operations."[10] However, local governments were required to cover one-third of any loss associated with land clearance.

This commitment of federal dollars to build public housing angered many in the private building sector and galvanized the National Association of Real Estate Boards (NAREB) against the 1949 legislation.[11] As urban scholar Colin Gordon concludes, areas that were labeled blighted were "driven not by objective urban conditions, but by the prospect of private investment."[12] Leading the charge to transform the 1949 legislation into a more agreeable act passed in 1954, the NAREB argued that public housing was unnecessary if more houses were built in the suburbs, making suitable housing available in the cities for low-income families who were affected by "slum clearance." The private housing industry would play an important part in the new legislation's application, as President Eisenhower noted in a statement on the Housing Act of 1954. The building industry was also opposed to any involvement by the "creeping socialism" of the federal government.[13] At the height of the Cold War, an indictment of socialism resonated with many influential citizens. In addition, NAREB proved effective in organizing a lobbying campaign in Washington, DC, and a marketing campaign called "Build a Better America."[14] The aggressive tactics used by NAREB were very effective in shaping popular opinion about public housing. The trade groups created colorful public relations materials aimed at fanning resentments of programs targeted for low-income people. One of NAREB's publications, for example, was titled "The World Owes Me a Living!" and demonstrated that "the enemies of public housing were not above attacking the program as socialist."[15] The result of this multipronged strategy was that the 1949 law was amended by the Housing Act of 1954.

However, the views of the private housing industry, especially its anticommunist sentiment, were in direct contrast to how the federal government viewed urban redevelopment. The initial 1949 law was an attempt to "reclaim the central city," restore downtown to business interests, and improve the community.[16] Instead, NAREB wanted to use the governments' money primarily on saving downtown instead of helping the residents living in "slum" areas.[17] Proponents of the 1954 law considered the diminution in the amount of public housing as an accomplishment and a blow to communism.

NAREB's claim that the federal government's actions were more symptomatic of socialism won out in the end. NAREB capitalized on the nation's fear of slums, "blight," and diverse populations to get a more aggressive law passed that benefited the private housing industry. One rhetorically effective way of doing so was, as political scientist Kevin Gotham points out, to change how the Housing Act of 1954 named the program—from the 1949 law's "urban redevelopment" to "urban renewal," which "empowered municipalities to redevelop blighted areas, and drastically reduced the funds to build public housing."[18] This subtle but key change in the language helped to construct the foundations of the master narrative.

This new approach to urban planning suited the needs of the private industries because "urban revitalization required the condemnation of blighted properties and the transfer of this real estate to developers who would use it more productively."[19] Private builders could take on projects that would generate more tax income, while those building public housing could not. Accordingly, in 1954, "the government amended the Housing Act of 1949 to include provisions for redevelopment, rehabilitation, and conservation of neighborhood."[20] But this change reduced the emphasis on building public housing while continuing to place emphasis on "the clearance and redevelopment of severely blighted neighborhoods."[21] The changes also meant that less low-income housing would be built as a way to limit blight, thus suiting the demands of NAREB, which argued as a rhetorical tactic that public housing was akin to socialism.

After vigorous debate in Congress, the Housing Act of 1954 was signed into law on August 2, 1954. Several parts of the law are important to note. First, the 1954 act prohibits demolition of "residential structures" if local governments determine that doing so would create undue housing hardship in the locality. The act stipulates that those living in new projects should be "low-income families in need of adequate housing." Also, discrimination is not permitted against "welfare cases," and "in no event may a project be undertaken which is of elaborate or extravagant design or materials."[22] Unfortunately, these stipulations lacked teeth because it was the local governments that decided how and, more important, where to implement urban renewal policies.

City governments would select an area for urban renewal that would later be approved by federal authorities in Washington. A public hearing would then be held during which city officials would argue for the urban renewal plan and citizens would be given the opportunity to speak for or against the plan. As Martin Anderson explains, "Once the project has been officially approved the authorities either persuade the owners of real estate in the area to sell willingly or force them to sell by invoking the power of eminent domain."[23] To persuade these owners, and the city more broadly, that urban renewal would create positive benefits for all, city officials drew heavily on the urban renewal master narrative.

The Master Narrative of the Lower Hill District

The master narrative of urban renewal in Pittsburgh created widespread support for the destruction of the Lower Hill neighborhood in 1956.[24] After the end of World War II, Pittsburgh leaders were concerned with remaking the city's image from that of a smoky, smog-filled town into one of a more "modern city." A 1947 *Pittsburgh Post-Gazette* article titled "City of the Future" signaled the beginning of redevelopment and the city's so-called "Renaissance."[25] On the heels of a successful urban development project downtown, the mayor of Pittsburgh and the Urban Redevelopment Authority wanted to create a "modern acropolis," which included a new arena to house the Civic Light Opera, a new symphony hall, a museum, and new, "modern" apartment buildings—all to be built in Pittsburgh's primarily African American Hill District (see fig. 2).[26]

The area first targeted for urban renewal was the Lower Hill in the Hill District, home to famous playwright August Wilson and jazz singer Lena Horne. The Hill District, situated between downtown and the University of Pittsburgh, was the heart of Pittsburgh's African American community, and the Lower Hill was its business center.[27] Although African Americans constituted the majority of its residents by the mid-twentieth century, the Hill District was still home to many Jewish, Italian, and Syrian residents and businesses as well, making it the most racially/ethnically integrated neighborhood in Pittsburgh.[28] During its prime, African Americans often referred to the Hill as "Little Harlem," and it was thought of as the "crossroads of the

Fig. 2. Proposed Lower Hill Cultural Center. Creator unknown. Allegheny Conference for Community Development, Detre Library & Archives, Senator John Heinz History Center Pittsburgh, PA.

world where there was 'never a dull moment'" and where "people never went to bed."[29] However, Pittsburgh's all-white city officials did not share the same view of the Lower Hill. In their minds, because the Lower Hill's primarily African American population and impoverished areas could not be reconciled as part of the ideal community, it had to be removed with the help of the Housing Act of 1954. That law provided the City of Pittsburgh with federal funds that covered over 70 percent of the total cost of demolition and redevelopment.[30] These funds included the expected $14 million cost of the "world's largest dome" auditorium. At the time, this project was one of the most dramatic in Pittsburgh's history.

Although ending "blight" and providing low-income housing (two goals that were often in conflict with each other but did not have to be) were the stated purposes of the Housing Act, Pittsburgh officials used the language of the 1954 law and the narrative of modernization to demolish the Lower Hill so new cultural sites could be built. It was a narrative that was repeated numerous times in the local media in the years prior to the Lower Hill's redevelopment. One of the first instances of the narrative was in a 1947 *Post-Gazette* article: "Like something conceived by Norman Bel Geddes for a World of Tomorrow is the plan for reconstruction of the Lower Hill District. . . . Instead of being a handicap, the sloping terrain on which the project was built has been made an asset."[31]

This narrative of the Lower Hill effectively shaped the public's thinking about redevelopment because it aligned with the master narrative of urban planning during the 1950s and 1960s. City leaders maintained that they must get rid of the "blighted" Lower Hill so that the city could "blossom" and become more modern.[32] As Andrew Herscher points out, "The status of 'blight' as a mysterious affliction and metaphorical figure was both traded on and transformed; blight became a problem eliciting the technical solutions of urban planning and opening up challenges and opportunities for real estate development."[33]

Although the "blight" metaphor encompassed different negative depictions of the Lower Hill, its use increased as more African Americans began moving to Northern cities from the rural South during the Great Migration.[34] The varying and expanding movement of "blight," as demonstrated in urban renewal discourse, created a space to which a person could attribute their greatest fear. This view distorted the view of communities and urban centers. Herscher notes, "As 'blight,' the impoverishment of the spaces to which the socially excluded were confined became an effect of their inhabitation rather than of urban segregation maintained by zoning, covenants, and violence alike."[35] In other words, the residents of the Lower Hill were the cause of blight instead of the victims of it. Therefore, the removal of these residents and the demolition of the "blighted" neighborhood would achieve the desired outcome—a new modern city.

In the examples that follow, notions of progress in the Lower Hill are presented as the positive consequences of overcoming the blight metaphor. In a 1950 brochure promoting the projects slated for the Lower Hill, for instance, the Allegheny Conference on Community Development draws on the ideal of a "modern" city: "At the present time, this area [Lower Hill District] is a welter of *substandard* housing, *obsolete* commercial structures and *narrow* cobblestone streets and alleys. It is *a blight upon our community* and nothing will do more to change the appearance and character of Pittsburgh than to *replace* this *old, worn-out* section with a park-like development, crowned with a great civic auditorium—and ultimately flanked with other *modern* structures."[36] This excerpt provides a more specific description of how housing, structures, and roadways of the Lower Hill were represented as blight that needed to be replaced. Negative adjectives such as "substandard," "obsolete," and "narrow" used to characterize the Lower Hill support the notion that demolishing this entire area would allow the city to take one step closer to being "modern." In a 1955 speech announcing the start of the plan, then mayor of Pittsburgh David Lawrence stated that multiple local, state, and federal agencies will "join hands soon to change the 103.6 acres of blight into an urban wonderland."[37]

"Blight" was also repeatedly used as part of the battle metaphors within the urban renewal discourse in Pittsburgh. For example, blight is sometimes personified within a battle metaphor as the foe or enemy to be defeated. This combined metaphor of battle and disease, where disease is the enemy, remains pervasive in American culture.[38] In urban renewal discourse, if one hundred acres of an area are blighted, then that area must be defeated through removal. The notion here is that blight was mysteriously infectious, suggesting that the only way to "fight" it was to remove it completely. A 1953 editorial on the urban renewal project in Pittsburgh's Lower Hill District neighborhood titled "The Fight on Blight" has several examples of this metaphor: "We have tolerated the Lower Hill district for a long time. Every Pittsburgher has known for years how badly this section was run down and how much it has cost us to do nothing about it. . . . *Combating blight* has been used with great success in other cities." This paragraph works in personifying the Lower Hill District as a foe that needs to be defeated through "combat." Blight itself may be difficult to understand, but a "fight against blight" indicates that blight is undesirable. Characterizing a neighborhood in this manner ignores the Lower Hill residents who would be adversely affected by the defeat of "blight." I do not mean to suggest that the editors of these pieces did not care about the residents, but the language they used fostered racist and white supremacist practices that worked by depopulating and then reanimating the Lower Hill as an enemy. Use of this metaphor focusing on the space as blighted obfuscated the people while still attributing the blight of the Lower Hill to them.

In addition to the battle or "fight" metaphor, blight is often depicted in various health-related metaphors. In the next excerpt, for example, the clearing of the Lower Hill District is a medical procedure performed by a doctor: "We're about to perform a *surgical operation* here. With the help of state and federal funds for slum clearance, the Lower Hill District's humble old structures are *scheduled* to come down and give way to a civic center bordered by modern housing."[39] The use of this medical-procedure metaphor implies that the clearing of the neighborhood will be precise and cause minimal damage. The City of Pittsburgh is a body that needs an operation to surgically remove "blight" and replace it with modern buildings. By referring to poverty and substandard housing as blight, the city's careful, "scheduled" removal (or relocation) would suggest that the community would thrive again.

Since blight is represented as a disease, other health-related metaphors about the Lower Hill were common in the Pittsburgh papers. In the next example, we see the Lower Hill characterized as an unsightly dead body part: "Now [the Urban Redevelopment Authority] turns its efforts to the Lower Hill District, for decades an *eyesore* and a *dead hand* on Downtown growth. One hundred *blighted*, slum-ridden acres in that area are to be cleared and redeveloped for modern civic residential uses."[40] What is problematic about this metaphor is not that "slums" should not be rehabilitated but rather that the metaphor suggests that there is only one way to solve the problem—removal of every "dead" building in the area. Another article extends this pattern, using the surgical-procedure metaphor alongside a gardening metaphor: "Slum clearance projects of the kind being planned for Pittsburgh's Lower Hill district are big and expensive. That's because the problem has been allowed to go *untended* for so long that *radical surgery* is needed to eliminate *blight*. But an application of some of the principles of the Pasadena plan could slow up the *creeping blight* that create slum areas."[41] This writer places the adjective "radical" in front of surgery, which gives the procedure a sense of urgency. The word "untended" suggests gardening—in this case, a situation in which the problem needs to be weeded out. The gardening metaphor is also used to promote ideas of progress, safety, and security, to which blight appears anti-thetical: "The plan for turning *blight* into *blossom* constitutes a far-sighted solu-tion. . . . The Lower Hill tuberculosis rate is triple, and its juvenile delinquency incidence is 2½ times higher than the City average."[42] The writer uses a plant metaphor to describe how the city will "bloom" with the removal of the Lower Hill and the construction of a "pleasure dome such as Kubla Kahn never dreamed of."[43] This article indicates the health of the Hill's residents and the actions of its youth as the target domain for "blight." This metaphorical con-struction suggests that getting rid of these problems will help save the "City."

In a 1955 speech announcing the start of the Lower Hill urban renewal plan, mayor David Lawrence shifted the meaning of "blight" and suggested that "blight" applies additionally to spatial design, uses of the land, the num-ber of people, and other factors in the Lower Hill. Lawrence stated, "The major objective of this project is the clearing of an area of massive *blight* which, due to a poorly designed street pattern, overcrowding, outmoded or completely lacking in sanitary facilities, improper mixed land use, has *dete-riorated beyond any point* where rehabilitation would be conceivable."[44] In this example, "blight" is all consuming, and nothing short of clearing the Lower Hill is possible. What is consistent across these metaphors is that the pri-mary focus is placed on the conditions of the buildings and rarely on the experiences of the people living in them. The language used to discuss the Lower Hill project insulates the readers from feeling compassion for the con-sequences that will befall the families affected by the project. As Herscher notes about blight removal in Detroit, "Race was never explicitly mentioned in any of these definitions of 'blight,' yet, in a city where wealth accumula-tion, education, employment, access to urban space, and other social and economic rights and rewards were structured by racial identity, race precisely contoured who and what these definitions applied to."[45] The same can cer-tainly be said for the Lower Hill.

The metaphor "blight" was also used as an official label, a designation that created access to federal funds. For instance, as described in a 1950 article in the *Pittsburgh Press*, the Lower Hill had to be designated as "blighted" by city officials so that federal money could be used for its demolition. This designa-tion was "preliminary to razing the entire area and replacing it with modern housing,"[46] This designation also highlights the rhetorical efficacy of the term "blight," including its varying and expanding metaphorical usages within the master narrative of urban renewal as it was deployed in Pittsburgh.

In many of the examples that follow, very little agency is attributed to city or federal government policies, evidenced by the widespread use of passive-voice sentence construction in which the subject of the sentence does not perform the action of the verb—the Lower Hill is blighted. This construction gives the sense that "blight" occurred naturally without any institutional causes. And, along these lines, the positive future of a modern city envied by others would also occur naturally.

This idealized future is another key feature of the master narrative in Pittsburgh's urban renewal projects, deployed, in part, by the constant use of the slogan "Renaissance." The Lower Hill District's development fell under the label of "Renaissance," which captured the desires of residents and the city government. Renaissance itself is defined as a renewal of life, vigor, or interest; rebirth; revival.[47] But when capitalized, the word harkens back to the movement in Europe that began in fourteenth-century Italy and lasted into the seventeenth century. The Renaissance was "marked by a humanistic revival of classical influence expressed in a flowering of the arts and literature and by the beginnings of modern science."[48] Scholars characterize this period as the transition from the medieval to the modern world. Given the historical significance of the term, to resist the Renaissance was to resist modernity and progress. In 1951, the *Pittsburgh Press* published an editorial on how the "new planners of Pittsburgh" have targeted redevelopment of the Lower Hill as part of the "spectacular civic Renaissance."[49] For the City of Pittsburgh, "Renaissance" functioned as a powerful euphemism for the urban renewal projects that displaced thousands of residents and businesses.

Another article published prior to the city council's approval of the plan noted that the Lower Hill project was "vital to Renaissance."[50] An editorial in the *Post-Gazette* reiterated a similar theme of urban redevelopment: "One hundred blighted, slum-ridden acres in that area are to be cleared and redeveloped for modern civic and residential uses."[51] Articles in these mainstream newspapers repeatedly concluded that to create a modern Pittsburgh, the city's redevelopment plan had to be implemented.

Urban renewal euphemisms, such as Renaissance, were employed by city politicians and newspaper editorials to provide a romanticized view of the city's future. For instance, in the following editorial, blight needs to be cleared first so that new modern buildings can be built in its place: "As detailed by the Urban Redevelopment Authority, 105 acres of the Lower Hill which planners call *a blighted area*, would be cleared. . . . Then the land would be cleared for some much needed buildings—an auditorium which could be used for summer opera, conventions, and sporting events. . . . All these things are needed and are desirable if Pittsburgh is going to keep up its *spectacular development* that is the *wonder and envy of many cities*."[52] This characterization of the project also places importance on the thoughts of people in other cities. This competition to create an ideal city, one that is a "wonder and envy" among other cities, is another reason for clearing blighted areas and displacing numerous residents. Similarly, in a 1955 speech, mayor David Lawrence stated that the multiple local, state, and federal agencies will "join hands soon to change the 103.6 acres of blight into an urban wonderland."[53]

This constant reinforcement of Renaissance and renewal by politicians, newspapers, and individuals established a narrative that demolishing one hundred acres of the Lower Hill was required for the city's rebirth. Mainstream newspaper editorials also argued for the need to build the civic assets that a city needs: museums, music halls, and so forth. For example, a mainstream Pittsburgh newspaper writer argued that "one hundred blighted, slum-ridden acres" of Lower Hill must be cleared and replaced with beautiful buildings for "civic and residential uses."[54]

Interestingly, the desire to renew the city by removing and replacing "blight" was reinforced in the African American newspapers as well, suggesting that the power of this narrative and the prospect of new housing may have initially persuaded the residents of the Lower Hill, many of whom did not resist the plan when it was first implemented. For example, the *Pittsburgh Courier*, one of the nation's most prominent African American newspapers at the time, printed the following in 1950: "Broken-down housing, overcrowded living conditions, lack of sanitary facilities and obsolete street patters and the general deterioration of the district were some of the factors reviewed by the Commission in determining officially what has long been known that the Lower Hill is blighted."[55] However, while the African American newspaper admitted the existence of blight, it also emphasized the need for better housing for the public residents. So, one of the key differences was how recognition of blight could create different pathways of response to it: the city's response was equal to "cut it out." The residents' response, in contrast, addressed why it was happening and where it was coming from, and considered the conditions through which blight could not grow or spread.

The *Pittsburgh Courier* featured a series of articles that reinforced the idea that redevelopment of the Hill was necessary, but the newspaper also questioned what impact redevelopment would have on the low-income residents of the area. African Americans in Pittsburgh associated modernity with better housing. One writer for the *Courier* described how Lower Hill residents could benefit from the redevelopment plan: "Many people who now reside in dingy, crowded back streets of the Lower Hill will be eligible for public housing. . . . For those who are found eligible, the entrance into a public housing community will be the first time in their lives that they have enjoyed a new home, one with adequate space and facilities. The street won't be their children's only playground. Wintry blasts will no longer make the inside of the house as cheerless as the outside."[56] For African Americans in Pittsburgh, it was the promise of improved housing that held the most importance for the city's redevelopment plan and overall renewal. Like the *Courier*, the Urban League of Pittsburgh first saw the federally supported urban renewal program as a "vehicle to improve housing and job opportunities for the African American community."[57] In short, for many within the African American community, the ideas of modernity and Renaissance meant better housing for residents of the Lower Hill.

Despite differences in emphasis, the effect of urban renewal's wishes and fears found its way into the discourse of residents of the Hill District. A 1954 essay contest titled "What Pittsburgh Redevelopment Program Means to an Eleventh-Grade Student" was held by Duquesne University, a private college located near the Hill District and a potential benefactor of one of the urban renewal projects. One of the winners was an African American student from the Hill District who ended his essay with the following: "Beautiful residential streets and modern houses will soon be available for just about everyone. The specially designed arena to be built in the Lower Hill district will provide great enjoyment for many years to come. . . . I shall tell one and all, whom I may meet, how our city has shown the rest of the world that it is not only the industrial giant of old but that it is also the most modern city in America."[58] But, of course, this vision of the future was not held by the city government. Not only was the housing that was built insufficient, but many African Americans also did not have the same opportunities to buy new housing in other mostly white neighborhoods. City officials did little to prevent African Americans' exclusion from these neighborhoods. For example, residents in the north side of Pittsburgh resisted the idea of public housing in their neighborhood. In a response to this resistance, an African American newspaper editorial stated, "We shall extremely regret the transformation of this housing issue into a political issue based on race. . . . We do not believe the best white citizens in our community want to see Negroes, or any other group, permanently restricted to a slum ghetto."[59]

This response from white residents suggests that their mythic images of a renewed Pittsburgh operated on the then present "racial divide"; these residents did not include African American residents in their imagined "City of the Future." Instead, they believed urban renewal would create a city center where people living in the suburbs (i.e., white people) would either return

to the city to live or at least come to the city to be entertained at a basketball or hockey game. In terms of race, the future ideal city as conceived by
1950s public officials should look no different than it looked prior to urban
renewal—racially divided; at best, with Black people occupying a smaller foot-
print in the city or, at worst, with Black enclaves having been removed and no
places provided for Black residents to go. Regardless, this ideal held a competing vision of divide and expulsion with anti-Blackness at the center of it.

In short, city officials and mainstream newspapers repeated the claim
that the Lower Hill was the central obstacle in the urban renewal narrative,
resulting in a belief among many Pittsburghers that the Lower Hill had no
redeeming qualities. While the blight metaphor helped politicians create a
policy for urban renewal by placing "blight" in opposition to the city's potential prosperity, the residents and business owners who lived and prospered
in the Lower Hill were almost entirely absent from this master narrative.
The power of the master narrative was made clear in the July 6, 1953, public
hearing before city council regarding the Lower Hill proposal. According to
city records, there was "little opposition" to the civic auditorium plan. On
July 12, 1953, the city council approved the plan. Three years later, in November 1956, the city invoked the policy of eminent domain, razing one hundred
acres of land and displacing nearly nine thousand people in the Lower Hill
District, some of whom were forced into public housing in three separate
parts of the city.[60]

Resisting Urban Renewal in Pittsburgh Through Rhetorical Strategies of Place

Prior to the demolition of the Lower Hill, Pittsburgh's Urban Redevelopment
Authority had promised new, clean public housing in other parts of the city,
as well as new, affordable housing built on the very acres that were razed by
the bulldozers and wrecking balls. Yet the city government, like those of many
other American cities in the 1950s and 1960s, failed to follow through on
these promises. After the destruction of the Lower Hill (fig. 3), many African
American residents in Pittsburgh soon felt betrayed by those who had urged
them to support the urban revitalization plan. To make matters worse, the city
government was now looking to increase redevelopment in the Middle and
Upper Hill as part of the city's "Renaissance." The proposed cultural district
that would connect downtown Pittsburgh with the University of Pittsburgh
would mean more destruction in the Hill District.

Fig. 3.   Demolition zone for the Civic Arena, with Marpec Construction Company Contract Hauling truck, in front of Bethel AME Church, possibly Elm Street, Lower Hill District, in Pittsburgh, 1957. Photograph by Charles "Teenie" Harris (American, 1908–1998). Black and white, Kodak safety film, 4 × 5 in. (10.20 × 12.70 cm). Carnegie Museum of Art, Pittsburgh. Heinz Family Fund, 2001.35.4091. Photograph © Carnegie Museum of Art, Pittsburgh.

When the city began looking at the Upper Hill neighborhood for future development, the painful lessons of the Lower Hill emboldened the remaining residents to organize a resistance to future urban renewal plans. Established organizations such as the Urban League and the Hill District Homeowners Association worked together to facilitate meetings with the city to discuss community interests.[61] To prevent any more destruction in the Hill District, neighborhood leaders Frankie Pace, Robert Lavelle, and James McCoy Jr. formed the Citizens Committee for Hill District Renewal (CCHDR). Frankie Pace was a community activist and owner of Pace Music Store (see fig. 4). Robert Lavelle, founder of the former Dwelling House Savings and Loan, "was as much preacher as banker in his evangelistic crusade to increase homeownership among the low-income residents of Pittsburgh who had trouble getting loans from mainstream banks."[62] James McCoy Jr. was a civil rights activist and worked to integrate the steelworkers union.[63]

Fig. 4. Portrait of Frankie Pace standing in front of Pace's Citizen's Committee for Hill District Renewal Office, ca. 1960–75. Photograph by Charles "Teenie" Harris (American, 1908–1998). Gelatin silver print, 10 × 8 in. (25.40 × 20.32 cm). Carnegie Museum of Art, Pittsburgh. Gift of the Estate of Charles "Teenie" Harris, 1996.69.326. Photograph © Carnegie Museum of Art, Pittsburgh.

To stop redevelopment of the Middle and Upper Hill District, residents and the CCHDR employed rhetorical strategies of place to counter the city government's claim that the entire Hill District was "blighted." As Harry Bray, the committee's coordinator, described, "It is most important that citizens of the Hill get organized and begin working on plans for their future area. We all know that the City Planning Department is working on a proposed plan for the Hill. Thus, this gives us an excellent opportunity to have a voice in the overall development of the new Hill."[64] Their responses are best interpreted through the lens of Black Rhetorical Citizenship, which centers place and cultural rhetorical traditions as constitutive. As discussed in the introduction, African American rhetoric, according to Maulana Karenga, is a rhetoric of community and communal deliberation, a rhetoric of resistance action, and a rhetoric of possibility oriented toward that which is good in the world.[65] These rhetorics are some of the discursive acts of citizenship that the BRC framework makes visible. Rhetorical strategies of place are specific tools that residents use to constitute these discursive acts. Further, because community suggests place, rhetorics of place are a fundamental aspect of African American rhetorics and BRC. Both symbolic and material (re)constructions of place have the ability to affect public discourse, specifically to resist the master narrative of urban renewal deployed by Pitts-burgh city officials. Thus, when we examine Hill residents' resistance to continued redevelopment as rhetorical strategies of place, we see how recon-structions of places within the community became a form of agency. As arguments against urban renewal, these reconstructed places help residents reclaim ownership of their community and create a place for community deliberation, unity, and civic action.

To stave off the threat of continued redevelopment of the Hill, the CCHDR and African American residents used rhetorics of place in two primary ways: (1) counternarratives to resist the city's master narrative of blight, including visual counternarratives of place that produced a map depicting their vision of a renewed and revitalized neighborhood that challenged the city's plans while simultaneously drawing from the ethos of nearby academic institu-tions by developing partnerships, and (2) the rhetorical (re)construction of "Freedom Corner" as a place for community unity and beliefs.[66] These strat-egies are not rigid in their categorization and often overlap during their exe-cution. But each strategy served as a form of civic engagement and allowed for residents "to consider new issues and see existing issues in new ways."[67]

Counternarratives of Place and "Home"

Counternarratives offer different and distinct perspectives from the master narrative and may encourage different forms of audience participation.[68] Thinking of counternarratives in this manner allows for narratives that are not overtly political to still serve a political purpose. For instance, narra-tives of nonpolitical events can still be viewed as political counternarratives because they bring attention or "presence" to events or issues that may unify or empower the audience. Chaïm Perelman and Lucie Olbrechts-Tyteca's concept of "presence" describes the selection of "certain events, facts, or information to present to the audience."[69] When the narrator simply brings these "elements" to the forefront, "their importance and pertinence to the dis-cussion is implied."[70] In an analysis of the effects of presence, Louise Karon suggests that presence focuses the audience's attention "while altering its perceptions and perspectives" and "disposes the audience toward an action or judgment."[71] Similarly, counternarratives can shift the focus of attention to overlooked events, views, and ideas that are excluded from or portrayed differently in master narratives. In addition, they can be viewed as a form of "counter-agency" when traditional agentive pathways are unavailable (e.g., speaking and being heard at a public meeting or hearing).

Counternarratives can also enable those hurt or oppressed by the master narrative to view themselves once again in a positive, empowered manner. Hilde Lindemann-Nelson's study on nurses suggests that a "counterstory" may undo the effects of a master narrative, which can "infiltrate a person's consciousness."[72] A counterstory can change self-understanding, resist the oppressor's viewpoint, and replace the oppressor's viewpoint with respect.[73] However, counternarratives need a venue or space where they can be read or heard. The constraints and affordances of racialized spaces (for Black and white residents) inform the aspects of BRC that allow us to see Black newspapers, Black churches, Black organizations, and Black social and literary clubs as spaces for these counternarratives to circulate in the community.[74]

COUNTERNARRATIVES OF THE LOWER HILL

As discussed earlier, many African American residents embraced the master narrative of urban renewal with a belief that redevelopment would be good for them and their city. Substandard housing owned and operated by slumlords was prevalent in many places, and the discriminatory housing policies at the time kept African Americans in one part of the city so that housing owners could take advantage of renters. Urban renewal, as it had been sold to the city, was going to change that dynamic and bring better, "bright, shiny" low-income housing. However, as the imminent destruction of neighborhoods became apparent, counternarratives that resisted the dominant narrative of blighted neighborhoods began to appear in the *Pittsburgh Courier*. Represented in the *Courier* was residents' shared belief that the Lower Hill was not as bad as city officials had depicted it, and no further changes to the Hill District would be permitted. These counternarratives were widely circulated within the African American community in "hush harbors," spaces within the community in which residents could speak their minds and make plans without fear of reprisal.[75]

A narrative analysis of these counternarrative texts allows us to see the oppositional relationship each has with the master narrative. These African American narratives directly countered the city government official's discourse of "blight" by providing another view of the Lower Hill. Personal accounts of events in the Lower Hill invoke empathy because the reader "sees" what the narrator wants the reader to see. By feeling sympathy for the former residents of the Lower Hill, the reader may also conclude that the Lower Hill neighborhood should not have been completely demolished. Finally, narrative analysis, when applied through the conceptual framework of BRC, reveals how narratives and counternarratives of place function as rhetorical tools that enable residents to enact agency; that is, to engage in forms of citizenship shaped by community identity, empowerment, and resistance, which are the constitutive elements of Black civic engagement.

For instance, narratives of reflection of a neighborhood's past can serve as a civic argument to preserve the neighborhood's present and/or future. In 1962, the *Courier* published Mary Burwell's memories of her life in the Lower Hill as told to a writer for the newspaper. The article does not state this elderly resident's importance to the community beyond her ability to describe specific events that took place in the Lower Hill. In this article, she tells numerous short narratives about people who lived, worked, or performed in the Lower Hill. She mentions more than 150 individuals by name. In analyzing this article, it is important to keep in mind what narrative theorist Mieke Bal describes as the different voices that speak in the text.[76] Since the narrative was told to a reporter, I refer to Mrs. Burwell as the narrator in my analysis (and in subsequent analyses).

The narrator begins by directly addressing the master narrative of the Lower Hill. The narrator states, "To one born and raised in the Lower Hill, the changes which have taken place, bring a touch of sadness, because the places we knew so well are no more. *Some people have the idea the 'Lower Hill' was a slum area*, always. This is not so."[77] With this introduction to her memories, the narrator has already created a framework signaling that the stories that follow will counter the belief that the Lower Hill has never been a vital part of the city. In the following excerpts, the narrator recalls one of the many families she knew in her neighborhood in the Lower Hill and their importance to the community: "The Halls, Sellers, Howard and George, lived with their housekeeper, Mrs. Russell after their mother died. Their father, George Williams Hall was the first president of the Loendi Club, which he organized while living on Pasture St. He also published a newspaper, the Pittsburgh Independent."[78] The readers of the *Courier* during this time would recognize the Loendi Club as an upper-middle class social organization for African Americans. The fact that this family was African American and had a housekeeper would also suggest an above-average income.

The narrator continues to make positive comments about the people she knew and grew up with in the Lower Hill. She writes, "I went to Franklin School on Logan St. . . . and some of my schoolmates became noteworthy citizens."[79] Some of the occupations and accomplishments of her friends and neighbors of the Lower Hill include grocery store owner, "colored school director," undertaker, jewelry store owner, "star" basketball player, barbershop owners, and several others.[80] Her sharing these narratives of the Lower

Hill challenges the notion that the neighborhood was not worth saving or rehabilitating. It affirms, rather, that the Lower Hill was a vibrant community full of African American business owners.

While Mrs. Burwell's narrative focused on the overwhelmingly positive features of the people in the Hill, other narratives provided insight regarding the nightlife and the colorful characters of the Lower Hill, which was also known as "Deep Wylie" by the residents. Most of the short narratives published in the *Courier* served the purpose of showing the importance of the persons mentioned: "Deep Wylie had its list of colorful characters . . . some good . . . some bad . . . some handsome . . . some homely clean to the bone. And its various establishments were equally colorful and unforgettable. Let's trip down memory lane."[81] This article also includes a host of characters whose actions are told through various multiple narratives. For example: "*Later*, W. H. (Pat) Patterson leased the entire first floor of the Star Theatre, *after* it closed in *1926*, for a general store in the front and a poolroom in the rear. He bought the three-story property a few years afterwards and continued in business until the Redevelopment Authority took over." These narratives demonstrate a strong form of presence as defined by Perelman and Olbrechts-Tyteca.[82] The characters may not be as prominent as the ones in Mrs. Burwell's narrative, but the telling of their stories gives them power and provides a human component that is absent from a metaphor-laden master narrative.

Examining the structure of the narrative also provides insight into its function as a counternarrative. For example, in the excerpt above, the clause "and continued in business until the redevelopment took over" is both a "narrative clause" and the resolution to the narrative. According to William Labov and Joshua Waletzky, a narrative clause cannot be placed anywhere in the narrative and still have the same meaning.[83] The location of this narrative clause signals to the reader how detrimental the actions of the Urban Redevelopment Authority were to Patterson's business operations. His story ends with this action because after this line is a short narrative about another business owner. This narrative also speaks to the chronological events that constitute the larger narrative.[84] Although this specific narrative text is about events in Patterson's life, it highlights the series of events in which African Americans owned and operated businesses in the Lower Hill that were later destroyed by urban renewal development.

The article ends with what could be described as a coda for the multiple narratives told in the article. Labov and Waletzky define coda as a "functional device for returning the verbal perspective to the present moment."[85] In other words, the coda provides the answer to the question of "what happens next?"

The article's narrator states, "And now, in 1962, colorful Wylie Avenue is DEAD! Urban redevelopment could not be denied."[86] As a coda, this declaration not only personifies the fate of the Lower Hill and names "who" is responsible for its demise; it also functions to bring the reader back to the ongoing consequences of urban redevelopment: the death of the Lower Hill.

In response to the Deep Wylie article reminiscing about the Lower Hill, a reader sent a reply listing his memories about visiting the Lower Hill as a child. On its surface, the collection of narrative fragments does not appear to present a significant political response to the master narrative about the Lower Hill as a "blighted" area. But taken together, these fragments help to shape an alternative identity for the Lower Hill—one that contrasts sharply with the master narrative of "blight." Because these narrative fragments are "filtered" through the narrator's consciousness, readers may be more able to see the Lower Hill in the same way that the narrator sees it.[87]

For example, the narrator of the article shares one of his earliest memories of childhood. "It was around 1925. . . . I remember my mother taking me to the old Star Theatre where I saw my first silent movie."[88] A like-minded person in the readership of the *Courier*, one who also remembers his or her first movie, may empathize with the narrator. The narrator continues telling the positive events of life in the Lower Hill: "I remember when Wylie Ave. and Fullerton St. looked like 125th Street here in New York, on a Saturday night. Gaiety and laughter everywhere, throngs and throngs of well-dressed people living it up as though there were no tomorrow."[89] But, in addition to these positive features, the narrator also names characters that did fewer positive things, which helps to humanize the neighborhood and make the account realistic rather than merely nostalgic: "The lower part of the Hill District had drama of every description. When 'Grey Eyes,' the gambler was slain, people talked about his death for months. He was one of the most feared men who ever walked the Hill."[90] By humanizing the neighborhood in this way, the narrator creates narrative verisimilitude, which is portraying an authentic life in the Hill to counter the inauthentic notions of her community. Throughout the narrative, events are told from the narrator's vantage point. This narrative situation, as defined by Suzanne Keen, may allow the reader to empathize with the author/narrator as he is telling these events and thus, in this case, to view the Lower Hill differently than it appears in the city's master narrative of urban renewal. In addition, this story may assist in galvanizing its audience in opposition to the master narrative, as appears to have been the case when Pittsburgh's urban renewal project later turned its sights toward the Upper and Middle parts of the Hill District.

The articles printed in the *Courier* begin to take a different tone against urban renewal in the early 1960s, signaling the Hill residents' growing resistance to the redevelopment of their neighborhood. A series of articles published in 1961 told the stories of people who were displaced by the Lower Hill redevelopment project. In the introduction to these narratives, the *Courier* makes extensive use of "judgmental commentary" on the events that took place in the Lower Hill.[91] For example, the following excerpt highlights the negative consequences of "renovation" that the city appeared unwilling to acknowledge: "When Pittsburgh (The Renaissance City) proudly displays its renovation of the Golden Triangle, highlighted by the $28 million Civic Arena, to many citizens and visitors . . . it has 'swept under the rug' its dregs of human misery'—these displaced persons, a majority of whom are Negroes, who either have not been relocated or unable to find suitable housing on their own."[92] Such commentary within a narrative text allows the narrator to take a stand in opposition to the master narrative of the Lower Hill. These counternarratives in the Black newspaper are functioning as rhetorical strategies of place to remind residents what was lost and prevent it from occurring again.

These narratives became a part of the urban renewal "discursive field," which is "comprised of local history, folklore, private conversations, and public rhetoric."[93] In subsequent years, other citizens and leaders in the African American community would access this field to organize resistance to future urban renewal plans. Recasting the Lower Hill as a place that should have been saved also resulted in the Hill residents' more aggressive approach to saving the rest of the neighborhood.

VISUAL COUNTERNARRATIVES AND A MAP OF THE HILL

The CCHDR developed a new rhetorical strategy to save their neighborhood with the help of a young white Carnegie Tech architecture faculty member named Troy West, who opened an office in the early 1960s in the Hill District.[94] West had already been taken under the wing of a group of African American artists, including painter Ewari Ed Ellis and budding poet and playwright August Wilson. Their interactions helped West understand the importance and the value of the Hill District to African Americans. With West's technical expertise, the CCHDR developed a three-dimensional architectural model of the Hill District with the purpose of opposing the city's plans. The model also argued that urban renewal should meet the community needs and make a better place for the residents, and that the desires of city government and real estate developers should not trump the needs of the residents.

The CCHDR presented the model and plan to the city in January 1965 at the Anna B. Helman Community Center.[95] According to CCHDR chairman Lorenzo A. Hall, the model highlighted the residents' attempt to bring more affordable housing to the neighborhood instead of the city's desire for "expensive housing which so far has invaded the Hill up to Crawford Street."[96] Schools, homes, and small businesses that residents could either buy or rent were taken into consideration when designing the model. During the presentation to the city officials, the CCHDR explained the model and the residents' plan:

> In this part of the city, life takes place on the street. There is interest here. The sidewalks were widened to 30 feet on the sunny side of the street. Deciduous trees shade the passing parade in the summer. Shops face the new sidewalks and open on to it. Above the shops are houses. Houses step up the steep hill on a series of gradations. Beneath these platforms are the cars, utilities, rubbish removal, storage, etc. These activities underneath receive light and air from a terraced flower garden. Above are the play yards and gardens. The houses orientate to the sunlight and the summer breeze from the southwest. The houses that look upon the street have porches. The school nestles into the little community and completes the level change up the hill. The kindergarten and the first grade face into a sheltered court yard. The other elementary grades look out to the community. After school hours the building becomes an adult community center.[97]

This narrative of the imagined neighborhood supports the idea that maps and models are a way of seeing and depicting a reality. The CCHDR offered a counternarrative to the city's claims that demolishing the neighborhood and building a new arts center was best for the city of Pittsburgh. The model emphasized family and community. The CCHDR's argument was that community-oriented development for the neighborhood would be better for the residents. An arts center would not best serve the community and only exacerbate the limited housing situation in the neighborhoods where African Americans were permitted to live. The model served as both a symbolic and a material argument against urban renewal: a visual depiction of civic ideals and a material object for civic engagement. Both the artifact and the images depicted served as an argument against the wishes of the city, and this argument was made explicit in the residents' presentation of it to city officials.

The city's urban renewal director, John Mauro, attended the presentation and was reported as sitting "without comment except to say that he and other city planners will discuss and look at the CCHDR's plans and model later."[98] Based on my research, the city did not respond to the CCHDR's proposal and none of the changes appear to have been implemented after this presentation. The residents, along with West's technical expertise, would collaborate on the creation of a large "room-size map" to continue their argument for a better Hill District. The maps projected an image that residents wanted city officials to recognize and respect.[99]

The collaborative production of the model and map is just as important to African American rhetoric's notion of community as the visual images they displayed. Enlisting the West's services to cocreate the maps provided another avenue to unify the community and resist the policies of the city. The CCHDR claimed that "the modern-day idea is to unite people, not to separate them with artificial boundaries." This claim highlights the importance of community and possibility in the communicative practices of African Americans enacting rhetorical citizenship. Since residents were instrumental in the model's design and the plans for their neighborhood, the designed building, streets, and schools allowed residents to take ownership of their community while developing a sense of belonging.

The production of the model and map also enabled residents to exert agency through an otherwise hopeless situation against the city and federal machine. As an act of rhetorical agency, the map created a space in which the residents could visually express their ideas to the city and increase their ability to have the city hear their desires for the Hill District. Enlisting the help of West increased the residents' ethos with the city because of West's status as an architecture faculty member at a respected institution. In other words, West appears to have created more legitimacy only within particular contexts/rhetorical situations—those in which the experience and expertise of residents "needed" to be legitimized by external sources that were ostensibly more recognizably authoritative for the primarily white people who maintained power/control of these contexts. West and his design team (which included both graduate students and several Hill District residents) were also able to provide the technical knowledge to depict the desires of the community, whose members simply wanted to protect their homes.

By producing a map of what they wanted to see for their neighborhood and the city in general, the residents participated in and performed a visual act of citizenship that permitted them to first deliberate on which urban plan would be best for their community and then to argue for it in a larger public sphere. Their model countered the city government's view that most of the Hill District neighborhood was neglected or blighted space that needed to be developed. Residents used this map alongside other rhetorical strategies of place to save their neighborhood. However, the CCHDR also put into practice the ideas of community that they were advocating through the models and maps.[100] They bought and rehabilitated a building to demonstrate to the city what "local organizations could do to eliminate blight in their neighborhood without handing the area over to wealthier, whiter residents."[101]

Rhetorical Construction of "Freedom Corner"

To stop redevelopment of the Middle and Upper Hill District, residents also employed material rhetorical strategies of place to counter the city government's claim that the entire Hill District was "blighted." According to Danielle Endres and Samantha Senda-Cook's theory of "place in protest," reconstructing a place can function as an effective argument and "repeated reconstructions over time can result in new place meanings."[102] In other words, the symbolic and material reconstruction of place can influence public discourse just as powerfully as other forms of resistance. As stated earlier, BRC helps us understand how reconstructions of place, as forms of resistance, were acts of citizenship for Hill residents, and these reconstructions of place included naming the intersection of Crawford Street and Centre Avenue in the Hill District and claiming it as a material site of protest. This corner in Pittsburgh, which became known as "Freedom Corner," symbolizes the larger struggle of African American residents against urban renewal and federal housing policies. The corner also represents a cluster of material rhetorical strategies—for example, erecting a billboard—which Hill District residents used to get their voices heard by the city government and to unify the community. Freedom Corner's geographical location personifies residents' resistance against the City of Pittsburgh, and subsequent protest demonstrations in the 1970s and '80s would invoke these "rhetorical performances" of resistance from the 1960s.[103]

One important rhetorical strategy of place for the residents of the Hill District was renaming the street corner, which created a centerpiece for resistance rhetoric against the city's urban renewal policies. In the early '60s, James McCoy, former chair of the Pittsburgh NAACP's labor and industry committee, first empowered the corner by giving it the name Freedom Corner.[104] Naming is a powerful ideological act, the rhetorical effects of which can "shape our shared reality."[105] The renaming of the intersection of Crawford and Centre to "Freedom Corner" tied urban renewal resistance to the larger national Civil Rights Movement and the discourse of "Freedom" used by African Americans during the 1960s—the Freedom Rides in 1961, Freedom Summer in 1964, and the March on Washington for Jobs and Freedom in 1965. The *Pittsburgh Courier*, an influential African American newspaper, regularly used the term Freedom Corner in its coverage of the events and protests held there, which cemented the symbolic meaning of the corner within the community.

The clearing of homes, businesses, and churches in the Lower Hill ended just before Crawford Street (the areas circumscribed by the red line on the maps shown in fig. 1), which made the geographic location of the corner of Crawford and Centre ideal. It became a symbolic representation of resistance for the remaining Hill District residents, serving as a natural site for community gatherings. Because Freedom Corner was next to downtown, it also became a convenient place to launch many citywide demonstrations.[106] This location offered an unobstructed view of not just downtown Pittsburgh but also the new Civic Arena (fig. 5), which, unsurprisingly, served as a visual reminder of the false promises of urban renewal and a stark reminder to the gatherings of the CCHDR, the NAACP, and the UNPC at the corner.

The location was suitable on a practical level, as well. The Church of St. Benedict the Moor, an African American Catholic church, was located on the other side of the corner and provided hospitality and support during demonstrations, including access to restrooms for protestors and use of the sanctuary itself for rallies.[107] The Church of St. Benedict the Moor also served as a reminder of the churches that had been demolished in the Lower Hill and the ongoing threat of redevelopment; this church and surrounding homes would be cleared if the city's proposed Center of the Arts was to be built.

The geographic location of Freedom Corner was additionally significant because Hill District residents claimed that it established a symbolic boundary between "Black Pittsburgh" and "White Pittsburgh." They saw that the new housing going up in the Lower Hill was not being built for low-income residents who had been displaced by urban renewal. The space that had previously been majority African American was now becoming a primarily white space. An official in a Hill District organization asserted that Freedom Corner "symbolized the demarcation of the black vs. white community."[108] Ralph Proctor, a longtime civil rights activist, stated that the location was a "demarcation zone between the ill-fated urban renewal and what was left of the Hill."[109] Activist and former city councilman Sala Udin stated, "Residents drew a line in the sand at Crawford Street."[110] Another activist declared that Crawford Street was the "end of the line" for urban renewal in the Hill.[111]

Fig. 5.   View of the Civic Arena in the Lower Hill, Pittsburgh. Freedom Corner is to the right of the church at the center top of the photo. Photograph by Robert E. Dick. Allegheny Conference for Community Development, Detre Library & Archives, Senator John Heinz History Center, Pittsburgh, PA. Image courtesy of dck Worldwide Group, LLC.

This language of boundaries, often used to indicate conflict between nations, constructs the corner as not only a boundary to keep Pittsburgh officials from overtaking the rest of the Hill District but also a place for residents to congregate and organize to protect the boundary. Within this language of place, Hill District residents described Freedom Corner similar to the way relations between sovereign nations are generally described. The language of demarcation for Freedom Corner had a unifying effect for African Americans in the city, creating an "us versus them" mentality that social movements sometimes require when trying to make policy change. This place-based resistance rhetoric against urban renewal created an impetus for residents to unify in determining the future of their neighborhood.

Freedom Corner was a symbolic site of resistance to urban renewal, but it also became an important material site for protest. One protest, in particular, centered on the ironic fact that not only were African American homes and businesses destroyed in the Lower Hill but also African Americans were excluded from the labor pool that was redeveloping these areas. The 1969 "Black Monday" march, organized by the Black Construction Coalition, protested the lack of construction jobs for African Americans in Pittsburgh. The march lasted two hours and wound three miles from Freedom Corner through downtown and back.[112] These incursions from "Black" Pittsburgh into the "white" downtown drew the attention of government and business officials.

Freedom Corner also served as a place for other political demands. In July 1965, a small march was led by several civil rights organizations, including the NAACP, to protest police brutality. The organizers intended to end their march with a sit-in at the county building, but all ten protesters were arrested before reaching their destination.[113] Three years later, in 1968, the local NAACP chapter planned a march at Freedom Corner in response to the assassination of Martin Luther King Jr. These protests reveal how African American activists and residents transformed the corner of Centre and Crawford from a site of urban renewal resistance into a site of broader social, civil, and economic protest. By rearticulating the meaning of this corner through protests, billboards, and meetings, the corner became a focal point of both symbolic and material sites of civic resistance, civic engagement, and community unification. This rearticulation of the street intersection as a place for civic engagement created what has since become known as Freedom Corner.

In 1969, members of the CCHDR, UNPC, Model Cities, and the Pittsburgh chapters of the Urban League and the NAACP erected a billboard at Freedom Corner. Overlooking the newly constructed $22 million Civic Arena, the billboard read: "Attention: City Hall and U.R.A.: No Redevelopment Beyond this Point! / We Demand: Low Income Housing for the Lower Hill" (fig. 6).

The billboard's location and message strove to accomplish three rhetorical goals. First, by claiming the corner of Crawford and Centre, it sent a clear message of resistance to Pittsburgh City Hall. The billboard faced downtown and was situated so that it was visible to anyone attending an event at the new arena. The text of the billboard also uses strong indicators of emphasis. The word "NO" is underlined and printed in larger and bolder type than any other word on the billboard. An exclamation point ends the phrase and further emphasizes the citizens' ultimatum that further redevelopment would not be supported. "We Demand" in the second section is also underlined. The verb "demand" is a performative verb often used when "it is important that a person's intentions in saying what he or she says be absolutely unambiguous."[114] The billboard's language is also consistent with the elements of revolutionary

Fig. 6.   Billboard inscribed "Attention: City Hall and U.R.A. No Redevelopment
Beyond This Point! We Demand Low Income Housing for the Lower Hill,
C.C.H.D.R., N.A.A.C.P., Poor People's Campaign, Model Cities," at Crawford
Street near the intersection with Centre Avenue, Hill District, Pittsburgh, 1969.
Photograph by Charles "Teenie" Harris (American, 1908–1998). Black and
white, Kodak safety film, 4 × 5 in. (10.20 × 12.70 cm). Carnegie Museum of Art,
Pittsburgh, Heinz Family Fund, 2001.35.9463. Photograph © Carnegie Museum
of Art, Pittsburgh.

rhetoric as defined by Arthur Smith (now known as Molefi Asante) in *Rhetoric
of Black Revolution.* According to Smith, revolutionary rhetoric is essentially
aggressive rather than defensive and becomes a unifying force.[115]

Second, the billboard both signals community unity and shows the community's endeavor to maintain this unity to stop redevelopment of the Hill
District. The four organizations that represented many of the residents in
the Hill District—NAACP, CCHDR, Model Cities, and Poor People's Campaign—had paid for the billboard. The language used on the billboard is
representative of the corner's function as a protest site for the residents of
the Hill District, reinforcing and unifying the community's resistive stance
against urban renewal. The sign also began to motivate more residents of the
Hill District to not only stop redevelopment of the Hill but also make other
political demands. A resident of the Hill District recalled, "That billboard

gave hope to those of us who had watched the demise of the Lower Hill. We had businesses and homes and we wouldn't give them up."[116] Essentially, the billboard unified the community by proclaiming resistance to the city government's continued urban renewal plans.

The third rhetorical goal of the billboard was to signal the African American community to take civic action. Since the new housing built in the Lower Hill was not affordable for those who were displaced by the construction, residents were determined that the Upper Hill would not become a "white space." However, they also simultaneously demanded that the Lower Hill become an integrated space and remained engaged in the developments concerning their neighborhood. The billboard complemented protest marches that would begin at Freedom Corner and end downtown; it also helped cement Freedom Corner as a physical place from which African American residents continue to communicate their views, ideals, and demands to this day. In other words, the corner of Crawford and Centre was transformed, as Yi-fu Tuan describes, from a "space" without significant meaning to a "place" endowed with value for the residents of the Hill District.[117] Freedom Corner and the billboard not only united residents of the Hill District to stop redevelopment of the Hill, but it also signaled the need for action on other community issues.

A Civically Engaged Community

In the end, the residents of Middle and Upper Hill saved their homes and businesses from mass demolition, but the damage to the neighborhood was complete with the loss of the Lower Hill. In 1967, the *Courier*'s Ralph Koger wrote:

> The promise to slum area Negroes at that time was that . . . no family was to be moved until new housing quarters are provided by the Urban Renewal Authority. . . . And then what happened? Only one luxury apartment building was built . . . which has windows on all sides except those looking toward the still slum-infested Hill District. Families were dumped wholesale into the Homewood-Brushton District and other parts of Pittsburgh, causing homes originally built for single-family occupancy to be pressed into service for two, three or more families. Instead of the jobs which the Pittsburgh Renaissance building boom was supposed to supply for Negroes and which were to be augmented

by the Lower Hill District urban renewal project, the rate of unemploy-
ment among Negroes in the remaining area rose to 18 per cent. . . . The
area was changed from a predominantly Negro territory to one which
is now almost all white.[118]

This narrative highlights how the master narrative of urban renewal helped
to both create and obfuscate the negative effects on the community. The narrative of urban renewal would continue among residents of the Hill District
and be deployed rhetorically in future city planning projects.

The language used in the 1949 and 1954 Housing Acts and subsequently
by city officials and newspaper editors bolstered arguments for urban
renewal policies that disproportionately targeted African American neighborhoods. These arguments illustrate how a master narrative is constructed
and repeated in order to implement a plan that fails to solve the problems of
the affected residents. As Murray Edelman notes, "Problems come into discourse and therefore into existence as reinforcements of ideologies."[119] The
ideology reinforced in the master narrative of urban renewal was that African American communities needed to be cleared out to create a prosperous
city or community.

As part of the master narrative, the "blight" metaphor was consistently
placed in opposition to the city—old versus modern, diseased versus prosperous, and sick versus healthy. Despite the verbal emphasis given to rehabilitation, "since 1954, less than two-tenths of one percent of the gross project cost
of urban renewal at the end of 1962 was for rehabilitation," strongly suggesting that, for all practical purposes, "the federal urban renewal program was
a clearance program."[120] As a result, the master narrative of urban renewal
informed the rhetorical strategies of resistance used by African American citizens who faced the implementation of new urban planning policies across
America during the 1950s and 1960s. In Pittsburgh, African American residents employed rhetorical strategies of place to resist urban renewal and
unify the community. These various uses of place—strategies made available in Pittsburgh because of segregation of both material and discursive
space—were also rhetorical acts of civic engagement in African American
residents' struggle for power with the city government. Residents circulated
narratives primarily through the *Pittsburgh Courier* since typical political and
deliberative pathways were less available, as Black people in Pittsburgh had
been excluded from government positions. Their efforts helped to halt the
mass destruction in the Middle and Upper Hill that had occurred in the
Lower Hill.

When we analyze through the lens of Black Rhetorical Citizenship the urban renewal policies and their targeting of Black neighborhoods, we begin to see the rhetorical significance of place, particularly in the ways in which African American residents established political and rhetorical agency against urban renewal. These textual, visual, and material counternarratives were forms of agency, acts of resistance informed by space and place that drew from a sense of community unity, civic rights, and oral traditions. BRC informs our understanding of citizenship enacted by African Americans and uncovers the conditions created for a different kind of agency that is outside of the mainstream acts of citizenship. The enactment of these rhetorical strategies of place in response to urban renewal highlights the connection between rhetorics of place and African American rhetoric. A BRC framework can bring visibility to the forms of citizenship enacted by African Americans who were segregated and needed to operate outside traditional discursive norms.

The next chapter considers how private and legal restrictions on Black mobility impacted the strategies available to resist the urban renewal master narrative introduced in this chapter. Because urban spaces were heavily racialized and imbued with social hierarchies, they determined the available actions of African American communities. Chapter 2 demonstrates how African Americans in St. Paul had to prioritize which battle to fight in response to the growing threat of highway construction. Their emphasis on open housing was intended to not only increase civic freedom but also to serve as a strategy to save their community.

2

"CAN'T SELL AND CAN'T MOVE":
RHETORICS OF PLACE IN ST. PAUL, MINNESOTA

The Negro will never be able to play his full part as an American citizen
and will never be able to develop his full potentialities as a human being
until he ceases to be segregated as to where he may live.
—Earl B. Schwulst, *New York Times*, January 17, 1960

Late in 1955, nine months before Reverend George Davis and his wife, Bertha Miller Davis, and his shotgun were forcibly removed from their home of more than twenty-five years, Reverend Floyd Massey caught word that the St. Paul City Planning Board would soon be receiving federal money for a proposed Twin Cities intercity freeway. A freeway, if built, would bifurcate the historically Black Rondo neighborhood, displacing all property owners between Rondo Avenue and St. Anthony Avenue. This devastation would eventually end with the removal of approximately nine hundred homes and businesses without full compensation to their owners.[1] Burdened with this information, Massey quickly reported back to his congregation at the Pilgrim Baptist Church, the largest Black congregation in St. Paul, Minnesota.

The rumors of a proposed highway had been floating around for at least a decade. In fact, Massey had used the rumors of a highway to lead a campaign to build a new elementary school because the old elementary school was located in the path of the rumored highway and any investment in the existing building would have been wasted. However, with the now looming passage of the 1956 Highway Act, the freeway shifted from rumor to imminent, and Massey knew that the Black community needed to respond quickly. Other urban renewal projects in St. Paul had displaced families in the densely populated "Negro District" and some of those families had difficulty finding homes in other neighborhoods.[2] It was becoming painfully apparent that if Rondo residents and business owners were displaced by the highway, they might not be fully compensated for their lost property or able to find other suitable housing.

In response to the highway plan, the Black community formed an organization that would be empowered to speak for the community, have conversations with city government, and keep residents informed of the progress. In January 1956, the Rondo–St. Anthony Improvement Association (RSIA)[3] was formed, "the first property owners' group to appear in connection with the proposed Twin Cities freeway routes."[4] This group assembled less than one month after Martin Luther King Jr. and the Montgomery Improvement Association achieved victory through federal courts in desegregating public buses in Alabama. But unlike the favorable federal court rulings in Alabama and the Deep South in general, the federal government was financing the efforts of Northern cities, like St. Paul, to disenfranchise African Americans by funding urban renewal and highway construction.

Understanding the great task at hand, Reverend Massey and the residents of Rondo also appointed Tim Howard to colead the RSIA. Howard was an owner and operator of a barbershop "on the same block on Selby Avenue" for nearly forty years.[5] These two men were already leaders in two important institutions in Black culture, a barbershop and a church—places where, on a varied scale, African American public deliberation often took place.

Because American communities have always been racialized through segregation, race is implicated in the contested spaces of urban renewal policies. Arguments over space via laws, policies, or violence are at the center of African American rhetorical history. As racialized "rhetorical spaces" in the urban North, African American neighborhoods informed the deliberative processes and rhetorical actions taken for the survival of the community. How might we understand the relationship between space, race, and rhetorical action? More specifically, how did residents in neighborhoods created, in part, by government-sanctioned racism and the discourse of segregation use rhetorics of place for civic engagement?

This chapter considers the origins, objectives, constitutive actions, and constraints of St. Paul's Black community response to the Twin Cities' (i.e., Minneapolis and St. Paul) highway plan in the late 1950s to highlight foundational attributes of Black Rhetorical Citizenship (BRC). It explores how the Rondo Community was organized through traditional African American leadership practices and highlights how Rondo community leaders and

residents used rhetorical placemaking (a strategy of rhetorics of place drawing from the historical, cultural, and economic importance of the community) to preserve a place for themselves and their community within a larger
place that did not want them. Rhetorical placemaking is both a concept and a
strategy to be utilized by a targeted community. As I discuss later in the chapter, rhetorical placemaking is the way in which African Americans create,
maintain, and try to preserve "sites of endurance, belonging, and resistance."[6]
The Rondo community wanted to create a lived experience in St. Paul where
they would truly have freedom, humanity, and "full citizenship." This would
mean rerouting the highway, receiving higher property appraisals, and creating open housing laws. Taken as a whole, the rhetorical actions and tactics of
the RSIA reveal a strategy of rhetorical placemaking: making a place in hostile, contested, and racialized spaces. This strategy, as highlighted through a
BRC lens, reveals how African Americans must employ rhetorics of place as
a central feature of enacting citizenship.

The placemaking strategy included community organizing, civic education on property rights, meetings with government officials, and, in some
instances, individual protests against forced removal. Rhetorical placemaking was residents drawing from their cultural and spatial history of Rondo,
which includes the joyful and celebratory part of their history, to resist the
actions of state and city government. Rondo was a proud community of what
Marcus Anthony Hunter, Mary Pattillo, Zandria F. Robinson, and Keeanga-
Yamahtta Taylor call "Black Placemaking"—"the ability of residents to shift
otherwise oppressive geographies of a city [St. Paul] to provide sites of play,
pleasure, celebration, and politics."[7] Many Rondo residents were not opposed
to the highway but instead wanted more input on how the highway was going
to affect their space. More important, they wanted to disrupt the borders
of racialized spaces so that Black residents could live anywhere in the city
through open housing laws. Rhetorical placemaking is a key feature of BRC,
which African Americans employed in response to the laws, the racist covenants, and the redlining that created racialized spaces in the United States.

Urban neighborhoods are rhetorical spaces that have material and cultural dimensions that affect the actions of residents. Race impacts not only
who can manipulate material spaces but also who can navigate or occupy
those spaces. As Roxanne Mountford describes, the concept of rhetorical
space helps us interpret how material spaces affect "the geography of communicative events."[8] Because rhetorical space has both material and cultural
dimensions, participants interpret the space through the social expectations
generated across the dimensions of a given space.

As a racialized rhetorical construct, urban space is often reflected in material boundaries (railroad tracks, highways, and even walls) that restrict movement.[9] The material and social boundaries of urban space reflect Blacks' long and troubled relationship to citizenship within the United States. Although the migration North was part of many African Americans' search for equality, the racist designs of the system attempted to limit the mobility of African Americans. Given restricted mobility, rhetorical action by African American residents was limited in the ways these residents could make arguments and have these arguments be heard. How could Blacks mingle informally or have casual conversations (a feature of public deliberation and where citizenship happens[10]) with whites if they did not live together? Mobility thus became a primary feature of the Black Freedom Movement's conception of citizenship, and the connection between mobility and freedom served as the backdrop for one of the arguments over urban renewal, open housing, which meant that African Americans had the right to live anywhere they could afford to live.

In America's urban environments, both material and cultural space plays an important role in the social and the political lives of its residents. Racialized spaces are often contested and defined by inequality and difference.[11] In St. Paul, racialized spaces had a considerable impact on civic actions, shaping the rhetorical actions residents employed to exercise citizenship. In particular, the central rhetorical actions taken by Black St. Paul residents drew from the African American leadership tradition and implemented a strategy of rhetorical placemaking in response to city plans and urban renewal racial narratives. These rhetorical strategies were informed in large part by the racial narratives surrounding urban renewal and highway construction. These narratives grew out of federally and locally circulated discourses of urban renewal that pitted progress against notions of blight and slum applied primarily to African American communities. The widespread circulation of these narratives created symbolic boundaries that reinforced the material boundaries of racialized space that the residents in Rondo sought to disrupt.

History of Rondo

The first African Americans arrived in Minnesota long before Minnesota was admitted into the Union. Dred Scott, one of the more famous African Americans, and his wife, Harriet Robinson, lived at Fort Snelling (near what is now the Minneapolis–St. Paul International Airport) in the 1830s, each "belonging" to different army slave owners. Their time in Minnesota and the fact that one of their daughters was born in free territory helped influence the couple to pursue their case for freedom all the way to the Supreme Court, where they lost the Dred Scott decision in 1857.

St. Paul, given its proximity to the Mississippi River, was also an important site on the Underground Railroad. William Taylor, "a barber with a shop on Third Street near the post office, used his daily contacts to help slaves wishing to escape."[12] One escaped enslaved person, whose raft was towed up the Mississippi River, would later become the founder of the Pilgrim Baptist Church in St. Paul, where Floyd Massey would later serve as pastor.[13] Barbershop owners would continue to have important roles in the Black community. S. Edward Hall, who owned and operated a barbershop for sixty-two years, founded the St. Paul Urban League in 1923, an organization that would later lead the fight alongside the NAACP and RSIA for fair and open housing in St. Paul.[14]

As a result of segregation, Rondo eventually grew to be the hub of the African American community. Between 1950 and 1970, the African American population would increase by 388 percent; many relocated from the Deep South as part of the Great Migration. Although Rondo did not have the size or the resources of African American communities in other Northern cities like Pittsburgh, Chicago, or Detroit, it grew into a proud working-class community. On any given day in Rondo in the early 1950s, a person could walk and get a bite to eat at the Booker T. Cafe and Tavern on the corner of Western and Rondo Avenue; buy groceries at the Credjafawn Co-op store on 678 Rondo Avenue (fig. 7); take their dry cleaning to Love Tailor Shop, located at 306 Rondo and owned by Morris Love, a Black proprietor who later added dry cleaning to his business; or walk east to see if any apartments were available to rent at the newly constructed Black-owned Rangh Court apartments.[15]

Although housing segregation and other racialized government practices restricted the majority of Black St. Paul residents to the Rondo neighborhood, the residents created a vibrant community for themselves. This vibrant community, however, was threatened by the impending urban renewal projects, particularly those supported and financed by the Highway Act passed in 1956.

Highways and Racial Master Narratives as Political Discourse

African American migration had a profound impact on urban redevelopment policies in places like St. Paul and Minneapolis (i.e., the "Twin Cities").

Fig. 7.   Credjafawn Co-op Store, 678 Rondo Avenue, St. Paul, interior view, 1940s. Permission granted by Minnesota Historical Society.

By 1970, more than seven million African Americans had left the South to live in Northern cities.[16] However, this massive influx of Southern immigrants increased cities' populations and placed extreme pressure on city governments to absorb the large population increases. The ensuing urban redevelopment policies were supported by not just the Housing Acts of 1949 and 1954 but also the 1956 Highway Act. However, unlike the Housing Acts, the Highway Act refused to address family relocation and housing demolition. Even though government officials often connected the construction of highways to other urban development and renewal projects, the Highway Act allocated no federal funding to city governments for families and businesses displaced by these projects. The lack of funding for relocating was a willful decision by the Eisenhower administration because of the anticipated costs. This decision, of course, would be financially detrimental to African American communities because city mayors and business groups "believed that the removal of low-income housing and 'blighted' neighborhoods would be good for their cities."[17] As historian Raymond Mohl notes in his analysis of federal highway planning, "the advocates of urban redevelopment and urban renewal operated on 'the basic premise that slums were in essence a problem of deteriorated buildings, rather than a problem of the low income of those buildings 'inhabitants.'"[18] As a result, city officials, like those in St. Paul, saw federal highway dollars as a way to get rid of slum (i.e., Black) areas without a detailed plan or the resources to assist the displaced families and businesses.

This plan to target Rondo and its Black residents was confirmed years later when Clause Thompson, an assistant to St. Paul city planner George Shepard, wrote that Shepard and the state legislature wanted to remove the "slums along Rondo Avenue."[19] Thompson claimed that the "freeway location was a political design—not an engineering one." These claims are consistent with the racial master narratives of urban redevelopment, which leveraged metaphors of the role of progress in overcoming blight and slum. Somewhat ironically, these narratives also avoided acknowledging the racial division—spatial and social—that existed in the United States during the 1950s and 1960s. Although Northern cities suffered from segregation, which was primarily enforced by racial housing covenants and redlining, part of what made the urban renewal master narrative so effective was the absence of this segregation or its causes from the master narrative.

As described in the previous chapter, racial master narratives are created by those with the greatest ability to deploy their usage, such as media organizations and government agencies. The depiction of urban renewal by city officials and editors in most mainstream city newspapers and even in many African American papers helped create an image of the ideal city, a mythical futuristic city that was either free of racial division or had greatly reduced the division, especially in the urban North. St. Paul residents valued this image of the ideal city. When St. Paul received the All-American City award in 1955, the *St. Paul Pioneer Press*, a mainstream newspaper, provided considerable coverage of the award and the capacity of the city to "increase its population by 100,000 without overcrowding."[20] What the article harkens to, without saying explicitly, is that St. Paul could march toward an idealized future with increased housing, but that this growth would not (and should not) include Black people.

By excluding existing racial division from the urban renewal master narrative, city governments and local media led many African American residents of St. Paul to believe that the new urban redevelopment plans could possibly help them by ending discrimination in housing and that the city could truly be ideal for everyone. The master narrative of urban renewal helped to create the myth of a better tomorrow for all city residents. When local newspapers repeated words such as "modern," "progress," "blight," and "slum," they reinforced the master narrative that urban centers could become better places when existing neighborhoods were torn down and replaced with new buildings or highways. Unfortunately, even though the hope for urban rede-velopment in the 1950s was the creation of an improved community, not everyone in the community would benefit when the laws were passed (e.g., the Highway Act in 1956). This exclusion illustrates what Celeste Condit has pointed out: "a sharing of community may not include all individuals who, territorially, might live within the boundaries of the community."[21] In North-ern urban spaces, race often determined who fit where within the "commu-nity" and who would suffer when large changes were made.

Yet, the repeated narrative that ridding the city of specific blocks would help the city to grow and prosper reflected a belief that many influential African Americans also initially identified with. This belief rested on the idea that urban renewal could help bring equality. Robert Clifton Weaver, an Afri-can American who served as an adviser to Franklin D. Roosevelt and as the first secretary of Housing and Urban Development under Lyndon Johnson, believed that urban renewal could be an "opportunity or threat" for African American neighborhoods.[22] Weaver himself suggested that urban redevelop-ment offered a way to change the living conditions of African Americans by providing more ways of integrated living in Northern cities, but only if the cities were also committed to open housing. In St. Paul, this notion was the grounds on which the RSIA, along with the NAACP and the Urban League, was fighting for an open housing ordinance.

One of the challenges that the RSIA faced, however, was that local govern-ments were primarily responsible for making urban renewal program and project decisions and these decisions did not necessarily take into account the concerns over racialized space raised in the federal government's assessment of future urban renewal programs. In some sectors, the federal government echoed and, in some ways, granted institutional backing for the concerns held by residents. However, because implementation happened locally, these con-cerns could be ignored. In a 1956 document titled "Urban Renewal in the Interest of All the People: A Racial Relations Service Document," B. T. Andrew of the Office of the Administrator Housing and Home Agency noted the expected consequences of the urban renewal policies. He writes:

> In the very nature and purpose of its operation, whether federally aided or not, urban renewal will inevitably and intimately involve dis-proportionately high percentages of Negroes and other racial minori-ties because of the highly-concentrated incidence of their residency in the very areas to be cleared or rehabilitated. Thus inherent in urban renewal are at once vast potentials for improving, as well as great

dangers for worsening, the housing opportunities of minorities. . . . A more negative approach to urban renewal runs the danger of eventuation in some dire consequences to minorities such as direct hardships upon the displaced families, about two-thirds minorities, increasing their overcrowding in other areas, and furtherance of their segregation and exploitation through differential treatment, to the general detriment of the community as a whole.[23]

This document recognizes how open housing was a needed response to urban renewal projects because of the decrease in housing opportunities. Federal government officials were aware of the potential effect on Black communities but still did not include open housing in urban renewal legislation. The document also prescribes ways in which minorities could protect themselves, including participating in the public hearings, which were required for all urban renewal projects, and any "voluntary rehabilitation program."[24]

The potential negative impact of urban renewal on African American communities was also not lost on legislators and the private housing industry. In a Hearing Before the Committee on Banking and Currency, the President's Advisory Committee on Housing was unhappy with the proposed changes to the previous Housing Act (of 1949). They felt that the bill did not provide enough housing for displaced residents and relied too heavily on public housing. James Thimmes, the chairman of the committee, believed that more affordable home purchasing options should be made available to displaced residents. Thimmes appealed to the congressional committee to recognize the problems for minorities to obtain suitable housing, writing in a statement: "To solve the minority housing problem, special attention must be given to making sites available for new construction of units available to minorities; the tendency to squeeze minorities into overcrowded, restricted areas must be successfully resisted; and the relocation of minority families in slum areas which are demolished must be provided in such manner as to provide better housing and more democratic neighborhood patterns."[25] As Thimmes's statement demonstrates, the negative impacts of urban renewal policies were not unknown or unknowable. Unfortunately, the problems described in these federal-level assessments could be ignored because the final determination of which projects would be implemented was made by local agencies. As was the case with St. Paul's city government, the planning processes of local governing bodies had specific agendas that focused more on "slum clearance" and removing blight and less on creating enough housing for displaced residents. Because Congress did not do enough to prevent predictions like Thimmes's, affected residents had to organize to get their voices heard and seek change at the local level. Creating this change meant resisting the racial master narrative of urban renewal, which ignored the needs of African Americans and instead focused on the perceived greater good of the city. BRC helps us see how community organizing and African American leadership are creative acts of citizenship in response to the rhetorical situation of urban renewal in St. Paul.

Community Organizing and African American Leadership

The segregation and isolation of African Americans in the urban North limited them from full participation in public deliberations, but it did provide crucial spaces in which they could organize and strategize. Thus, it was no surprise that the Rondo community selected a preacher (Floyd Massey) and a barber (Tim Howard) to represent them and lead the Rondo–St. Anthony Improvement Association. The preacher is the traditional social justice leader in the Black community, and the barber is an obvious choice to lead business owners who are rooted in the community. As Quincy Mills notes, "Unlike churches, barber shops are profit-generating institutions that various classes of men enter, for grooming services or to socialize, without much at stake; no professions of faith or obligations of membership are required."[26] It is in these Black public spaces where civic dialogue takes place.

When Floyd Massey and Tim Howard began working to save their community, the political and social environment was strongly influenced by fears of highway construction and displaced community. While both men knew it would be difficult to stop the highway, they believed there was a slight chance they could dissuade the city planning committee from building the highway through Rondo and St. Anthony.

As part of their organizing the community against the highway, both men brought their own version of the African American leadership tradition. Whatever the community's response to the highway construction would be, they knew that it had to be organized and unified. As a Baptist preacher, Reverend Massey drew from the Afro-American jeremiad tradition to unify and organize the community. The jeremiad style of leadership draws from narratives of the Bible to unify African Americans, as well as to find understanding with a moderate white Christian audience, an audience that was crucial when building political community.[27] Given that a large portion of the African American community in Rondo was churchgoing,[28] this leadership style would appeal to many residents as well as garner allies outside of the community. Massey, a North Carolina native, received his divinity degree from Colgate Rochester Divinity School in Rochester, New York, and served as the pastor of Pilgrim Baptist Church from 1944 until 1965. By 1956, he had already served as the first vice president of the St. Paul Urban League and was a member of the Rent Control Advisory Board and a mayor-appointed member of the Planning Board of St. Paul.[29] He routinely integrated religion and social justice in his sermons during the time of the freeway crisis. For example, on "Race Relations Sunday" at the Pilgrim Baptist Church, he gave a sermon on "Brotherhood in Our Time."[30]

Drawing from the Bible for social justice reasons is also a feature of what Manning Marable calls a "messianic" style of leadership, a rhetorical style that is rooted in the Old Testament, where figures such as Moses and Joshua are "deliverers of an oppressed, enslaved people who found themselves in a foreign land."[31] Historically, Martin Luther King Jr. and Frederick Douglass practiced this style of leadership. As Marable notes, the merger of the secular and the spiritual "expressed itself as the ability to communicate effectively programs that in some measure represent the interests of most blacks, while also constructing bonds of collective intimacy through appeals to the spirituality and religiosity among many African Americans."[32] What Marable is suggesting is that merging the spiritual and the secular allowed African Americans to organize around social justices issues, like open housing, because they were simultaneously religious causes. The spatial analogies of the messianic style of leadership also apply to African Americans' lived experience of urban renewal. Many African Americans were immigrants from the rural South now living in the strange landscape of the urban North. For many in the Rondo community, open housing represented freedom and full citizenship. Massey's rhetorical leadership style drew from this spiritually focused tradition; as a minister, he was leading a large congregation, and as a community leader, he was actively working within mainstream organizations to achieve goals of equality.

The biblical leadership style was not shared by Timothy Howard, owner of "Howard and Gonzalez" (his pet chihuahua) barbershop. Described as a "vehement" critic of racial discrimination, Howard strongly supported his "constituents'" interest in trying to save their homes from urban renewal policies.[33] After an angry exchange between St. Paul Black leadership and city councilman Milton Rosen over comments Rosen had made about "rabble rousers" misleading Northerners about the treatment of African Americans in the South, Howard demanded an immediate apology from Rosen and replied: "Not only has this trust been apparently misplaced but the intelligence of the community has been belittled by the statements that the negroes of the south are not being mistreated or suppressed. Who is Mr. Rosen trying to fool?"[34] Howard's unapologetic and "unrelenting" approach toward city officials regarding the freeway would prove beneficial in obtaining the RSIA's main objectives of fair housing prices and input on highway design. A few years after the battle over the freeway, Frank Marzitelli, the deputy highway commissioner, said of Howard: "If every community had a Rondo–St. Anthony Highway organization and a Tim Howard to guide and direct it, the stupendous task we face would be more satisfactorily accomplished for the mutual benefit of all involved."[35]

Massey's and Howard's dual leadership of the RSIA was also reflective of the community spaces they were responsible for. The church and the barbershop/salon are vital Black spaces for political, social, spiritual, and economical discourses in a segregated community. Many Black people will spend significant time in at least one of these places where deliberation takes place, especially when important events are affecting the community. Cities, for African Americans, were not the civic ideal described by the ancient rhetoricians of Greece, in which, more than a mere place, a city "was also a people, bound together by shared ancestors, values, customs, institutions, and language."[36] For African Americans, this ideal may have held true on a neighborhood level, but common spaces among Black and white people were few and far between in segregated Northern cities.

Redlining was one tool that reinforced segregation and limited informal interactions between Black and white people while also leaving Black people vulnerable to urban planning decisions. According to a report by the Urban Land Institute: "During the 1930s, Rondo was disparaged through mapping. The Home Owners' Loan Corporation's residential security maps, otherwise known as redlining maps, label Rondo as 'hazardous,' the lowest-ranked category, while sociologist Dr. Calvin Schmidt created a map in 1935 labeling Rondo as the 'Largest Negro Section of the City.' Among other targeted policies, these maps paved the way for routing I-94 through Rondo."[37] Given these mapping practices, African Americans did not live in the neighborhoods or belong to the organizations of government leaders and other influential persons in the city. Thus, informal places for deliberation on city issues that affected African Americans were rarely accessible to members of the African American community.

Still, the inaccessibility of white spaces did not mean public deliberation failed to occur among African Americans in the community. Instead, the community created and relied on safe spaces or "hush harbors." Vorris Nunley's examination of hush harbors, for example, highlights how safe spaces, like the barbershop/salon, enabled African Americans to discuss politics, pop culture, and other issues that affected their community. Because race is based primarily on exclusion, space becomes "an ideal means of creating and asserting racial identities."[38] Since African Americans owned and operated these places in the community, they created a forum in which residents could employ a "hush harbor rhetoric" that critiqued the actions of city officials on policies regarding urban renewal and discuss their ideas and proposed actions. A hush harbor rhetoric is constructed through Black public spheres with a distinctive relationship to spatiality (material and discursive), audience, African American nomoi (social conventions and beliefs that constitute a worldview or knowledge) and epistemology.[39] The barber shop and the church are just some of the spaces where hush harbor rhetoric took place. We can assume that the rumors and discourses of the St. Paul highway construction and its potential effects on the Black community had been circulating within these spaces for years.

Rhetorical Placemaking in Rondo

The objectives of the RSIA in response to the proposed highway highlight the civic component of belonging to place, specifically to Rondo and more broadly to St. Paul. Urban renewal policies and their targeting of Black neighborhoods help rhetoric scholars think about spaces rhetorically—that is, to consider how actions were constrained or afforded within these spaces. African Americans drew from their sense of autonomy, civic rights, and oral traditions to argue for their community. However, because these community spaces were segregated and imbued with social hierarchies, the spaces themselves helped determine the acts of citizenship available to Black residents: what they could and could not do, what they could and could not say, and what constitutional rights they could or could not express.

Meetings for the RSIA, as well as community meetings about the proposed highway, were held at Pilgrim Baptist Church. The leaders used these meetings and the Black newspapers the *St. Paul Recorder* and the *Minneapolis Spokesmen*[40] to share plans, warn of real estate dangers, and inform the community of the latest developments in the construction plans. In addition to participating in all public hearings about the highway, the RSIA leadership also invited city government officials to the church to answer questions about the highway. These actions were necessary because Black neighborhoods were (and continue to be) materially and rhetorically comprised from the outside in. In other words, Black neighborhoods are often places in which those living outside of the community seemingly know and argue for structures or plans that *they think* are best for those living in the community.

To resist these impinging external forces, RSIA leadership and Rondo residents enacted placemaking strategies that were rooted in consistent acts of civic engagement and rhetorical citizenship. Definitions of placemaking tend to differently emphasize who makes a place and how. For example, according to Arijit Sen, placemaking is a "powerful role played by local, regional, state, and federal institutions in constructing social and physical worlds."[41] This view prioritizes institutions rather than communities and thus loses sight of the people who live in the communities. Another view of placemaking more closely aligned with a notion of *rhetorical* placemaking is that of critical geographers: "the set of social, political and material processes [and rhetorical processes] by which people iteratively create and recreate the experienced geographies in which they live."[42] This sense of placemaking, which highlights the creative roles of people within communities, better encompasses the ways in which African Americans lived, worked, and created institutions in their community to inform the meaning of the place. Their history of a place, their culture of a place, and their experiences of a place all create the meaning of a place. In other words, rhetorical placemaking is a collective placemaking.

Urban renewal in St. Paul, particularly the highway project, called on Rondo residents to respond with a placemaking strategy to either save Rondo or provide more places where African Americans could live. Thus, rhetorical placemaking is a form of democratic participation, an enactment of Black Rhetorical Citizenship, highlighted across several key features. First, rhetorical placemaking is the process through which residents organize to shape outcomes and create change for their community and the spaces within them. Second, rhetorical placemaking is the creative construction and reconstruction of place through discourse and materiality, which is manifested in civic actions. And third, rhetorical placemaking invokes place through narration, human connection, and personal experiences. These features of BRC were enacted by the leaders of the RSIA through their public language and by the community as a whole working together and sharing information to save their community.

In the sections that follow, we see how the RSIA tried to save the Rondo neighborhood through rhetorical placemaking while simultaneously seeking equal access to the larger community of St. Paul through an open housing ordinance and fair property appraisals. We also see the constraints of racism, segregation, and devaluation of Black spaces, which made the community's chance for success difficult.

The RSIA's Process of Deliberation and Community Organization

When the RSIA met on April 12, 1956, at the Pilgrim Baptist Church, the association was developing a placemaking strategy to save the vibrant Rondo community—a community created through Black agency and autonomy. By the time of this meeting, the association included "nearly 100 percent of threatened property owners and quite a few others as well."[43] The purpose of the meeting was to accept an invitation and issue a response to correspondence they had received from the St. Paul Chamber of Commerce about the proposed Twin Cities Freeway. The Chamber of Commerce had "invited this organization and other civic, commercial and governmental representatives to a public meeting at the Hotel Lowery."[44]

The meeting was long. Some thought the "perceived choice of objectives" was difficult.[45] But one thing was certain: the proposed highway would split their community down the middle and "force one seventh of its residents to leave their home."[46] By 1953, urban renewal had already displaced many residents in the densely populated community, many of whom were unable (or not permitted) to find places to live in other neighborhoods. The highway project would put even greater pressure on the limited housing supply and cause more overcrowding in the "Negro District."

After a long discussion, the group voted to oppose the highway plan that would come through their community, noting the difficulty in obtaining housing in surrounding neighborhoods and the devaluing of their property, which would make selling difficult. The association appointed Timothy Howard, George Brooks, and Charles Rogers to argue their position at the Chamber of Commerce meeting held on April 12. They made the following arguments at that meeting, as quoted in the *St. Paul Recorder*:

1) We are now and have been, consistently, limited in area which we can buy property.
2) No provisions for social planning, in regards to relocating displaced home owners, has been made by responsible officials.
3) Approximately 50% of the homeowners directly affected are 50 or more years old and for some of them the acquisition of another

home, the incursion of further indebtedness, is undesirable. In view of age, income and job status, ability to secure mortgage loans readily is a matter of question, under current practices.

4) Rumors for the past ten years about the highway coming through the area have been intensified, causing much confusion. The property owner has been strongly discouraged from making major repairs on his home, and in some cases forbidden to make major improvement; his property therefore is running down. The resale value of the property is practically nil because of the highway threat. The property owner is hampered, can't sell and can't move.

5) Business men are equally concerned because it is feared restrictions by zoning codes may put them out of business for good unless something favorable is forthcoming.

6) The proposed highway system would divide the residential area into smaller segments and cause inconvenience and disturbance because of noise and fumes.

Given these arguments, the RSIA called for the following:

What the Organization Favors

1) Compulsory open-occupancy to ensure suitable landsites and homes, i.e., make it possible for displaced property owner to relocate without restrictions. . . .

2) The organization also favors the recommendation of the Urban Renewal proposal to relocate and subsidize fairly the owner whose property is declared by authorities to be blighted or substandard.[47]

These objectives and requests outline the unfairness of the consequences of living in racialized spaces and of the mobility restrictions to African Americans seeking to live wherever they could afford.

Trying to save neighborhood life, property owners, and Black businesses in Rondo, the RSIA's objectives and arguments invoke placemaking as a rhetorical strategy to the proposed freeway through narration, human connection, and personal experiences. The objections to the freeway proposal capture the triumph and struggle of Rondo business owners, who had created economic opportunities for themselves despite not being granted federal or private loans or other resources to build and maintain their properties. In addition, the RSIA creates human connection by accurately noting the difficulty older residents would have purchasing a new home comparable to the one they currently owned. Their displacement would cause great financial difficulty. Therefore, the only hope in preventing the highway, at best, or limiting its disruptive effects, at worst, was the community unifying around the efforts of the RSIA. Organizing within the neighborhood was key in any hope of helping property owners to either save their property or give them fair payment. Rhetorical placemaking in a time of redlining and urban renewal meant that creating arguments to preserve Black spaces was paramount, as was continuing the larger Civil Rights Movement to argue against housing segregation because of its adverse emotional and financial effects.

The Northern Route and RSIA's Placemaking Arguments

The primary goal for the RSIA was to prevent the highway from bifurcating Rondo and destroying its main business street. One hope to save Rondo was the discovery of another option for the highway that could be used in their argument to state officials. The Minnesota Highway Department (MHD) and other civic organizations began planning for expressways as early as the 1940s, but the RSIA did not become aware of the plans until the 1950s.[48] Two different highway routes were proposed to connect St. Paul with Minneapolis: the "northern route" and the Rondo / St. Anthony Avenue plan. The northern route would have minimal effects on the residents of Rondo because it would travel north of their community along railroad tracks. This route was less populated and included more farmland, but it would add a few more miles to the trip between St. Paul and Minneapolis (fig. 8). The Rondo / St. Anthony route connected St. Paul directly to Minneapolis, but it would travel through the heart of the Black community. Although advocating for the northern route was the first option of solutions chosen by RSIA, the leaders knew it would be the most difficult to achieve because of the traffic data produced by the highway department.[49] What they did not find out until much later, however, was that the St. Paul City Council (a government body that would not have a Black member until the 1980s[50]) had approved MHD's Rondo / St. Anthony Avenue plan in 1947.[51]

One influential St. Paul city planning engineer, George Herrold, was opposed to the Rondo / St. Anthony Avenue highway plan; however, his opposition relied on external (and racist) assessments of the detrimental effects of the highway rather than the value of the places that Black residents had created within the Rondo neighborhood or the ways that residents might maintain these spaces or re-create them in other neighborhoods (i.e., through an open housing ordinance). Herrold maintained that highways

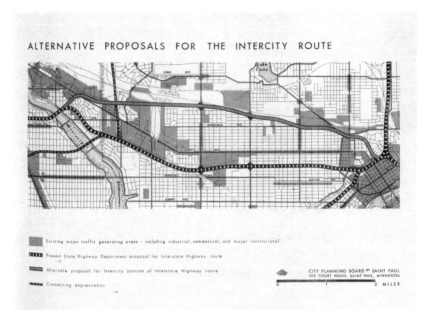

ALTERNATIVE PROPOSALS FOR THE INTERCITY ROUTE

Fig. 8.   Alternate proposals for the St. Paul intercity freeway route. Permission granted by Minnesota Historical Society.

built in urban environments would displace "negro neighborhoods,"[52] and he proposed, developed, and argued for the northern route of the intercity freeway plan in 1945.[53] According to Altshuler's history of the construction of Minnesota highways, Herrold argued for the northern route because two scenarios were likely if the Rondo / St. Anthony plan was chosen: "(1) displaced Negroes might try to move into other neighborhoods, public reaction would be extremely unpleasant and Negroes would find it virtually impossible to buy or rent homes in the neighborhoods to which they aspired; or (2) the Negroes might remain within their ghetto—reduced in size, more crowded, more completely Negro in composition."[54] In other words, because less housing would be available to Black residents, they would either overcrowd current Black housing or spill over into white communities. In objecting to the Rondo / St. Anthony Avenue plan, Herrold wrote, "the freeway idea . . . requires the moving of thousands of people, who must give up their homes, churches, schools, neighbors and valued social contacts, who lost the institutions they have built for their pleasure and profit."[55] In short, Herrold was a friend to the preservation of Rondo for the racist reason that he wanted to maintain white neighborhoods and not disrupt Black ones.

Although the RSIA agreed with this reasoning of not building highways through cities (but not the racist premise it relied on), convincing the St. Paul civic leadership would be difficult and time was an issue. Massey and Howard decided to split their labor; Howard would pursue the northern route objective, and Massey would concentrate on the open housing and fair property appraisal objectives. Both objectives feature the narrative of the possible plight of the Black resident after highway construction. Their strategy was first to argue for the toughest objective to achieve—the northern route—with the hope that at least the other objective would be met as consolation.

The leadership of the RSIA had a distinct interconnected argument strategy against the Rondo / St. Anthony route that could only be made by Black residents of St. Paul because only Black residents faced housing restrictions. The northern route provided an opportunity to argue against the racial practices of urban renewal. The highway plan and previous urban renewal projects were a constant and consistent opportunity to argue for open housing ordinances so that Black residents could live anywhere in St. Paul. The deliberative goals in response to the highway construction included the following:

1. Stop the highway by convincing the planning board to select the northern route to avoid bifurcating the Rondo community.
2. Provide open housing so that Black residents would be free to move where they wanted to within the city.
3. Compensate home and business owners with fair value for any property in the path of the highway.
4. Build the highway underground if they could not convince the planning board to select the northern route. An underground highway would at least limit some of the disruption to Rondo.

This argument strategy revealed itself at a state Senate committee meeting on February 27, 1957. Howard argued that the current highway plan was "causing great mental and financial concerns to persons affected by the freeway program."[56] Howard understood that the importance of Rondo to the residents was more than just financial, but also a way of life. Although he was a proponent of the northern route for the highway, Howard also maintained that "if the Rondo route was decided upon, his organization wanted immediate appraisals, and other relief measures because of the peculiar problem facing members of the organization who are Negroes."[57] Howard's argument shows the RSIA's awareness that saving Rondo would be difficult and other objectives must be met for the well-being of the community. Placemaking as a rhetorical strategy in this context means limiting the damage that will be inflicted on the community.

The RSIA's efforts to stop the northern plan would prove to be futile. Once federal funding became available to the states, the Minnesota Highway Department gave each local government one year to finalize plans and provide cost estimates to the Bureau of Public Roads for highway segments that passed through their jurisdiction.[58] Although St. Paul government officials would listen to community groups, their decision for the highway had already been made. The northern route was not seriously considered by the city because "the additional travel time beyond Saint Anthony Avenue to the Northern Route meant that Herrold's option would carry less traffic than their plan."[59] So, with the seeming failure of argument for the northern route, the push for open housing became even more important to the residents of Rondo. Freedom to live anywhere in the city would alleviate the housing shortage problem.

An Open Housing Ordinance and the RSIA's Appeal for Place Without Segregation

To save their neighborhood, the RSIA enacted a placemaking strategy in response to the city's desire to transform the cityscape into a place more convenient for white commuters. The RSIA's argument was that if we can't save Rondo as a place made for and maintained by African Americans, then all of St. Paul should be made available to us. This argument was a placemaking strategy because residents were attempting to dismantle the segregated boundaries of Rondo through civic action since less housing would be available in Rondo. Black residents wanted the freedom to live wherever they wanted in St. Paul and the surrounding areas. This argument raised questions of mobility and agency and demanded that segregation in housing come to an end. The association recognized the highway project as an excellent opportunity to push for open housing in St. Paul and allow African Americans to relocate to any neighborhood that they could afford to live in. Because the highway construction did not provide federal dollars for relocation, the RSIA called on the St. Paul City council to pass an ordinance to desegregate housing.

The issue of open housing brought the local chapters of the NAACP and the Urban League, along with the Citizens Committee for Open Occupancy, to work together with the RSIA. Given the experiences of families displaced by the highway, the president of the St. Paul branch of the NAACP maintained that "housing has become the number one problem facing non-white citizens in St. Paul today."[60] All groups met on Sunday April 18, 1958, at Pilgrim Baptist Church to discuss the housing situation, and each organization explained what they were doing to alleviate the housing problems. But, more important, community members were invited and asked to share the problems they were facing. This community meeting indicated the need for public deliberation among the Black community. And the Black church provided them a space in which to do so with the purpose of developing an effective strategy.

But the opposition to open housing was deeply entrenched in the legal and social practices of St. Paul, as it was in nearly all urban Northern cities. The Black newspaper the *St. Paul Recorder* highlighted these practices when it reprinted an excerpt from an April 1956 article of *House and Home*: "In northern cities, where Negro groups now object to all-Negro projects, the difficulty is compounded. Open occupancy requires choice sites if it is to attract any white tenants. Few communities have shown readiness to earmark these for anything but white tenants, though the method is subterfuge rather than segregation."[61] This excerpt shows how "subterfuge" was used as a euphemism for segregation in Northern cities. The suburbs were hostile toward African Americans, and the RSIA's strategy was to disrupt the practices that maintained segregated neighborhoods.

In addition to social barriers, the real estate industry erected institutional and legal barriers. Walter White revealed in his famous 1955 book *How Far the Promised Land* how the National Association of Real Estate Boards (NAREB) actively pursued and maintained segregation. Quoting NAREB's training materials, White writes:

> There is a natural inclination of the colored people to live together in their own communities. . . . Property values have been sadly depreciated by having a single colored family settle down on a street occupied exclusively by white residents. . . . Segregation of the Negro population seems to be the reasonable solution. . . . Frankly rigid segregation seems to be the only manner in which the difficulty can be successfully controlled. . . . The colored people certainly have a right to life, liberty and the pursuit of happiness, but they must recognize the disturbance which their presence in a white neighborhood causes, and forego their desire to split off from the established district where the rest of their race lives.[62]

This racist viewpoint, according to White, was taught to realtors across the country and implemented in various ways. St. Paul and Minneapolis followed this practice vigorously. A 1910 editorial in the *Minneapolis Journal* demanded that the Real Estate Board address the problem of the city's "considerable negro colony." It stated, "No one wants to do the negro an injustice. But residents will not tolerate African Americans moving into areas where they are unwelcome."[63]

The advent of restricted housing covenants was the most effective legal mechanism for maintaining segregation and keeping nonwhites out of certain neighborhoods. A covenant is a type of contract included in a property deed referring to the conditions attached to housing or land. In the first half of the twentieth century, racial covenants prohibited nonwhite people from buying or occupying housing and certain parcels of land in US cities for segregationist purposes. The Twin Cities landscape of segregation was certainly no different. In St. Paul, as in many Northern cities, racial segregation was enforced and maintained by the extensive use of racial housing covenants. For many in the private real estate sector, space and race intertwined with the language of housing covenants and the economic practices of redlining, which created material and cultural racialized spaces. The creativity that the Rondo community employed to navigate these covenants illustrates the importance of rhetorical placemaking in reconstructing community spaces lost to highway construction.

Racially restrictive covenants began appearing in deeds with greater frequency at the turn of the twentieth century, becoming commonplace and withstanding court challenges throughout the 1910s, '20s, and '30s.[64] The use of racial covenants became more widespread after racially restrictive zoning was struck down in 1917 (*Buchanan v. Warley*) and following a 1926 case (*Corrigan v. Buckley*) that validated and upheld their use.[65] By 1928, half of all homes owned by white people in the United States were covenanted.[66] Though racial covenants often included language identifying a range of racial, ethnic, and religious groups prohibited from occupying properties, in practice they primarily targeted Black Americans.[67] In 1948, a key Supreme Court case (*Shelley v. Kraemer*) determined that restrictive covenants were legal but not enforceable. However, racial covenants continued to be registered well after 1948.

Although racial covenants were often written into deeds by private developers and homebuilders and drew on language and examples developed by the real estate industry, they were enforced by the courts and endorsed and encouraged by the Federal Housing Administration (FHA).[68] The implementation of racial covenants required the mutual cooperation of a number of parties: white property owners agreeing not to sell or rent to nonwhite people; federal, county, and municipal authorities enforcing and supporting the covenants; and the real estate boards, neighborhood associations, and property developers that enacted and applied the deed restrictions. The violation of covenant conditions came with the risk of foregoing a property.

As a mechanism explicitly designed to separate urban populations by race, racial covenants were widely implemented in the Twin Cities. For instance, one housing covenant in Minneapolis read, "Premises shall not be sold, mortgaged, or leased to or occupied by any person or persons other than members of the Caucasian race."[69] Another Minnesota covenant read, "Housing sites could not 'be conveyed mortgaged or leased to any person or persons of Chinese, Japanese, Moorish, Turkish, Negro, Mongolian, Semitic or African blood or descent.'"[70] This language of racism not only restricted African Americans to specific urban neighborhoods but also reinforced a social hierarchy. As Roxanne Mountford notes, the racialization of space can have a "heuristic power over their inhabitants and spectators by forcing them to change both their behavior (walls cause us to turn right or left; skyscrapers draw the eye up) and, sometimes, their view of themselves."[71] Because spaces have a hierarchy tied to race, certain locations are valued and protected when others are not.

Racial covenants, as well as the racial hierarchies they deployed, had to be carefully navigated by the Rondo community. The Union Gospel Mission, a St. Paul nonprofit religious organization rooted in the Rondo neighborhood and engaged "in social work and rehabilitation of people," purchased a lot from the city on which to build a playground for Rondo children.[72] The proposed highway would cut off children's access to existing playgrounds and the boys' club. The members' proposal to the city stated that "the continued operation of the Club is essential to the welfare of the general community."[73] However, before the purchase could be made, the deed had to be clear of any racial restrictions. In a memo to the board, the president of the Union Gospel Mission reported, "The restrictions beginning on page 9 [of the contract] as to use of the property, diligent construction of the improvements, and no discrimination or segregation in respect of the property, should give us no difficulty."[74] The group had to review the deed carefully for any embedded racist language because Black children would be the primary users of the playground. These restrictions indicate how Rondo was a place surrounded by legal racist barriers that financially affected African Americans. The rhetorical placemaking strategies employed by the RSIA not only sought to dismantle those boundaries through an open housing law but also to preserve Rondo for the current residents and businesspeople.

Race-based spatial restrictions were why the RSIA emphasized open housing alongside stopping the highway project. Yet, their argument for open housing would not be overtly contested by city officials. Instead, the highway engineers at the Chamber of Commerce said that the open housing ordinance was a matter for the city council. City council members refused to take up the issue and said it was a matter for the state. In summer 1956, Massey and Howard set up a meeting with governor Orville Freeman to argue that the relocation process and its decisions should be removed from local government. The governor stated that "he would refer the problem to the state commission on Human Rights . . . a commission that had no legal power of any kind and no budget."[75] With little movement on the open housing ordinance, the next battleground objective was getting relocation funds for residents and ensuring fair appraisals of their property. The rhetorical placemaking strategy here was to expand the segregated boundaries of Rondo so residents could live anywhere.

Fair Appraisals and Racial Narratives of Property

In the 1940s when the Black men of St. Paul came home from their day jobs as railroad porters, shoeshine "boys," waiters, and other service-related employees, they "ran clubs and conducted business with all the class and decorum of any businessman."[76] Five of these men, Ira Rawls, Miles Newlen, L. A. Anderson, B. M. Henderson, and Clyde Gillmore, formed the Twin City Negro Development Co., Inc. With a construction loan of $247,000 ("the largest loan made to a Black organization at that point in time"[77]), they built the Rangh Court housing development on Rondo Street in 1947. The property was open "to anyone regardless of race, color, or creed." They built twelve side-by-side units, and according to their advertisement, "the design [was] simple and modern with horizontal window lines."[78] Every apartment was rented out, with two of the owners of the property as residents. Unfortunately, the property also stood in the path of the proposed highway.

The RSIA was adamant in its pursuit of fair property value for the residents and business owners whose properties, like Rangh Court, were in the way of the highway. The success of the RSIA's strategy relied on educating the residents on real estate practices and getting their cooperation in a unified front for obtaining the best appraisals for their properties. This process, as stated previously, depicts a key feature of rhetorical placemaking where

residents organize to shape outcomes and create change for their community. Thus, financial property education by the RSIA was key to this strategy. In August 1956, Tim Howard urged residents affected by the freeway to
"avoid hurried plans and to resist any attempts by special interest to exploit
their situation."[79] The RSIA leadership had conducted a door-to-door survey,
which indicated that 1,523 people and twenty businesses and clubs would
be displaced by the highway. They issued a statement through the *St. Paul
Recorder* that warned residents to be alert to exploitation, "avoid high pressure
salesmanship," and "secure a reputable realtor" for property appraisals.[80]

Racialized spaces created numerous opportunities for wealth production for unscrupulous realtors who leveraged the racial master narrative of
progress versus blight to undervalue property. As discussed in the previous
chapter, metaphors of disease undergird urban renewal racial narratives; the
word "blight" was often used in conjunction with slums and slum clearance,
which helped justify the undervaluing and seizure of private property. The
"blight" metaphor rarely allows buildings, structures, or people to be seen
individually. If two structures on a block are blighted, then the entire block
may receive the label. Spaces designated as "blighted" or "slum" by city governments were most often inhabited by Black residents.[81] As a result, this
labeling of blight for Black spaces made it easier for city governments to
reclaim these spaces to create white spaces and simultaneously undervalue
the property.

Because place and race were often interchangeable within urban renewal
discourse, the label blight (and often slum) was also applied to Black people
themselves. The racial narrative in which Blackness equals blight affected how
the value of properties in Black neighborhoods was assessed. For example, the
NAREB manual *Fundamentals of Real Estate Practice* describes the "undesir-
ables" who can blight a neighborhood: "a bootlegger who would cause considerable annoyance to his neighbors, a madame who had a number of call
girls on her string, a gangster, . . . a colored man of means who was giving
his children a college education and thought they were entitled to live among
whites."[82] In other words, the mere presence of a Black person in the neighborhood could cause the property and its building to be considered "blighted"
and, by this logic, render property within the neighborhood less valuable.
Homeowners could then hide their racist practices of not selling to Black
people or harassing those who did by claiming they just wanted to preserve
their property values. Worse still, the NAREB statement indicates how overt
Jim Crow racism was systematized in the real estate industry, including in
Northern states.

This racist narrative by NAREB also suggests why community organizations like the RSIA found it difficult to get fair appraisals of Rondo residents' properties. Accordingly, the State of Minnesota seized the Rangh Court property via eminent domain in 1956 and claimed that the property was "inferiorly constructed,"[83] a label, like "blight," that justified tearing down or seizing the property without fairly compensating the owners. Yet, according to Marvin Anderson, a son of one of the owners, the buildings were "sawed in twos, [threes] and in four parts, placed on trucks and they were transferred throughout the city of Saint Paul. They're still standing to this day, [almost] fifty years later."[84] After battling the decision in court and eventually running out of funds, the men dissolved their corporation and abandoned their plans to build a hotel and shopping center. The Black owners of Rangh Court were never paid what the property was worth. Not only did the families who lived in those apartments lose their homes, but the owners lost economic gains, which has affected generations.

However, Massey and Howard were able to get some favorable appraisers for other Rondo properties. They worked vigorously arranging meetings with the city council and the governor. Howard doggedly researched and worked toward finding suitable "appraisers in the Negro community who were sympathetic to the Negro plight and who would let it affect their awards."[85] He also sought out "real estate men" who would deal fairly with the residents. The effort to get favorable property appraisals had mixed results. Although some buildings were fairly appraised, many were seized (i.e., stolen) through eminent domain despite objections of the owners. Many business owners had nowhere else to relocate and subsequently lost their businesses.

The open housing ordinance fight would continue well past the building of the Twin Cities freeway. In fact, it was not until 1968 (after a decade of organizing and protesting by Blacks in the urban North) and the passage of the Fair Housing Act that discrimination on the basis of race in the sale and rental of housing was outlawed. The efforts of Howard and Massey, especially those to organize the community, highlight a rhetorical placemaking strategy. The results may have been mixed; however, their efforts illustrate their community organizing to exert ownership of their community—even as their actual ownership of property was being threatened.

Saving Place

At the same time that these open housing efforts were taking place, the RSIA was also attempting to limit the damage that would be done to the neighborhood by the highway project. Although the primary objectives of the RSIA had essentially failed—the state and local city planners were not persuaded to go with the northern route—there was one objective that the leaders of the RSIA felt was achievable. By mid-1957, the argument strategy now centered on *how* the highway would be built in Rondo: as either an elevated or a depressed highway. In the original plan, the state highway department had proposed that the highway would be elevated over "two major north-south streets in the western half" of the neighborhood.[86] Drivers for the most part would not ever see Rondo, whereas the raised highway would be an eyesore to the residents. But, worse than that, the leaders of the RSIA knew that a raised highway would disrupt any chance for a maintained community and create a "massive ugly barrier running through their neighborhood."[87] The noise and fumes would be problematic, as well. Alternatively, if RSIA leaders could persuade city planners to build a depressed highway, they believed that property near the highway would not have a significant decrease in value. The reason being that in an ideal scenario for Rondo, a depressed highway would allow residents to remain connected through a series of bridges and perhaps maintain some sense of community.

Howard campaigned vigorously for the depressed option of the highway. On discovering that a "high bureau official" was in town, Howard confronted him about how the highway should be built—that is, depressed and not elevated. The official said that "the bureau would not object to the expenditure if the Highway Department recommended it."[88] With this information, Howard then informed city highway coordinator George Shepard of the conversation, who then promised to investigate it. Shepard found Howard to be an informer and passionate leader for his community. He would later remark in an award ceremony for Howard that Howard "knew as much about the various highway and freeway terms as some of the engineers employed by the city."[89] After the conversation with Howard about a depressed highway, Shepard reached out to a city engineer friend in Detroit about the issue. Detroit had built elevated highways earlier. Shepard learned from his friend that the elevated highways had created "serious noise, fume, and crime problems."[90] With this new insight, Shephard became a stronger ally of Howard and the RSIA and would argue for a depressed highway to the state highway department. Black Rhetorical Citizenship highlights the persistence of African American residents in shaping their communities— to make a way out of no way. The leaders of the RSIA had argued how their quality of life would have been affected by the raised highway, which would further disrupt the harmony of the Rondo community. These arguments were part of a rhetorical placemaking strategy enacted through Black Rhetorical Citizenship.

Whereas the planners, politicians, and engineers were thinking of the highway from aesthetic, financial, and engineering perspectives, the residents of Rondo were arguing from a value of perspective. In other words, Rondo was their home, and its value was measured emotionally and historically. This measurement was vastly different from those of the urban planners, politicians, and engineers who had the civic power to change Rondo. The language and discourse of "progress" influenced state and city officials' understanding and meaning of Rondo. But the language and the rhetorical action from the RSIA and the residents of Rondo shaped their meaning of their neighborhood. Sen notes that placemaking "denotes the production of a site that is material and tangible not only by its physical characteristics, but also by much less explicit symbolic and socially constructed boundaries."[91] These symbolic and socially constructed boundaries of Rondo produced opposing views of what was best for the city and its residents.

Howard's and the RSIA's insistence and persistence on the issue persuaded the highway department to build a depressed highway through the neighborhood (fig. 9). This decision was among a number of small but important victories for the organization, which also included some more favorable appraisals for residents' properties and in some cases one-year

Fig. 9. Interstate 94 construction at Dale Street and St. Anthony Avenue, St. Paul, 1966. Permission granted by Minnesota Historical Society.

rent-free occupancy for some relocated families. Still, nothing could compare to the impact on community life that the highway would have or the personal wealth lost to the families. For some residents in Rondo, the highway "created two separate and distinct communities without the infrastructures to support either one."[92] In her work on race and architecture, Adrienne Brown asserts that "race is always shaped in some way by the built environment."[93] It should not be surprising that the urban highways in Northern cities generally indicate the geographic locations of Black neighborhoods. Still, the efforts of the RSIA and Rondo's community members and leaders illustrate how the Black residents were not passive when their community was under threat of major change. Instead, they enacted agency through BRC and made material changes to the planned highway forced on them.

"The Last Time You Force Anything"

Of the RSIA's primary concerns were the difficulties Rondo residents over the age of fifty would face in having to start over. In response to the RSIA's arguments, alongside those made by Rondo residents, against the highway and housing plan, one city official said, "We know that you are reasonable people and understand that someone has to pay the price of progress."[94]

Standing in the doorway of his St. Paul home with a shotgun, George Davis was not ready to pay this price. Progress was not on his mind when he attempted to hold off the police and city officials who wanted to tear his home down. Davis's "fleeting moment" of agency offered "resistance but not revolution" to the dominant ideology of urban renewal and the rhetorical space of Rondo.[95]

Davis was born June 15, 1875, barely a decade after the Southern states surrendered in their war to maintain enslaved labor and human trafficking. The Black son of a former slave master, Davis fled Jim Crow Texas like so many other African Americans during the Great Migration. According to Isabel Wilkerson, from 1915 to 1970 more than six million African Americans fled the American South to live in the urban North.[96] Some left for economic reasons. Some left for educational reasons. All left because they believed almost anything was better than their dehumanizing lives in the Jim Crow South. According to his grandson Nick Davis Khaliq, Davis left Texas because "he had had a conflict down there and supposedly killed a White man, and they got him out of there and he ended up here in St. Paul."[97] He met his wife, Bertha, in St. Paul, the place she had migrated to from Tennessee along with some of her siblings. Together, they would raise more than ten children. Their house had a "Union Gospel Mission" sign out front, and "[Davis] would have little church services and maybe one or two neighbors would come besides the family."[98] As a self-ordained minister, Davis used their home also as a place of worship. Davis, seeking a better life in Minnesota, was trying to maintain his place in the world—a place where he and Bertha were landowners, a place where he could employ agency and autonomy.

When the police arrived to remove him and his family, Davis was over eighty years old and had lived in the house for more than twenty-five years. The Davis family was one of the last of the 650 families in the Rondo Avenue neighborhood that were displaced by the construction of I-94. Based on his no-nonsense mannerism, it was no surprise to his family or the neighborhood that Davis was one of the last to leave his home.[99]

Standing in resistance to the shifting urban racial boundaries, Davis said to the police and housing authorities when they arrived to evict his family, "If you force your way in here it will be the last time you force anything."[100] While it could be argued that Davis was employing a rhetoric of violence in his response to the police, I suggest that he was enacting a rhetoric of equality, if momentarily. The goal of BRC is to be treated fairly and equally even when the law does not indicate such. Civic action can mean individual resistance, which can inspire other residents. For Davis, he, city officials, and the police were standing on equal ground. Of course, the city had the power of the federal government and eminent domain, but Davis created a rhetorical situation that forced others to deal with the reality that they were intruding on the small place in the world that he had carved out for himself and his family. His actions were a rhetorical placemaking strategy indicating his ownership of the property. He had to be willing to go. He would not be forced. Although a decade early, Davis's public display of resistance and empowerment harkens to the discourse of Black nationalism, which "emerged in the response of Blacks to their American experience of alienation"[101] and would be articulated through the phrase "Black Power" in the mid- to late 1960s.

More important, Davis embodied a material manifestation of resistance rhetoric; his refusal to leave disrupted, albeit temporarily, the state and local governments' attempt to commodify and transform the urban space for a highway.[102] His actions in 1956 would be continuously told and retold in present-day discussions about urban planning in St. Paul. His tactical act of resistance reconstructed Rondo as a "place-in-protest" and challenged the "slum area" view some white city officials had of Rondo.[103] During the stand-off, Davis briefly created autonomy within a racialized space that was in the process of becoming a non-Black space. The construction of the highway was shifting the racial boundaries and forcing African Americans into new areas and into defeat. The $3,000 "condemnation award" given to Davis for his property was not enough to buy another home, and even if he could afford another home, he still would be limited to where he could buy because of segregation. Davis was eventually convinced to leave his home and relocate his family to an apartment set aside for him. But as Mindy Fullilove explains, the forced relocation had a substantial effect on Davis's "emotional ecosystem" and delivered a "root shock."[104] Davis would die a year later.

In the end, many St. Paul families were forced to move because of freeway construction and the highway program. Some were not able to find suitable housing in St. Paul, so they relocated to the Black neighborhoods in Minneapolis where more housing was available. Unfortunately, a few years later, a different highway named I-35W would find them there, too.

The rhetorical actions of the RSIA and Davis's protest were acts of Black Rhetorical Citizenship that in practice were not able to stop the highway but that, importantly, laid the groundwork for future urban planning victories. Their actions and instrumental objectives in saving their home help us understand how rhetorical acts of civic engagement from the Black perspective are important despite the lack of "success" of the outcome. What is valuable is understanding—which BRC as a method can provide—how a community can deliberate, organize, and strategize in their fight for social justice. This fight will be duplicated and modified over time within the Black Freedom Movement.

Conclusion

On a Monday evening, January 21, 1957, Floyd Massey introduced to the Minnesota State Pastors Conference held in St. Paul the "courageous young leader" of the 1955 Montgomery Alabama bus boycott campaign. In his speech on the "cancer of segregation," a twenty-eight-year-old Martin Luther King Jr. argued, "If you [the US] are going to be a first class country, you can't afford to have second class citizens."[105] The Rondo–St. Anthony Improvement Association was determined that the Black residents of St. Paul would be treated as first-class citizens—a central theme of this chapter. Unfortunately, mid-twentieth-century policies and practices regarding property in the United States did not view African Americans as such, highlighting the importance of Black Rhetorical Citizenship in reframing urban renewal as a rhetorical situation. Because BRC theorizes rhetorical agency, deliberation, and place/space/mobility within the African American community, we are better able to take full account of racialized spaces that, as David Fleming points out, inhibit the ability of Black, Brown, and other marginalized groups to have full access to places of deliberation.[106]

The everyday practices of rhetorical citizenship carve and mold the meaning of any given place. Examining the role of rhetoric in the Rondo / St. Anthony freeway debate illustrates how placemaking is a rhetorical act of citizenship rooted in the Black Freedom Movement, which the RSIA employed in response to the laws, racist housing covenants, and redlining that created racialized spaces in St. Paul. Davis's standing in the doorway of his house and the actions of the Rondo neighborhood association, which included civic deliberation, financial property education, and community organizing, invoked rhetorical resistance to the construction of a highway through their community. In response to eminent domain, these rhetorical actions at the neighborhood level illustrate residents' efforts to make a better place in the city/country for themselves by enacting citizenship through leadership and placemaking.

Centering St. Paul's urban renewal rhetorical history on the agency of the residents involved and their cultural and spatial histories allows for better understanding of the histories of the highways and the actions of government officials. But, more important, it helps us understand the ways the residents enacted citizenship through rhetorical resistance, illuminating not just the injustice they faced but also the creative ways in which they responded. African American residents were not passive victims to urban renewal. Instead, they created organizations and alliances that continue to impact urban planning. These events were another struggle against white supremacy because urban renewal was an act of both economic and social injustice that adversely affected the Black community on a large scale, particularly in terms of the wealth gap and homeownership. What happened in St. Paul provides insight into the prominent role of urban renewal resistance in the Northern Black Freedom Movement. At the same time, urban renewal in St. Paul demonstrates, especially in comparison to Pittsburgh, how rhetorical acts of citizenship emerge in response to the material and symbolic places that people inhabit. The next chapter explores a different model of African American rhetorical leadership and the response to urban renewal in Milwaukee.

3

"CITIZEN AND SOCIAL ACTION" IN MILWAUKEE, WISCONSIN

Democracy is not a gift of power but a reservoir of knowledge. Only the soul that suffers knows its suffering. . . . The people alone are the sources of that real knowledge which enables a State to be ruled for the best good of its inhabitants. And only by putting power in the hands of each inhabitant can we hope to approximate in the ultimate use of that power the greatest good to the greatest number.

—W. E. B. Du Bois, 1915, from the *Boston Globe* writings

In 1963, the Milwaukee city government, led by mayor Henry Maier, initiated the Hillside Neighborhood Redevelopment Program, which "displaced 69 individuals, 116 families, and destroyed over 200 buildings."[1] This urban renewal project was the opening salvo directed at the Bronzeville neighborhood and the heart of Milwaukee's African American business community (fig. 10). Although the project replaced old and dilapidated housing, the urban renewal project cleared many of the Black-owned businesses that operated in the business district, and those businesses able to relocate did not survive very long after their move.[2] At a city council hearing about the project, a business owner remarked, "It took me 27 years to build this business, now where am I supposed to go?"[3] The Hillside project built within the "inner core" of Milwaukee was the first step in the displacement of the African Americans in Milwaukee. What began with the Hillside project in the early 1960s later evolved into the construction of the North-South Freeway (I-43), which would destroy more businesses and institutions in Bronzeville by the end of the decade.

Fig. 10.   Businesses on 12th and Walnut Streets in Milwaukee, 1958. Image courtesy of Historic Photo Collection / Milwaukee Public Library.

The NAACP Milwaukee Chapter was well aware of the potential problems urban renewal would bring to the African American community in Milwaukee. As NAACP Milwaukee Housing Chairman Bernard Toliver wrote in a 1957 letter to Madison Jones, special assistant for housing in the NAACP national office, "We anticipate discriminatory practices by real estate groups in the relocation process because these groups have placed rental and sales listings at the disposal of the relocation agency. It is at this point that much of the discrimination is liable to occur."[4] The Milwaukee NAACP believed that the building of new public houses would be problematic because "public housing here is identified as Negro housing and is bitterly opposed by certain elements."[5]

Even those African Americans who could afford to make private housing purchases in other neighborhoods would meet resistance. The housing list created by government relocation officials was made available to all affected families, but African American families had to deal directly with the real estate organizations that would prevent them from moving into white neighborhoods. With this growing threat of "clearance and redevelopment"[6] to their neighborhoods, the residents of the targeted communities soon realized that active organizing would be the only way to either stop the perceived destruction of their neighborhoods or create more housing opportunities for themselves. As a result of the planned development, the Milwaukee NAACP and the Milwaukee Urban League provided rhetorical education to African American residents in preparation for the proposed housing policies and city plans for urban renewal. The rhetorical education program developed for community members by the local Black social justice organizations amplified community voices surrounding the growing housing crisis. I explain below how the leadership seminars provide a meaningful opportunity for residents to learn leadership, enact citizenship, and distribute agency, all of which are features of the Black Rhetorical Citizenship (BRC) framework.

The BRC framework highlights how the exigencies of the Black Freedom Movement, such as segregation and housing discrimination, changed the conditions of leadership and the distribution of agency within many Black communities. These exigencies resulted in African Americans creating a model where leadership operated as "intercommunal reciprocity."[7] In other words, given the role of racism in constructing rhetorical situations, African Americans required a broader range of political responses based on the different skills and talents of the people. This cultural model of leadership differs from the traditional model of leadership where one person directs strategy or manages a group of people. Cultural leadership, in contrast, accommodates the larger role that followers play in leadership, making room for more widely distributed rhetorical agency.

African American residents reconfigured the traditional understanding of leadership to strengthen the community's rhetorical agency in the face of the city's usage of eminent domain. In rhetorical situations where race is involved, the question of agency is not whether agency resides within an individual but how agency is distributed. When a group of people are in a setting that systemically, legally, and culturally constrains their full exercise of agency, what are the opportunities for agency afforded to them under these conditions? What are the local, internal processes of a social movement, and how do these processes maintain, strengthen, or deteriorate the movement?

This chapter describes the history of urban renewal in Milwaukee, its effects on the African American community, the efforts by Black leaders to distribute agency, and the creation of a community program that educated citizens about urban renewal and supported them in becoming leaders in their neighborhood. I discuss the importance of critical rhetorical education to informing and organizing citizens and the necessity for a counterhegemonic space to provide conditions for distributing rhetorical agency throughout the Milwaukee African American community. By distributing agency, this program served as a rhetorical strategy of resistance and response to the actions of the city and the racial narratives circulating in Milwaukee politics. Rather than locating the origin of rhetorical agency within individual speakers and writers, this chapter argues that leaders of the Black Freedom Movement in Milwaukee distributed agency through rhetorical education, and demonstrates how distributed agency is an attribute of Black Rhetorical Citizenship.

Milwaukee Politics and Racial Narratives

Black Milwaukee's experience with urban renewal policies was different from that of Pittsburgh and St. Paul because Milwaukee's more devastating policies occurred later in the 1960s. This later implementation was due in part to Milwaukee's shift in political identity during the mid-1950s and to a newly elected mayor in 1960. Although Milwaukee had a socialist mayor at the start of the policies, most of the urban renewal projects occurred during the Maier administration, whose perspective on the African American community was more adversarial than the previous administration.

Socialist party mayor Frank P. Zeidler is remembered by historians as being more sympathetic to the housing conditions of the African American community than his successors. However, because of his support for progressive public housing projects, Zeidler was challenged by conservative Democrat Milton J. McGuire in 1956. McGuire was an alderman in the third ward where many Irish and Italian immigrants lived. The Third Ward was also slated for urban renewal projects.[8] According to historian Kevin D. Smith, this contentious 1956 political race centered on urban renewal and "race," setting the stage for a shift in political identity in Milwaukee from class-based to race-based politics.[9] Zeidler was accused of advertising to African Americans in the South to come to Milwaukee and "take advantage of its public housing and liberal social-welfare policies."[10] McGuire, in contrast, supported the free enterprise system and the "need to stand firm against 'Negro Lovers.'"[11] According to Patrick D. Jones, McGuire's mayoral campaign was called the "Shame of Milwaukee" by *Time* magazine because of the overt racist claims made of Zeidler's critics, including that Zeidler posted a billboard throughout the South that invited Black people to move to Milwaukee.

Many white Milwaukeeans had come to associate public housing with the influx of new Black residents and urban decline and so opposed "public housing." Real estate brokers exploited these fears by circulating rumors that Mayor Zeidler planned to import African Americans into their neighborhoods. During the campaign, McGuire revived these old rumors and added new ones. One smear claimed that Zeidler's oldest daughter was married to a black man. During a debate on public housing, McGuire—whose campaign used the slogan "Milwaukee needs an honest white man for mayor"—opposed building more low-income housing units, stating, "I will call a spade a spade. If there is more housing, more people will move into Milwaukee. The only thing that has kept . . . Negroes from coming up here is the lack of housing."[12]

Although McGuire lost the election, the racial critique of Zeidler's Socialist Party had its effect and began racist white citizens' ardent resistance to integrated public housing and neighborhoods in Milwaukee.[13] Although the African American population was much smaller in Milwaukee than in other Northern diaspora cities like Chicago and Pittsburgh, many working-class whites were threatened by the growing African American population immigrating from the Deep South. They wanted to protect their neighborhoods from the "Negro invasions," which limited the ability of the Zeidler administration to implement its public housing policies. Without an increase in public housing, the overcrowded African American neighborhoods continued to deteriorate.[14]

The increasing number of African Americans residents in Milwaukee—which grew from 8,821 in 1940 to 21,772 in 1950 and to 62,458 in 1960[15]—heightened the "racial anxieties" of the city and brought Milwaukeeans' racial prejudice to the forefront of racial politics. The anxieties of white Milwaukeeans were further increased with the election of African American politician Velvalea "Vel" Phillips to the Milwaukee City Council in 1956 and by the growing national Civil Rights Movement.[16] Although African Americans constituted less than 9 percent of the city's population, Phillips provided African American residents one representative voice in the city's political arena.[17]

Milwaukee's shifting political identities led to Zeidler's failed fourth bid for mayor and saw the rise of Henry Maier's administration in 1960. Under the Maier administration, three important political decisions made it easier for the City of Milwaukee to acquire property by eminent domain. First, Maier campaigned heavily to the state legislature "to repeal the state constitutional requirement that a jury must rule, in each instance when the city sought to acquire land by eminent domain, that the particular piece of land in question would serve a public purpose and that its condemnation was necessary to effectuate that public purpose."[18] The second was Maier's creation of the Department of City Development, which consolidated the staff of both the executive director of the Housing Authority and the executive secretary of the City Plan Commission. Finally, Milwaukee became the first large city to endorse the federal Community Renewal Program (CRP), which sought "to identify and measure in broad general terms the total need for urban renewal action in Milwaukee, to relate this need to the available resources and to develop a long-range program for urban renewal action."[19] The CRP would proceed with urban renewal plans that fit the city's larger plan, prioritizing projects that focused on blighted areas and were meant to prevent "the creation of slums due to poor planning."[20] These events by the City of Milwaukee put the urban renewal program on a direct collision course with the city's African American neighborhoods.

The Maier administration was aware of the impact on African American families and seemingly wanted to minimize the negative effects. For one, Maier seemed deliberate in wanting to avoid rushing the start of new projects without measured urban planning. In fact, he claimed he wanted to save old neighborhoods, as opposed to letting them succumb to block razing. However, while Maier emphasized comprehensive planning to his approach to urban renewal, the construction agencies and real estate agents disagreed with this measured approach. In addition to dealing with the private industry's pushback, Maier's primary political support was from the white working class of Milwaukee, which meant they expected their neighborhoods to be treated differently from African American neighborhoods under all urban renewal projects.[21] In a 1961 speech Maier stated, "We have been concerned for some time that the convention and tourist business has suffered because we lack modern attractive and large enough facilities in which to conduct tourist and convention activities."[22] For Milwaukee, urban renewal meant an economic turnaround, but for the African American community, urban renewal meant forced relocation and lack of affordable housing.

Although Mayor Maier was an important proponent of urban renewal projects and the general improvement of the city, his language clearly indicates how he viewed Milwaukee's African American neighborhoods. Maier's administration engaged in the racial narratives of urban renewal, which included blight and sickness metaphors. "Blight" was framed repeatedly as an antagonist against progress in Milwaukee within arguments and discussions surrounding urban renewal. Early in the urban renewal phase, a free movie about blight titled "Our Living Future" was shown to Milwaukeeans so they could have an opportunity to penetrate the problems of blight and see how they are being combated.[23] Following the mayor's lead, a local editorial stated, "The hope is that at last we're on the way with a program that will take in the whole city and get some effective work done on the blight that is destroying tax values, creating bad health and social condition and driving people into the fringe areas."[24] Here "blight" is playing a larger menacing role in Milwaukee, directly affecting the economy, health, and citizenry of the city. To stop the blight and make way for progress, the families and businesses in the affected area would have to relocate.

For some, urban renewal was not just about attracting people to the city; the spirit of the city was also at stake. Urban Renewal Commissioner William Slayton took a spiritual stance toward the future of the city after urban renewal. In a 1962 speech given at an urban affairs seminar in Los Angeles, Slayton stated, "Urban renewal has given a new impetus, a new meaning, and a new practicality to planning."[25] The repeated use of the word "new" in that sentence can only invoke positive feelings to those in the audience listening to the speech. Slayton concludes the speech by saying, "If we are to rebuild our cities, we must rebuild them so that the spirits of men will be uplifted as they contemplated their handiwork. . . . We must strive to make men consciously proud of their other accomplishments."[26] Slayton, who would later become a planning analyst and special assistant to the mayor and city council in Milwaukee, situates urban renewal as a source of dignity and gratification.

Local newspapers and government officials also frequently used words like "modern," "Renaissance," and "civic asset," reinforcing the belief that redevelopment was the only way for city centers to become better places, even though redevelopment often meant the demolition and relocation of African American homes and businesses to make way for new buildings or highways. For example, Milwaukee government officials, just like those in Pittsburgh, used the term "Renaissance" to describe the desired effects of urban renewal. In 1953, the then mayor of Pittsburgh, David Lawrence, stressed "civic Renaissance" as the main goal in his successful reelection campaign of 1953.[27] Likewise, in a 1966 letter to the mayor of Corpus Christi, Texas, Milwaukee mayor Maier wrote that urban renewal "has been an important key to Milwaukee Renaissance."[28] This use of the word "Renaissance" was prevalent in creating the belief that urban renewal would create an idealized community. For both these cities, Renaissance was a euphemism for the destruction of homes and businesses standing in the way of urban renewal. To resist the Renaissance was to resist progress and the projects important to many city leaders. The constant reinforcement of renewal by politicians, newspapers, and individuals established a narrative that demolishing neighborhoods, primarily African American neighborhoods, was required for a city's rebirth.

Initial Effects of the Master Narrative

As stated in previous chapters, the initial effects of the urban renewal master narrative in the Black community resulted in early support of the urban
renewal programs because, at least for a short time, urban renewal represented equality. In Milwaukee, the Hillside urban renewal project was initially
supported by the lone African American on the city council, Vel Phillips, who
said that she was "wholeheartedly in favor of urban renewal in this particular
project."[29] Although some businesspeople were "irritated" about losing their
businesses, the city promised that residents affected by the urban renewal
project would be relocated to "decent housing at a comparable rent anywhere
in the city of Milwaukee that such facilities can be found."[30] This promise of
living anywhere in the city appealed to many African Americans. Unfortunately for Phillips and the affected residents, dreams of plentiful housing and
equality were not immediately realized. The project displaced more than a
hundred families, and not enough housing was built to replace what was lost.[31]

The Black newspapers in Milwaukee also saw the potential benefit of the
urban renewal program. However, unlike the predominately white newspapers that employed the master narrative of health and progress of the city,
African American newspapers focused on the people who would be directly
affected by the policies. An editorial in the *Milwaukee Defender* drew a direct
connection between blight and the human beings living in the dilapidated
buildings, focusing on the effects of poor housing on residents, especially
juveniles, in the city.[32] Renewed housing could mean better living conditions
for residents. Many residents lived in poorly maintained homes owned by
white property owners. As the editorial states, the "urban renewal program
will also result in the human rehabilitation" of the affected citizens.[33] These
were lofty goals, of course, and after witnessing how the master narrative
of urban renewal framed "blighted" African American neighborhoods as
inhibiting the city's Renaissance, African American residents quickly concluded that the program would not be beneficial to them. These conditions
presaged the move for the leadership seminars to be created and educate
residents of their rights.

Racism in Milwaukee Housing Covenants

Similar to St. Paul, municipalities and private actors in the Milwaukee metropolitan area supported real estate practices and lending patterns that further
guaranteed the racial homogeneity of neighborhoods. Restrictive housing

covenants were just one mechanism explicitly designed to separate urban populations by race, which led African American communities to be disproportionately affected by urban renewal. These housing covenants worked in conjunction with an array of other federal policies, patterns of lending, municipal ordinances, and private practices that ensured the racial segregation of American cities.

On a national scale, concerted opposition to integration on the part of white homeowners, together with federal and local policies, strengthened urban racial boundaries and intensified wartime and postwar housing crises in cities across the United States. Housing shortages for growing Black populations in the urban North were particularly acute due to the "double barrier"[34] that they faced: deteriorating and limited housing stock combined with entrenched racism that prevented access to affordable, decent housing and that intensified overcrowding. Landlords exploited these conditions through rent increases targeting Black families with few other options for housing.[35] In 1926, a Milwaukee Urban League (MUL) report found that 99 percent of the city's Black residents were renters and had faced rent increases of 30 to 200 percent.[36] In the early 1940s, NAACP attorney George Brawley made a survey of the plats filed with the Register of Deeds Office of Milwaukee County, finding that approximately "90 percent of the subdivisions which had been platted in the City of Milwaukee since 1910 contained some type of restrictive covenant that pledged the owner not to sell or rent to anyone other than Caucasian [sic]."[37]

For instance, Wauwatosa, like many other suburban neighborhoods in Milwaukee County and across the nation, relied on racial housing covenants to restrict any nonwhite persons from living in the community. One covenant in the Washington Highlands section of Wauwatosa read: "At no time shall the land included in Washington Highlands or any part thereof, or any building thereon be purchased, owned, leased or occupied by any person other than of white race. This prohibition is not intended to include domestic servants while employed by the owner or occupied and [sic] land included in the tract."[38] The language of the covenants served to restrict the mobility of African Americans who could afford to move away from intrusive urban renewal projects.

However, one Black Milwaukee resident was able to subvert this racist practice. Zeddie Hyler asked his white friend to buy a covenant-restricted property and then sell it to Hyler, who became the first Black person to buy property in Wauwatosa. But soon after construction began on his new house "800 dollars' worth of damage was inflicted on his property, and he received 75 threatening phone calls, telling him to 'stay where you belong.'"[39] Still, none of this deterred Hyler. He personally submitted his permit to build on his lot at 2363 N. 113th Street. "I went right to City Hall and applied for all the permits in person so they wouldn't have to guess who was coming to dinner," said Hyler in an interview in 1987.[40] Despite harassment from the white community, Hyler built his house in 1955 and remained there until his death in 2004. Many other covenant-breaking families faced different outcomes, including mob violence and loss of their homes.[41] Efforts to overcome these covenants and other housing restrictions included protest, proposals for open housing legislation, and individual attempts to buy or build homes.[42] Despite such efforts, these policies ensured that Black communities would be disproportionately affected by urban renewal and served as an additional catalyst for residents to organize in response to urban renewal and highway construction.

Black Milwaukee Responds with Open Housing as a "Rebirth of Our Inner City"

The mechanizations of racism in housing were well known to Milwaukee civil rights leaders and the general African American population. The threat of urban renewal was only one of several issues confronting Black Milwaukee. Led by the Milwaukee United School Integration Committee (MUSIC), the Black Freedom Movement was already engaged in fighting against de facto segregation in the public schools, which is the more widely known civil rights issue in Milwaukee.[43] In the 1960s, numerous protests led by Lloyd Barbee were held over the segregation of schools and school buses. But the challenge of integrating schools was exacerbated by the less publicized problem of de facto segregation in Milwaukee's housing sector. Affordable housing in the city was difficult to find for many African Americans because of urban renewal and the growing African American population immigrating from the Deep South. More leaders were needed in the community to fight the battle of segregation.[44]

There were two central responses to the increase in population and the threat of urban renewal. First, African Americans fought for an open housing law, an effort that was led by Vel Phillips. Second, local chapters of national African American organizations, such as the NAACP and the Urban League, offered programs to the Milwaukee newcomers to help them adjust to urban life and make them aware of their citizenship rights.

Beginning in 1962, Vel Phillips gave a series of speeches during city council meetings, an effort that did not end until the passing of the 1968 Open Housing Act. Having access to the papers of Black elected officials helps provide the Black perspective of housing constraints and urban renewal. In 1962, Phillips championed a bill to alleviate the housing pressure within Milwaukee's African American neighborhoods. If passed, the open housing bill would have prohibited "both formal and informal discrimination in the renting or selling of housing within the city."[45] However, due to the lack of African American voting power in the city, the measure was "defeated overwhelmingly year after year during the mid-1960s."[46] Although the majority white common council voted against the measure (18 to 1), Phillips's actions helped to invigorate the community and increase involvement in the struggle against housing restrictions.[47] In Phillips's 1966 papers for economic concerns, we see in her typewritten speech and handwritten edits how she envisioned the potential of urban renewal for the city of Milwaukee with an open housing measure. She argues that "without a fair housing ordinance, the deterioration of the central city will continue."[48] To make her argument, she first confronts the racial narrative of "white persons" who believe segregated housing provides them with housing security. However, Phillips notes that because of segregated housing, prices are made high for whites. But if a Black person moves in, everyone rapidly sells (at a loss) and the neighborhood becomes segregated again. Phillips writes, "'Fair Housing' will correct this because it will allow an orderly integration of all neighborhoods. The fluctuation in property values will end, since no area will be immune from Negro families. There will be little reason for a white property owner to sell if a Negro moves next door, because there will be no assurance that the new neighborhood will remain white. Real Estate speculation will end. Houses will sell for their real worth."[49] Phillips's goal here is to make an appeal to the financial desire of white people to not pay higher prices for housing. This appeal counteracts the then common argument that white people's actions were not racist but instead reflected concern over investment in their houses. Phillips believed that white homeowners would not sell if they knew Black people would be in any neighborhood they moved to, thus creating more stable neighborhoods. For Phillips, this stabilization would cause a "rebirth of our inner city," and more important, "with freedom of movement for Negroes and gradual dispersment [sic] throughout the city, this area could become a good investment area."[50] For Phillips, only the freedom of Black movement to live anywhere in the city could make urban renewal beneficial to the city and end neighborhood deterioration.

For two hundred consecutive days from August 1967 to March 1968, local civil rights activists protested racial discrimination in housing in marches across the city.[51] And, of course, any movements toward social justice will inevitably be followed by a "whitelash."[52] Cries for fair housing or open housing were met with chants of private property rights by white residents. But worse than the dueling phrases, open housing marchers were sometimes met with physical violence. Mary C. Arms, former member of the NAACP Youth Council, recalled in a 2008 oral history interview that an angry mob was "on top of those cars throwing light bulbs at us besides the bricks, and bottles, and sticks, and anything, and spitting. . . . Little kids with t-shirts on saying 'Go home nigger.'"[53] But the civic action enacted by the African American community stemmed from their firm belief that the dominant notions of progress in Milwaukee could only be achieved by fair and open housing.

Phillips also recognized the power of the media in her cause. Like Martin Luther King Jr., who understood how Bull Connor would be a good foil for protests in Alabama and draw media attention, Phillips understood how Father James Groppi, a strong advocate of the open housing movement, could serve as an active ally in Milwaukee's Black Freedom Movement and draw more media attention to the fight for fair housing. Whereas Connor was using his bullhorn, water hoses, and attack dogs to terrorize Black people, Groppi used his voice to chant slogans of freedom and march with the NAACP Youth Commandos. Both events were media spectacles. In 1967, Phillips coordinated with the NAACP Youth Council to rally for citywide housing laws, creating a visual ethos to push for open housing.[54] In an interview, Phillips explained:

> Groppi didn't join [the fair housing fight] until '67. And he called and asked . . . if he could join my cause in '67. But after Groppi got in it, it got more attention than when I was doing it all by myself. I have to give him his dues. Here was a white priest and these little, black kids who were sort of ghetto kids, and it was just too movie-like for them [the media] not to be attracted. And Groppi, even though I'm sure he enjoyed the attention, never ever tried to pretend like he was the main show. When they'd come up to him, he'd said, "Hey, we're cool. We're just here to support Vel."[55]

Groppi's participation in the open housing movement increased media coverage, including in the national outlets. His allyship to Phillips's cause proved to be an important development in Milwaukee's long Black Freedom

Struggle. His participation brought significant media attention to the open housing marches.

For Phillips and her followers, the strong push for open housing laws was one way to combat the lack of housing caused by urban renewal projects and highway construction. But Milwaukee residents developed other strategies in response to the city's use of eminent domain for new development and highway construction.

Leadership Seminars and the Distribution of Agency

Sometime in early 1964, Lucinda Gordon, community director of the Milwaukee Urban League, contacted Leo Ryan, director of continuing education at Marquette University, and Roger Axford of the University of Milwaukee's extension division, requesting help in developing three leadership courses for "individuals working in our neighborhood organizations and in civic groups."[56] Gordon, formerly of the NAACP, spearheaded the creation of the seminars. Noting the coordinating roles of the two organizations, she stated, "The League's role is to help the Negro citizen prepare himself for the opportunities which the NAACP secures for him."[57] The seminars were part of the Urban League's "Emerging Leadership Training for Minority Groups" offered "to citizens of the Milwaukee area and for the benefit of the whole community."[58] The program was open to minorities who had lived in the Milwaukee area for "at least 18 months and who are between the ages of 18 and 45."[59] The participants had to be recommended by the Urban League, clergy, youth organizations, or schools.[60] According to the 1964 proposal, the leadership program had several aims:

1. Provide qualified, socially conscious persons for leadership positions the community
2. Contribute to the upgrade of leadership standards and provide more vehicles to enable minority peoples to interpret community actions
3. Encourage youth to expand their goals, perhaps even to include a college education
4. Introduce participants to a more perceptive and sensitive awareness to social problems
5. Help participants prepare for a more effective role in community development[61]

As the proposal suggests, these courses were designed to foster active participation by African American residents in civic activities within a community
that was just beginning to experience the negative impacts of urban renewal.
The aims of the leadership seminars reflect the rhetorical placemaking that
is central to Black Rhetorical Citizenship in the sense that these aims provided residents with an awareness of city renewal plans and how to advocate
for the neighborhoods in which they lived.

In March 1964, the Milwaukee Urban League, cosponsoring with United
Community Services, the Committee on Community Relations, and the University of Wisconsin–Milwaukee Extension, held an evening course titled
"Neighborhood Organizations in Government" as was part of the "Citizens
and the Public" course series. Thirty-one people enrolled in the course,
which was led by UWM Extension professors A. Clarke Hagensick and Sara
Ettenheim.[62] The success of this initial course led Hagensick, a Milwaukee
native who had previously served as assistant director of the Institute of Governmental Affairs for UWM Extension, to write a letter to senior university
administrators requesting continued liaisons between citizen groups and the
university in June 1964. He writes, "The emergence of voluntary neighborhood councils has been dramatic in many urban areas. At least seven such
groups have been created in Milwaukee, and their membership includes
persons who are dedicated to the notion that their neighborhoods should be
improved and preserved. They represent an excellent vehicle for citizen participation on local problems. Some have been formed in predominately Negro
residential areas, some in racially-mixed areas and others in areas populated
almost exclusively by whites."[63] Hagensick's letter illustrates how the African
American community was rapidly organizing to meet the existential threat of
urban renewal. He recognized the agency enacted by community groups performing Black Rhetorical Citizenship as they try to save their communities.

Civic participation led to in an increase in numbers of community groups
springing up as a result of residents' response to the urban renewal and
housing crisis.[64] Some groups were intent on simply cleaning up the neighborhood, while others were more aggressive about finding suitable housing for residents. But the Milwaukee Urban League and others recognized
that more citizens needed to be informed about how urban renewal policies
worked in order to increase rhetorical leaders—residents who could organize and speak to the growing threat of urban renewal. On the heels of a
successful partnership between UWM and the Milwaukee Urban League,
the leadership seminars were created to meet this need for more rhetorical
leaders in the community.

The Urban League and the Northside Community Inventory Committee, an "organization of 60 religious, civic, education, social, professional and other organizations in the city's north side,"[65] wanted to equip citizens in the movement to become better leaders in the community. The goal was to increase the numbers of active citizens in various neighborhoods by creating the leadership seminars. The local chapters of the NAACP and Urban League desired more "socially conscious" citizens with expanded knowledge of who could speak for the community, organize others in the community, and be aware of issues in the community. This type of leader/citizen, produced by the leadership seminars, would practice "ethical leadership," another tenet of African American rhetoric where the rhetor sees the African American community "as agents in the world rather than objects or victims."[66]

As part of developing the leadership seminars, Gordon received a syllabus titled "Effective Speaking in Group Situations" by Professor Joseph M. Staudacher of the School of Speech at Marquette University, which appears to be the original plan proposed by the university.[67] Staudacher's syllabus was part of an overall outline the university had for the seminar. His course was set up in ten parts, with the last three sections dealing directly with organizing and public speaking. Topics in the syllabus included teaching students how to present a proposal to a panel or forum and how "to answer questions and objections, to clarify and persuade, to maintain poise and composure in the face of possible heckling."[68] The final section of this course was called "Make Your Final Plea." Its purposes include:

1. To learn the hard lesson that "you can lead a horse to water, but you can't make him drink" or "a man convinced against his will is of his own opinion still"
2. To learn how to get the other to want to do what you want them to do
3. To answer the big question in the minds of the listeners, "What's in it for me?"
4. To learn how to use basic motivation in persuading others to your way of thinking and doing
5. To strengthen motivation with clearness, showmanship, and sincere enthusiasm, watching your tone of voice and body in your sensitive to others[69]

Although it's hard to say how much of this syllabus was actually taught in the leadership seminars, we can see the importance and value of rhetorical education for understanding leadership during this time. Rhetorical education is "any educational program that develops in students a communal and civic identity and articulates the rhetorical strategies, language practices, and bodily and social behaviors that make possible their participation in communal and civic affairs."[70] But, more important, teaching these principles to residents would give them the ability to recruit and train more people for community organizing.

The collaboration between Gordon and faculty from two Milwaukee universities resulted in the creation of three separate leadership seminars: (1) "The Citizen and Social Action," (2) "Adult Volunteer Service with Youth Groups," and (3) "Family Life Leadership."[71] Each seminar was to be offered in six weekly sessions between September and October 1964.[72] Gordon characterized these leadership seminars as "Seminars for Community Service."[73] She lamented that the Urban League needed more help in the community but noted, "We [Urban League] can't afford to pay for it."[74] Although the first seminar centered directly on the problems surrounding urban renewal and how to address those problems, all three seminars spoke to citizenship education.

Michael J. Reese of the Milwaukee Urban League was the coordinator for the first leadership seminar, titled "The Citizen and Social Action," which directly addressed the policies, plans, and issues surrounding urban renewal, and provided strategies for how to address those issues.[75] There were thirty-two participants in this seminar.[76] The course content for this seminar included the following classes, each taught or administered by faculty from UWM or a representative from the city:

1. Government Structure
2. Citizen Preparation for Involvement in Public Hearings
3. Services of the Department of Public Works
4. Ordinance of Landlord-Tenant responsibilities
5. Community Renewal Program
6. Organization for Public Action[77]

The titles of these classes reveal that this seminar taught an understanding of city government, rules, and policies, which could prove valuable when challenging specific policies.

Analyzing the background of the instructors also helps us understand their effectiveness in the classroom. The first lecture, titled "Government Structure," was taught by A. Clarke Hagensick, a University of Wisconsin–Milwaukee political science instructor. He was a native of Milwaukee and earned his PhD from Johns Hopkins University. Hagensick's class explored how the government was structured, which could presumably help a person craft an argument based on which government body the argument would be addressed to.

Sarah Ettenheim taught the second class, titled "Citizen Preparation for Involvement in Public Hearings." According to her file, Ettenheim was an "energetic organizer" for these citizen programs and a "dynamic speaker." One of the University of Wisconsin–Milwaukee annual reports notes that Ettenheim "was called upon for an unusually large number of speeches in recognition of her superb speaking talents."[78] Not only was she a dynamic speaker, but she was also heavily involved in other social causes. She had received awards from the National Conference of Christians and Jews and the Women's Municipal League for public service.[79] Her teaching this class would provide not only a rhetorical education to African American students taking the lecture but also potentially another bridge on which African American residents resisting urban renewal could build a political community and strengthen their citizenship rights.[80]

The third class, titled the "Services of the Department of Public Works," was led by Herbert Goetsch, commissioner of the Department of Public Works. This and the fourth class, "Ordinance on Landlord-Tenant Responsibilities" (instructor not listed), offered participants a foundation for making arguments concerning urban renewal and housing policies. The fifth class, "Community Renewal Program," was taught by Richard Sinclair, a member of the city development staff. The City Renewal Program was established by the Department of City Development in 1961.[81] These classes provided residents with information that could better serve them when developing arguments in city hearings.

The final class of this seminar, "Organization for Public Action," was taught by Warner Bloomberg, professor of urban affairs at UWM. Bloomberg was also very active later in Milwaukee urban politics regarding housing policies. In a 1966 memorandum to the Milwaukee Metropolitan Area Social Scientists Specializing in Community Analysis and Community Problems, Bloomberg campaigned to help raise money for the Organization of Organizations, or "Triple-O," in order to develop "indigenous leadership and organizations among the people of inner core North."[82]

The information provided to the African Americans in these classes would allow them to organize and participate in the debates regarding their neighborhoods. A UWM report noted the high level of interest in the purpose of the meetings.[83] In addition, Ettenheim wrote a report of the leadership program, although a "decision was made not to publish the manuscript but to use [it] as a basis for further study by a UWM political scientist."[84]

The second and third leadership seminars, held at Marquette University, focused on organizing youth and family life leadership; they are noteworthy because Milwaukee youth played a large role in the Milwaukee Civil Rights Movement. The course content included several lectures on leadership, including "Leadership through Logic," which was taught by Marquette faculty member Edward Simmons of the philosophy department, and a lecture titled the "Dynamics of Leadership," which was led by communication specialist Robert C. Niss.[85] By the late 1960s, the NAACP Youth Commandos were on the forefront of the fight for open housing laws. Their 1968 march into the predominantly white southern neighborhoods of Milwaukee ended in violence and the destruction of the NAACP youth headquarters, "Freedom House."[86] The youth group also assisted in construction and security patrol for houses rehabilitated by neighborhood organizations.[87]

As acts of citizenship, the leadership seminars enabled Milwaukee's African American community to resist housing policies while creating a foundation of civic leadership in the community. Because the Hillside urban renewal project disrupted the economic and housing life of the Milwaukee African American community, some leaders believed that an organized and distributed response to the policies was necessary.[88] Therefore, the organizing and planning at the community level was, in part, a tactical response aimed at taking on public policies at the city, state, and federal levels. These civic rhetorical strategies of resistance helped create more organizations and enable citizens to participate in civic activities that centered on urban renewal and changes to their neighborhood.

Distributed Agency and New Rhetorical Leaders

The Milwaukee leadership seminars were noteworthy not only because they offered spaces for citizens to learn about urban renewal policies; these spaces also connected the idea of leadership with civic engagement in the African American community. It is through this direct connection that we can understand the distribution of agency among the residents of Milwaukee. Blurring the concepts of leadership and citizenship became effective and necessary to organize resistance to the Milwaukee housing policies.

The coalitions between the African Americans and individuals at the University of Wisconsin–Milwaukee and Marquette University provided resources that assisted the residents in shaping the discussions of their community. In addition, these partnerships provided a space where African Americans could learn about urban renewal policies and thus develop strategies to resist them. While racialized urban spaces can limit the full exercise of agency because of systemic legal and cultural constraints, they can also allow for opportunities for agency to permeate through racial barriers to engage that system in somewhat tactical ways. The leadership seminars provided a "counterhegemonic"[89] space for the creation of rhetorical leaders in the community, people with basic training in rhetorical skills who could work to represent their community in complex and politically charged situations. In short, the leadership seminars demonstrate the significance of rhetorical education in creating leaders in the community who could then organize others for civic engagement. The development of these community leaders was a result of rhetorical agency distributed through the leadership seminars.

These local acts of citizenship invite us to reconsider traditional notions of rhetorical agency.[90] Whether the goal of rhetoric is defined as persuasion or something else, rhetoric seems to imply the ability to do something or make something happen. What rhetoric produces, and what powers it uses to produce this, are among the classic problems of rhetorical theory. In the late twentieth century, as rhetoric appeared to be an account of representations that reflect social and cultural matrices of power, questions arose about its efficacy—specifically, its account of agency. In light of the acknowledgment that we are more often spoken by language than speaking it, how could we claim that rhetors "do" things?

The traditional view of rhetorical theory and agency centers on the individual rhetor.[91] Gerard Hauser notes that agency deals with voice, power, and rights.[92] For Hauser, agency is the ability to act and make a change in the world; however, this view still tends to privilege the individual rhetor. Marilyn Cooper views agency as being "based in individuals' lived knowledge that their actions are their own,"[93] and that people can make a difference in the world "without knowing quite what [they] are doing."[94] While Cooper shifts focus away from agency based in "the subject" toward "agency as an emergent property of embodied individuals,"[95] this work still tends to prioritize the perspective of the singular rhetor. In fact, Michael Leff has noted that "among contemporary rhetorical scholars, one of the most widely accepted judgments about traditional humanistic rhetoric is that it contains a strong, almost totalizing, emphasis on the agency of the rhetor."[96]

But the conditions of agency—means and resources—and the question of who gets to be heard are also important features of rhetorical agency, especially when those means are constrained to racist urban policies. Organizing within the Black Freedom Movement highlights how agency is circulated within social movements and distributed within the community. Instead of agency as a possession of an individual rhetor, more distributed forms of agency are prevalent in the deliberative forums of the Black Freedom Movement, such as churches and civil rights organizations,[97] where leaders and followers freely change places and the rhetor and audience stand in a distributed relationship as they sustain the social movement. Distributing rhetorical agency is a necessary tactic to help sustain the movement. The leadership seminars demonstrate that scholars should not regard agency as simply the success or failure of an individual's words or actions, but rather as the circulation of empowerment needed to sustain social movements. This approach expands what Christian Lundberg and Ioshua Gunn recommend—rhetorical scholars should focus not on whether a rhetor possesses agency or creates it but rather on tracking the rhetorical effects of agency.[98]

The organizations that developed in the wake of the leadership seminars provide a model of how community groups distributed agency and leadership among themselves. One organization in particular, the Walnut Area Improvement Committee (WAICO) had a large impact on Black Milwaukee by providing a "self-help" approach to the stated goals of urban renewal. With the threat of I-43 expressway looming over Bronzeville, which "housed three-fourths of Milwaukee's African American population," WAICO was founded in early 1965 by James Richardson, Jimmie Davidson, Katherine Brewster, Wesley Hutchins, and Eugene Walker.[99] At least one of the founding members of WAICO was a product of the first year of the leadership seminars. Quickly gaining new members, the organization became an important player in the community renewal policies of Milwaukee and was very active in other housing issues in the Milwaukee area. The mission of WAICO was a "self-help action program in neighborhood rehabilitation," which meant cleaning up empty lots as well as buying and rehabilitating homes.[100] The organization was also committed to community organizing and "made consistent efforts toward the preserving and improving of their area."[101]

WAICO was intent on showing Milwaukee that the neighborhoods could be rehabilitated and offer low-income housing for residents. In early 1966, WAICO created their "Five Point Conservation Plan,"[102] which included providing low-interest rate loans to residents, buying and repairing homes, razing buildings unfit for habitation, engaging in "greening unsightly lots," and influencing "city legislation pertaining to neighborhood upkeep."[103] The plan aimed to reclaim the neighborhood and have a direct impact on its future. With these goals as the foundation for their organization, WAICO formed Operation Green and Operation Remove All Trash (RAT) to begin beautifying the neighborhood and reinforce community pride.[104]

By 1968, membership had grown to well over one hundred. WAICO had built and sold homes with help from a Federal Housing Administration program. Two members were architects who had designed some of the low-income homes built by WAICO. One two-home project had assistance from UWM landscape design students. Other accomplishments include painting one hundred buildings in their area and conducting trash removal drives.[105] The mantra for WAICO and other neighborhood groups was the same as that of the Urban League Leadership Seminars: active participation in your neighborhood is a requirement for citizenship.

This rhetoric of "self-help" was part of the shifting view of some African Americans during the mid-1960s. The phrase "Black Power" started to take root after Stokely Carmichael's use of it at a rally in Mississippi in 1966. In his book *Black Power: The Politics of Liberation*, Carmichael defines Black Power as "a call for black people in this country to unite, to recognize their heritage, to build a sense of community. It is a call for black people to define their own goals, to lead their own organizations."[106] WAICO was representative of this call.

With a growing membership and a clear plan, WAICO's self-help mantra also meant speaking directly to city officials. In 1967, WAICO worked with city officials "to locate owners of vacant buildings" and "to tear down these properties or establish that they be kept to a certain standard of upkeep."[107] Concerned about how the spread of "blight" in the community would give the city more cause to propose detrimental projects in the community, WAICO presented a plan to Milwaukee's Common Council to prevent this from happening. The plan added the establishment of a WAICO office to keep residents informed of projects and initiatives. The plan also included the creation of "a formalized in-depth survey of all structures included in the area."[108] If accepted by the Common Council, WAICO's plan would allow them to participate in a housing program that enabled low-income families to purchase homes that had been rehabilitated to last a minimum of thirty years, allowing WAICO members to become property owners.[109] The accomplishments of WAICO and its self-help approach were informed by the rhetorical education received by its founders in the leadership seminars.

African American Rhetorical Leadership as
Intercommunal Reciprocity

Since the majority white population in Milwaukee isolated African Americans in certain parts of the city, African Americans created and patronized many of their own institutions and businesses. This isolation also forced African Americans of different socioeconomic status to live alongside one another. Joe Trotter, in his famous book *Black Milwaukee*, highlights the socioeconomic differences of African Americans in the community.[110] These socioeconomic differences within the Black community also enabled other forms of leadership, especially those that allowed communities to leverage different kinds of knowledge and action. These more distributed forms of leadership, what I refer to as "intercommunal reciprocity," reveal how leadership is a dimension of citizenship.

Not all forms of African American rhetorical leadership during the Black Freedom Movement, especially in Milwaukee, conformed to traditional definitions of leadership as one person directing strategy or managing a group of people. The "messianic" leadership style, as discussed in the previous chapter, helps audiences see leaders as delivering African Americans from the hardships they are facing during their respective times.[111] Since great orators were often found in the Black church, an institution that African Americans had complete control over, the church became central in organizing the African American community. Black leadership existed outside the church, as well. Malcolm X and Stokely Carmichael invoked a "Black revolutionary rhetoric" that engaged a new ideology among some African Americans during the 1960s.[112] This revolutionary rhetoric took a more aggressive stance than the traditional civil rights arguments. For instance, the phrase "Black Power," coined by Carmichael, was confrontational and demanding rather than conciliatory. Instances of these oratorical styles and leadership were present in St. Paul, Pittsburgh, and Milwaukee during arguments over urban renewal projects.

Although scholarship on these leadership forms and styles is fundamental to the African American rhetorical tradition, examining the role of "followers" is also important to recognizing other forms of leadership driving the Black Freedom Movement. Within local communities, leadership also operated through *intercommunal reciprocity*, meaning that leaders are followers and followers are leaders. Kathryn Olson offers a similar concept when she suggests "one may function as a leader in some areas of life and as a critical follower in others and may move in and out of performing a leadership role in the same arena across time."[113] Similarly, as Robert Kelley notes, "followers" are not only more important to an organization than leaders, but they also determine whether or not a leader will lead.[114] When leaders are given too much credit by rhetoric scholars, the complexity of what it means to be a follower gets overshadowed. True "followership" is a person who participates with "enthusiasm, intelligence, and self-reliance."[115] Essentially, Kelley debunks the myths that leaders are primary to an organization's success and that followers are "passive sheep."[116]

This certainly holds true within the African American rhetorical tradition. Extending Kelley's argument one step further, I contend that followers and leaders can be one and the same depending on the rhetorical situation they are facing and the acts of citizenship these situations call for. Urban renewal is a rhetorical situation in which African American residents had to practice leadership—follower and leader—within their community with the hope of saving their community. The Milwaukee leadership seminars invite us to reconfigure leadership as acts of citizenship informed by intercommunal reciprocity. Throughout the Black Freedom Movement during the 1950s and 1960s, the model of leadership had to be different because of the national and local scopes of segregated spaces. Leadership for community organizing required a diversity of strategies in relation to power as ways of realizing its conceptual leadership. Accordingly, leadership was reconfigured to mean organizing, where organizing meant empowerment, or as rhetoric scholar Charles Payne has noted, "helping others to develop their own potential."[117] The leadership seminars, along with citizenship schools in the South, were part of that process. Thus, when leadership is reconfigured as acts of citizenship through intercommunal reciprocity, more informed and situationally adaptable citizens are prepared and ready to oppose policies that are disproportionately discriminatory.

Leadership as intercommunal reciprocity operates closer to the African American rhetorical practice of "call and response," adding a spiritual component to the rhetor's message that can only be validated by the audience's participation through utterances of "teach," "that's right," "preach," "Amen," and "go ahead on" to obtain a "spiritual and harmonious balance."[118] Given the specific exigency of the African American community, a model of leadership that is strongly oriented around a hierarchical figure is not sustainable in all situations. Harmful public policies sometimes require that marginalized people see leadership as a reciprocal relationship, which means bringing your gift, serving your talent, or sometimes stepping aside for the sake of the whole.

Perhaps not surprisingly, leadership as intercommunal reciprocity appears to have been fostered by women of the Civil Rights Movement, including Ella Baker and Septima Clark, who believed that leaders create other leaders. Septima Clark states the goal of leadership is "broadening the scope of democracy to include everyone and deepening the concept to include every relationship."[119] Clark is best known for her creation and operation of the Sea Island Citizenship Schools in South Carolina. Of these schools, Clark stated, "The basic purpose of the citizenship schools is discovering local community leaders [with] . . . the ability to adapt at once to specific situations and stay in the local picture only long enough to help in the development of local leaders. It is my belief that creative leadership is present in any community and only awaits discovery and development."[120] Ella Baker, in her work with the Southern Christian Leadership Council, endorsed the same philosophy. Joshua H. Miller argues that "Baker's rhetoric of empowerment, leadership style and eloquence allowed her to revitalize and rethink the Civil Rights movement by positioning her audience as leaders."[121] Clark's citizenship schools in South Carolina and Stokely Carmichael's Freedom Schools in Mississippi emphasized the importance of leadership among citizens.[122] Not only did these schools emphasize a model of expanding the number of leaders across the community; they also operated as sites for distributing agency. When leadership is democratized in this way, we can move away from the civic republican sense of the citizen as simply a voter. Instead, the simple act of voting by a Black person in the Jim Crow South becomes both a civic act and an act of leadership within the Black Freedom Movement. In other words, within the African American community during the Black Freedom Movement, leadership is citizenship and citizenship is leadership.

Although Milwaukee's leadership seminars were not of the same size or scope as the Sea Island Citizenship Schools, they operated under the same premise. Lucinda Gordon and the Urban League repurposed the traditional understanding of leadership and reconfigured it to mean service to the community, a form of citizenship. Gordon's desire for community strength and well-being is reflected in her letters, where she emphasized the need for active citizens in the community. The seminars were designed to foster active participation in civic activities in the community and eventually led to the creation of influential neighborhood organizations in Milwaukee.

This idea that all citizens are empowered to act enabled the African American community to better resist discriminatory policies, simultaneously creating a foundation of civic leadership in the community, which strengthened their resistance to changes in their neighborhood and bolstered their fight for better housing.

Leadership Seminars as a Counterhegemonic Space

The location of the seminars was just as important as the course content for several reasons. First, holding the seminars at the University of Wisconsin–Milwaukee and Marquette University gave credibility to the seminars in the minds of the members of the community and the city at large because of the expertise provided by the university faculty. And, importantly, because of their recognized importance and educational contributions to the City of Milwaukee, UWM and Marquette provided legitimacy to the arguments concerning urban renewal made by residents who attended the seminars.

The second reason is that the seminars at UWM and Marquette provided an environment that could protect the voices of leadership who do not have recognized authority like that granted to government officials or business leaders.[123] In his research on the Freedom Schools in the South, Stephen Schneider writes that we must "take seriously the role of location—physical and institutional—in the development" of citizenship pedagogies.[124] According to Schneider, "Freedom Schools, being located in community buildings and directed toward concrete goals such as voter registration, asserted an educational model centered not around assessment or standards but rather around action and community organization."[125] Although the leadership seminars were held in places of higher education, they, too, were focused on a community goal of understanding the policies of urban renewal and educating citizens to speak to these policies.

Understanding the spaces where rhetorical education takes place is especially important for marginalized people. The Milwaukee leadership seminars provided a "counterhegemonic public" for African Americans to learn about housing and community renewal policies. Lorraine Higgins and Lisa Brush define counterhegemonic public as "a separate rhetorical (and often literal) 'safe space' for building and expressing identities, analyses, solidarity, leadership skills, and other basic social movement capacities."[126] In their study of a community writing project, Higgins and Brush describe how welfare recipients use "personal narratives to enter into the public record their tacit and frequently discounted knowledge," creating the sort of public in which "people on the margins need to constitute themselves."[127] In other words, a counterhegemonic public offers a space where oppressed individuals can learn and express their perspectives with confidence and competence to a larger community in order to better serve as a more effective "counterpublic."[128] In the case of the Milwaukee leadership seminars, these safe spaces were located at the University of Wisconsin–Milwaukee and Marquette University. What made these safe spaces safe was the absence of outsiders; they were organized by the Urban League and advertised by the African American newspaper *The Milwaukee Defender.*

These spaces served as a training ground or practice area for marginalized rhetors to develop their rhetorical skills before entering a white-majority-dominated public sphere. According to Higgins and Brush, the members of a counterhegemonic public must "connect enough with the rhetoric of others to be intelligible and persuasive, yet they must rebut rather than reproduce commonsense understandings."[129] In other words, they must develop the rhetorical ability to produce discourse that may appeal to the majority, but not lose the power of their own experiences, in order to contribute new knowledge to the public. Leadership seminar attendees could have developed this rhetorical ability in, for example, Ettenheim's lecture, "Citizen Preparation for Involvement in Public Hearings." While no documents reveal whether seminar participants could practice presentations, sitting through a lecture or watching a demonstration on public hearing discourse could improve a citizen's rhetorical skills in connecting with others and resisting and rebutting dominant views of urban renewal.

The leadership seminars were both a material and a psychological safe space for learning about urban renewal, discussing civic issues, and doing so without having their positions publicly challenged. I would also suggest that at times, depending on the instructor, these spaces also served as sites for "hush harbor" rhetoric,[130] where participants of the seminars could discuss controversial ideas with comfort and little pressure while improving their rhetorical skills. This space also set the conditions for future actions regarding urban renewal and open housing policies. Attendees would later have the opportunity to organize with the community and "disseminate their perspectives to ever-wider" audiences.[131] WAICO's efforts on the implementation of urban renewal policies highlight the impact that the leadership seminars had on providing spaces for critical inquiry.

The Success of the Seminars

Because of the policies of urban renewal, Milwaukee's African American community was faced with the question of what they must accomplish for their community to survive. One tactic to resist or modify implementation of urban renewal policies was to create more rhetorical leaders in the community—not a leader in the traditional top-down orator sense, but adaptive leaders, people with basic training in rhetorical skills who could work to represent their community in complex and politically charged situations. In short, the leadership seminars helped create the conditions for a transformation of African American leadership to serve as intercommunal reciprocity with an emphasis on the circulation of rhetorical agency across the community.

The Milwaukee leadership seminars illuminate the methods of rhetorical education made available to citizens in the African American community that would result in more active leaders/citizens. These seminars represent just one way African American residents in Milwaukee were becoming critical citizens, or "individual[s] who recognize her or his situation within a political community and who engages in the discourses that define both that situation and the parameters of her or his political community."[132] In other words, the leadership seminars helped to empower citizens with the knowledge of how the local government worked and the rhetorical skills necessary for leadership in their community. By disseminating necessary civic information and rhetorical education to citizens, the seminars created the conditions for distributed agency in the fight against urban renewal and restricted housing in Milwaukee. By providing a safe space for residents, the leadership seminars empowered Milwaukee residents to take control over their own circumstances. These seminars also helped residents establish relationships with other organizations and individuals outside the community, leading to the creation of empowered organizations within the African American community. These partnerships provided additional space where African Americans could learn about urban renewal policies and thus develop strategies to resist them. The success of these seminars resulted in increased resident participation and a greater demand for more such courses.[133] This study of Milwaukee's leadership seminars helps us understand the importance of the connections among leadership, citizenship, agency, and rhetorical education. These seminars provided African American residents in Milwaukee a path to become critical citizens who can engage in trying to make change in the community.

The next chapter explores how the memories of urban renewal and highway construction inform urban planning decisions, and provides another way for African American communities to enact rhetorical agency.

4

CRITICAL MEMORY OF URBAN RENEWAL

We must realize that we are tied together—white and black Americans—
in a single garment of destiny. There cannot be a separate black or white
path to power, there cannot be fulfillment for one group that does not
share in the other's aspirations. The black man needs the white man to
save him from his fear; the white man needs the black man to save him
from his guilt. I still believe in the future. Our goal is freedom, and we'll
get there because the goal of America is freedom.

—Martin Luther King Jr., 1966 speech given at the
University of Pittsburgh

The fight over housing—urban renewal and desegregation—in Northern
urban cities was the catalyst for a significant part of the Black Freedom Movement in the North. Martin Luther King Jr., whom many scholars center as
the primary leader of the Civil Rights Movement, recognized both the importance and the struggle of African Americans living in the segregated North.
In 1966, King finally joined the ongoing civil rights struggle for housing
decades after it began with the 1949 Housing Act.

King visited several Northern cities, including Pittsburgh, Milwaukee, and
Chicago, to protest unfair housing policies and school segregation. In doing
so, he showed the rest of the country the level of hatred and animosity many
whites had for African Americans living in Northern and Midwestern cities.
Accurately assessing these intense levels of animosity in the Northern Civil
Rights Movement, King said of Chicago, "I have never seen, even in Mississippi and Alabama, mobs as hateful as I've seen here in Chicago."[1] As part of
his 1966–67 nationwide tour of the United States, King gave several speeches
on the fight for equal rights in housing. In one speech delivered at the

Unitarian Universalist Association General Assembly in Hollywood, Florida, King sought support for new civil rights legislation that would end discrimination in housing. He urged the audience to write their congressional representatives and mobilize support within the community to pass the legislation: "[Civil rights legislation] means that discrimination in all housing will be federally non-sanctioned. It involves the sale, the rental, and the financing of all housing. This is the difficult one because there still are many fears around. There are stereotypes about Negroes, Puerto Ricans, Mexican Americans and others. Studies reveal that there are numerous forces both private and public which make for the problem, because they are profiting by the existence of segregation in housing. I am convinced that if we are to have a truly integrated society we must deal with the housing problem."[2] King recognized that the plight of African Americans centered on housing. His tour would include stops in Pittsburgh in 1966 and St. Paul and Milwaukee in 1967.

During these visits, King would see the psychological, physical, and economical damage urban renewal and highway construction had on these cities, actions that had exasperated the crowded conditions. He would also meet, or in some instances meet again, the well-organized local civil rights organizations that had been in constant battle over destructive urban redevelopment plans. And he would observe the rising influence of a younger generation whose goals were the same but who used different methods, as manifested in the chants of "Black Power!"

Sadly, it was not until a week after King's assassination in 1968 at the Lorraine Motel in Memphis that Congress finally passed the Civil Rights Act of 1968, which President Lyndon Johnson signed into law on April 11. The Civil Rights Act of 1968, commonly known as the Fair Housing Act, made "discriminatory housing practice" illegal, including sales, rentals, and financing.[3] Because the Fair Housing Act gave all people the legal freedom to live in any part of the city, housing shortages in African American neighborhoods could now be alleviated. The act served as a legal reminder to white Americans that African Americans had the freedom to live wherever they could afford to live, including the suburbs or other previously race-restricted areas. The Fair Housing Act of 1968 was the same type of law that Vel Phillips had proposed repeatedly in Milwaukee Common Council meetings throughout the 1960s that was repeatedly voted down by other council members. Unfortunately, the Fair Housing Act was much too late for those African Americans already displaced the decade prior. Just a few months before the passage of the legislation on December 9, 1968, the Minneapolis St. Paul Inter-City Freeway had been completed.

Five years after the passage of the act, the federal government's urban renewal program ended. Across the United States, hundreds of thousands of African Americans had been uprooted, and the social and economic fabric of their neighborhoods destroyed. As noted by historian Jon C. Teaford, between 1949 and 1973 "more than two thousand construction projects on one thousand square miles of urban land were undertaken. Roughly six hundred thousand housing units were demolished, compelling some two million inhabitants to move."[4]

Within these square miles sat Rondo, the Hill, and Bronzeville, segregated spaces with populations limited as to what control they could have over their community. Essentially, they were quarantined communities, like other Black communities in the United States "whose physical area failed to expand proportionally to the dense growth" of the city's population.[5] In Milwaukee and St. Paul, this disruption was caused by construction of a series of interstate highways. In Pittsburgh, the source of disruption was a new arena and shopping districts.

Yet the memories of the events, protests, places, and civic actions held by those affected of what happened, how it happened, and where it happened have significance. All of these events are informed by both the memories of what happened to these communities and the community members' resistance to the urban renewal projects that inspired these events. This resistance, while not successful in preventing the development, succeeded in its maintenance of community organizing and reminding the public of what happened to the communities. In some situations, resistance to urban renewal modified and transformed to repair the damage—physical, financial, and emotional—of urban renewal and its subsequent consequences (e.g., overpolicing). In this chapter, I demonstrate how African American rhetoric of resistance and community persists through critical memory as a tactic of persuasion, emphasizing how shared goals of unity and civic engagement can sustain movements predicated on social and economic justice and calling attention to the role of Black Rhetorical Citizenship in current and future discussions of race.

Tracing how material and discursive critical memory of urban renewal in St. Paul, Pittsburgh, and Milwaukee transmits shared struggle, mutual lost, and a sense of identity, this chapter illustrates how critical memory of urban renewal is deployed as both symbolic and material rhetorics through language and visual symbols, including memorials and plaques. These rhetorics demonstrate that even the profound losses experienced by African American communities can be a means of sustained civic engagement through rhetorical agency. Close attention to the creation and usage of memorials for lost neighborhoods and new organizations formed for remembering, for civic actions, and for economic development makes clear how critical memory functions as a rhetorical tactic of African American rhetorical citizenship within the ongoing Black Freedom Movement. In this way, critical memory maintains unity in the community and serves as a "place for invention" for present and future urban policy deliberations.

Critical Memory as Rhetorical Agency

On the heels of the Great Migration, the spaces occupied by African American communities were first a place for hope but too often became places of "drudgery and hopelessness."[6] Yet, in between, African American residents organized and developed skills to maintain their dignity and their city block. They pushed for more inclusive housing and more power on city urban planning boards. They held city officials accountable for their actions and highlighted the inconsistencies and hypocrisies of those same city officials.

That social movements enact rhetorical agency in different ways ought not be surprising in light of the arguments and analyses advanced in previous chapters, which have demonstrated how the racial exigencies and geographies that inform African American civic engagement are varied and adaptable. The rhetorical actions that constitute this engagement also make them foundational to critical memory because the memory of what happened to these communities fuels the arguments of what *should* happen in the future. In his essay "Critical Memory and the Black Public Sphere," Houston Baker Jr. explores the role of critical memory in counteracting nostalgia.[7] According to Baker, critical memory

> is the very faculty of revolution. Its operation implies a continuous arrival at turning points. Decisive change, usually attended by considerable risk, peril or suspense, always seems imminent. To be critical is never to be safely housed or allegorically free of the illness, transgression and contamination of the past. Critical memory, one might say, is always uncanny; it is also always in crisis. Critical memory judges severely, censures righteously, renders hard ethical evaluations of the past that it never defines as well-passed. The essence of critical memory's work is the cumulative, collective maintenance of a record that draws into relationship significant instants of time past and the always uprooted homelessness of now.[8]

Baker's understanding of critical memory is not rooted solely in past events, but it is active, ongoing, and "always in crisis." Through the lens of critical memory, resistive actions taking place in the Black community today communicate with the events and actions of the past. Critical memory inoculates against nostalgia by actively resisting the ways that nostalgia frames the past in rosy terms, choosing which events should be remembered.

The concept of critical memory has a direct relationship with rhetorical agency. As Baker explains, critical memory within the Black community "focuses the historical continuities of black-majority efforts, strategies and resources for leadership and liberation [and] demonstrates the ever-renewing promise inherent in the contiguity between majority and leadership remembrance."[9] In other words, when Black leaders and their followers remain committed to critically recalling past events, they are drawing on these events to enact rhetorical agency in the present. Consequently, critical memory is not limited to those events in the past; it is situated in the present and foreshadows events to come. Lessons learned from racialized spaces and restrictions on Black mobility in the urban North continue to inform current and future civic engagement in these spaces. Many public deliberations about urban spaces in Pittsburgh, St. Paul, and Milwaukee must pass through the Black public sphere and its "hard ethical evaluations of the past."[10] African American residents continue to contest space in ways that reflect their culture, their rhetorical tradition of arguing for "full citizenship," and an increasing assertion of ownership of their community. These actions reveal how critical memory is an important form of rhetorical agency within the Black Freedom Movement, serving as a source to argue for social justice and highlight past injustices.

To be clear, critical memory is different from *public* memory. As Sara Vanderhaagen notes, public memory is "employed as a critical lens" and "foregrounds the ways in which individuals or groups interpret and represent the past in order to act in the present."[11] Although the two concepts are similar, public memory generally applies to a much larger public and is greatly influenced by those with power to shape the narrative. Vanderhaagen notes the difference when she writes that "both black American public memory and public memory overlap" but "diverge at key moments."[12] This difference between public memory and critical memory has also been explored by Cynthia Duquette Smith and Teresa Bergman in their study of public memory of Alcatraz Island. They argue that because the US National Park Service has greater power in shaping the collective public memory of Alcatraz Island, the land is projected primarily as a site of federal prison memory with little attention to the memory of the Native American occupation of the island and their liberation movement.[13] Critical memory, in contrast, originates within the marginalized group, so their values will be reflected when deployed rhetorically through memorials. Similarly, African American neighborhoods in Pittsburgh, St. Paul, and Milwaukee are places of critical memory for urban renewal and serve as sites for deliberation, reflection, and action.

Because public memory does not always incorporate the Black experience or realities, the concept of critical memory is more applicable in examining how urban renewal's past shapes the future. Yet, as Mary Triece notes, memory is a site for struggle and "public memory may serve as a rhetorical resource for legitimating a course for future action."[14] Critical memory contributes to and draws from public memory to assert the Black community perspective, especially when this perspective challenges and resists widely accepted public memory.

Critical memory allows for marginalized communities and/or groups of people to critique and question, while public memory may tend to be more hagiographic, representing an idealized or nostalgic version of past events. Their lived experience surrounding historical events, like urban renewal projects, animates critical memory. The effects of urban renewal and highway construction on these communities, their descendants, and those living in the neighborhoods construct memory that is often different from a city's public memory. Critical memory may contribute to public memory, but Black communities' emotional connections to past events, as well as their experiences of being Black in America, produce interpretations of the past that are different from those of whom do not identify as African American.

Critical memory can function as a signpost for navigating current civic discussions about how local and national Black histories have shaped the Black Freedom Movement. As Pero Gaglo Dagbovie learned from his conversations with elderly African Americans, "Black America's past and present are inextricable."[15] Yet Dagbovie laments that many Americans' understanding of Black history has been "strikingly impacted by popular culture, journalists, political pundits and politicians, Hollywood films, and of course, information from the easily accessible internet."[16] My own experiences teaching in Milwaukee and Pittsburgh have revealed how unaware many students are of the local histories and events of the Black Freedom Movement, especially in these cities. For many students of all racial backgrounds, Black history tends to begin and end with Martin Luther King Jr., with a sprinkling of Rosa Parks and John Lewis. Expanding Dagbovie's call for "professional historians" to help shape public memory of Black history, I maintain that the persons, communities, and organizations experiencing these histories should also play a critical role in shaping local Black histories. Although these local histories may not appear to have a national import, collectively they are a vital part of the fabric of the Black Freedom Movement. At a time when the American Dream of homeownership was being widely touted and advertised in popular culture during the 1950s and '60s, the absence of Black folk in popular culture and government marketing materials revealed how distorted that dream really was for African Americans. What presently remains in urban North communities, overbuilt with new buildings and intrusive highways, are the memories of communities and relationships lost, a palimpsest of memories, lives, and buildings lost that continues to radiate within the community. But what also remains in displaced Black communities are the people who worked hard to maintain community with reunions and memorials even after displacement. People and communities did manage to survive, if in very different forms and places.

Understanding the ways in which critical memory enacts rhetorical agency requires more than acknowledging or reminiscing on historical events. Critical memory brings active African Americans to bear witness to their lived experience in the urban North through a variety of means. As Vanderhaagen notes, "Because memory can in some sense belong to everyone and anyone, it is often understood as a repository of power, namely the kind of power necessary to challenge and subvert hegemonic narratives about the past . . . and can draw our attention to the dynamics of power at play in representations of the past."[17] Rhetorical agency, in this sense, is enacted from critical memory through "historical narratives, memorials, cultural productions, and what these representations may mean to people in the present."[18] The representations of urban renewal presented in the narratives of the devastation of the Hill, Rondo, and Bronzeville get told and retold by residents.

Agency is enacted by these narratives, impacting current decision-making in urban planning. As Justin Mando points out, narratives of place get uttered by citizens in deliberative hearings about public policy decisions.[19] To persuade decision-makers to avoid repeating past mistakes, citizens invoke problematic past actions. These narratives bring the rhetorical force of both memory and place into deliberative discussions of current urban policies. Because the policies of urban renewal have affected a wide swath of African Americans' cultural, economic, social, educational, and personal lives, the narratives highlight the parts of critical memory that are ever present in policies currently affecting African American neighborhoods.

In this way, critical memory is a rhetorical tactic that resists those who attempt to do what Eddie Glaude calls "disremembering events," which distorts histories and blots out loss: "When we disremember an event, an egregious moment in the past, we shape how we live in the present." Drawing on Toni Morrison's depiction of "haunting memories that come to consume" in the novel *Beloved*, Glaude highlights how "disremembering enables the characters in the novel to ward off, temporarily, the pain of past events. Disremembering blots out horrible loss, but it also distorts who the characters take themselves to be. Something is lost. . . . Disremembering is active forgetting."[20] Glaude suggests that some in the United States, both Black and white, are active in trying to forget or to not acknowledge historical events in support of white supremacy that in some situations continues to occur. Baker, too, emphasizes the effect of public forgetting in his discussion of Martin Luther King Jr., writing, "Only a colossal act of historical forgetting allows envisioning the King of 1967 as anything but a black political radical of the first order."[21] This public forgetting or misremembering of important events and figures within Black history usually serves the dominant ethnic group. In contrast, critical memory is active remembering by African Americans to hold American institutions and African American institutions accountable. Baker and Glaude both remind us that *all* groups of people, even African Americans, must be vigilant against misremembering important events, especially the pain and horrible loss unequally distributed across communities.

Critical memory of urban renewal will not allow the general public or local governments to adhere to the selective memory they choose to embrace. Urban renewal was not simply a loss of buildings and the dislocation of residents. Urban renewal was the "root shock" of forced displacement, lost relationships, and economic hardship, which continues to resonate within the community and generationally.[22] The people of Bronzeville, the Hill District, and Rondo want to remind people of how families were disrupted, relationships were lost, and that a way of life is forever gone—events and disruptions they had limited control over when they were taking place. In the present, the African American community deploys critical memory of urban renewal as a rhetorical tactic to inform political discussions surrounding the future of their community. These present discussions must be weighed against and interacted with past events, actions, and narratives.

Critical Memory as a "Place of Invention"

After the urban renewal era and the implementation of civil rights legislation, African American communities exercised their new civic power by forming new civic and economic organizations to protect their communities' interests, keep alive the history of places lost to urban renewal, and inspire present and future generations. These community organizations invoked critical memory to "define their place in society through creative means, asserting their own agency in the process."[23]

In this way, critical memory of urban renewal is a tactic of Black Rhetorical Citizenship that engages both placemaking (as described in chapter 2) and historical "placekeeping." Drawn from cultural activist Roberto Bedoya, placekeeping is a concept that puts a greater emphasis on a connection with the cultural memory of local people.[24] This strong connection with, and respect for, the cultural memory of place emboldens community members to stay connected with the past, retell its narratives, and shape actions in the present. Critical memory thus assists residents in actively remembering what was lost through their present-day actions. Current community and cultural events surrounding these historic neighborhoods serve as occasions to create and maintain community unity.

Because the spaces affected by urban renewal remained contested even after the construction of highways and the removal of buildings, and deliberations on what to do with and around them continued, these contested spaces also became "places of invention" for the African American community.[25] Situating material places as sources for arguments in "local politics and contested publics," Candace Rai explains how "places of invention" are "those stock arguments, words, ideas, symbols, and discursive structures that circulate with force within a social space and that yoke the rhetorical, the ideological, and the material. The emphasis of place as it pertains to invention, therefore, is intended to: (1) capture the literal, concrete, material aspects of place that affect rhetorical invention and action and (2) highlight the competing rhetorical frames that circulate within and are tied to literal places."[26] The concept of "places of invention" thus highlights how material and literal places in the *present* are sources of developing arguments. Drawing on Rai's concept, I am suggesting that the historical places that were destroyed by urban renewal can also serve as places of invention for African Americans *in the present*. The past deliberative actions of neighborhood residents in response to urban renewal have become sources of present urban planning deliberation. These arguments follow overlapping lines of community discomfort over the lack of affordable housing, the political intentions of city government, assumptions of what is best for the community, cultural connections to historical past, and residents' power over community decisions. Community leaders draw from this critical memory to leverage arguments about the community's present and what actions should be taken for the future.

Another way that critical memory informs the future of the community is by articulating an alternative understanding of the material and spatial logics of historical events. Material manifestations of critical memory can serve a rhetorical function in memorials and other sites as remembrance. As Victoria Gallagher and Margaret LaWare note, a memorial "evokes and intensifies emotions" and "highlights certain values and experiences, making those values concrete and visible to a wide audience."[27] In other words, memorials are created to reflect public values. Unfortunately, many memorials are funded by sources outside the community to serve external values and purposes, as Gallagher and LaWare point out was the case with "The Fist," a memorial to Joe Louis in Detroit. But material sites of *critical* memory tend to serve the local community because this community produces the site from its perspective— a perspective that includes racism and discrimination and may differ from public memory. In the pages that follow, I highlight the ways that communities in Pittsburgh, St. Paul, and Milwaukee draw on local critical memory of urban renewal to shape the future of their respective communities.

Critical Memory in Pittsburgh

In the subsequent years after the destruction of the Lower Hill and the successful fight of the Citizens Committee for Hill District Renewal to save the Middle and Upper Hill, several subsequent community organizations emerged in the Hill District. Most of them were concerned with economic development in the community. These organizations include the Hill District Project Area Committee, the Hill District Citizens Development Corporation, the Uptown Community Action Group, and the most recent organization, the Hill Community Development Corporation (Hill CDC).[28] Formed in 1987, the Hill CDC's goal has been to direct funds from the Urban Redevelopment Authority to various projects in the community. They describe their mission and philosophy as being one of "placekeeping," which they explain in their mission statement: "Placekeeping is the active care and maintenance of a place and its social fabric by the people who live and work there. It is not only about preserving buildings but keeping the cultural memories alive, while supporting the ability of local residents to maintain and improve their way of life, however, they see fit. A 'Placekeeping' approach can help to prevent the negative outcomes associated with redevelopment, such as displacement of disadvantaged residents, real estate speculation, and systemic racism, which are often inherent in traditional neighborhood planning and development practices."[29] By implementing placekeeping, the Hill CDC incorporates the memory of the Hill and the injustices of the past as significant reasons to preserve the neighborhood. The Hill CDC envisions the cultural memories of the Hill District as working in harmony with planned economic projects. All projects should include an appropriate level of community involvement to ensure that stakeholder issues are relevant to the natural, social, political, economic, and cultural environment of the community.

The Freedom Corner Memorial

Hill District residents have also worked to ensure the "cultural memories" of the Hill District and Black life in America are enshrined in a memorial site at the corner that has become the symbol of race-relations activism since the early 1950s.[30] Because of the significance of the sign placed at Freedom Corner in Pittsburgh, the residents wanted to maintain permanent images of the local Black Freedom Struggle. To visually capture the language of resistance and struggle of African Americans, a permanent memorial was built at the corner of Centre and Crawford in 2002, in precisely the location of the 1969 billboard. James McCoy, former chair of the Pittsburgh NAACP's labor and industry committee who is credited with naming the intersection, was the first to suggest raising funds for a permanent memorial. In 1992, city councilman Jake Milliones worked to have a sculpture built at Freedom Corner and ensured the space was kept accessible when the nearby Crawford Square housing development was built.[31] After Milliones's death in 1993, Sala Udin headed the committee that raised more than $682,000 in public and private funds to have the memorial built.[32] The public funds included $175,000 from the Allegheny Regional Asset District, $110,000 from the city's Urban Redevelopment Authority, and $25,000 from the city planning department.[33]

For over thirty years, the location has become a place for multiple types of civic discourse and action. Between 1965 and the memorial's dedication in 2002, Freedom Corner served as the starting point for more than fifty marches, protests, and prayer vigils. While these events varied in their goals, from protesting police brutality to fighting for more economic opportunities in construction work, they all shared a foundation in the goals of the Civil Rights Movement of the day. The repetition and variety of marches, protests, and events constructed and reconstructed the meaning of Freedom Corner.

The site ceased to represent merely resistance to urban renewal; it also came to represent other important messages of the Civil Rights Movement, such as fair hiring practices and ending police brutality. When Freedom Corner was mentioned by members of the community or written about in the newspapers, it usually meant that a protest or gathering was taking place. Therefore, any memorial built at the location needed to incorporate the practical idea of Freedom Corner as a meeting place for community action, as well as capture the community's message of "not another inch" in response to urban renewal.

With this weighted importance by the community for the memorial, Hill District natives were best suited to design and build the memorial. Carlos F. Peterson was the artist responsible for the monument's overall concept, design, and images. He grew up on Crawford Street and witnessed the destruction of the Lower Hill.[34] Howard K. Graves, also from the Hill, was the architect who was responsible to make Peterson's design a reality. Together, both men saw the Freedom Corner memorial as what Peterson describes as a "way of preserving African American heritage as well as reinforcing the community values of freedom and unity."[35]

The Freedom Corner memorial was designed to both commemorate the struggles of the Civil Rights Movement and create a place to honor the "fallen heroes" who were active during that time. Organizers of the Freedom Corner memorial designed it to be a living landmark to educate young people on the Civil Rights Movement, incorporating into the memorial an interactive video component explaining the Black Freedom Movement in Pittsburgh. According to Ralph Proctor, a longtime civil rights activist in Pittsburgh, "The memorial is a place to feel uplifted. We saw [the memorial] as a place where people could go to that actually work in the movement. There is no other place like that in Pittsburgh."[36] But what *is* different about Freedom Corner, as compared to other African American cultural memorials, is that it was designed not only to educate visitors about the local Civil Rights Movement but also to serve as a place to stage future gatherings. According to Peterson, "Freedom Corner is a starting place, a beginning of our past, and a living landmark for those who were in pursuit of justice yesterday and all who seek justice today and tomorrow."[37]

The physical layout of the memorial was designed to enable citizens to use the space for demonstrations, declarations, and deliberations (fig. 11). A raised platform is provided for a speaker to address a crowd. More important, the speaking platform faces downtown. When addressing those who are gathered at the memorial, the speaker will be sending his or her message

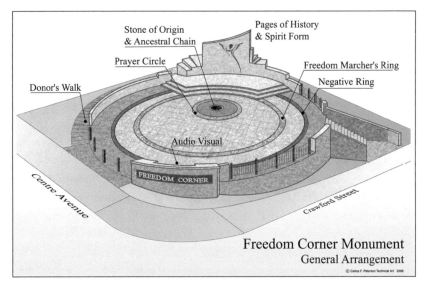

Fig. 11.   Design of Freedom Corner Monument by Carlos F. Peterson. © Freedom Corner graphics used with permission of Carlos F. Peterson, artist.

in the same direction as the billboard planted by Hill District residents more than fifty years ago. This orientation allows the site to act rhetorically in future protests and for protestors to stand on the shoulders of previous speakers who were standing up for their community against city powers.

The memorial also serves as a material embodiment of African American resistance rhetoric, capturing visually the struggle for civil rights. A human-like figure with its arms spread out as if flying and head tilted back looking upward to the sky provides the most prominent feature of the physical memorial. The design provides an image of the figure floating upward (fig. 12). The figure is referred to by Peterson as a "spiritual form which commemorates the courage of those who applied the principles of nonviolence and hope."[38] But the image also provides a sense of moment, of transcending place. Consequently, when a speaker uses the platform to speak, the figure sends a symbolic message of nonviolence to whatever messages might be spoken by future protestors at Freedom Corner.

The Freedom Corner monument space consists of four concentric rings, "which combine hostilities of the past with a sense of purpose for the future."[39] Each ring attempts to capture a part of African American history, including images from slavery and the local and national Civil Rights Movement. The images reproduced in figure 13 are located within the outermost

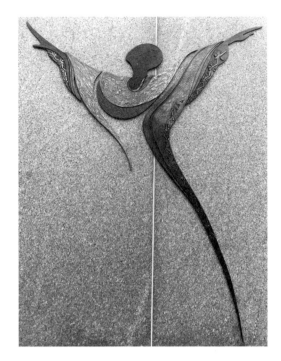

Fig. 12.   Freedom Corner figure. Photo: author.

"negative ring" of the memorial and printed in the *Lessons of Freedom Corner* document. Each image was designed by Carlos F. Peterson.

The first set of images (fig. 13, top) represent shackled slaves (male on left, female on right). According to the learning guide, these stones "create a chain and bondage motif." The second set of images (middle) depict scenes from the more recent Civil Rights Movement and the "brutality" activists met during this time, including the use of police dogs on marchers in Birmingham, Alabama. The final image of the negative ring (bottom) depicts the 1963 bombing of the Sixteenth Street Baptist Church in Birmingham that killed four girls.

These images connect the rhetorical history of the Freedom Corner with the long-term African American struggle for civil rights. Although no Pittsburgh-related images are depicted in the memorial, the "Circle of Honor," which surrounds the "Stone of Origin" and "Ancestral Chain" at the center of the circle (see fig. 11), lists the names of twenty-five "fallen heroes" of Pittsburgh's civil rights movement. When protesters gather at the memorial, they are standing symbolically on the shoulders of those activists that came before them. The center "Stone of Origin" is made of "polished granite from Zimbabwe."[40] According to Peterson, the African stone symbolizes the "origin

Fig. 13.   Images in Freedom Corner's "negative ring." © Freedom Corner graphics used with permission of Carlos F. Peterson, artist.

and power" of African Americans and is at the center of the prayer circle. These symbols pack the Freedom Corner memorial with a strong visual narrative of the African American struggle for freedom and civil rights in Pittsburgh and the United States. By doing so, the monument increases the significance of its geographic location and the community's original struggle to halt redevelopment of the Hill District. In addition, the site serves as place-keeping for the Hill District and informs the critical memory of the events that occurred there.

As a site of critical memory, Freedom Corner is a physical reminder of past resistance rhetoric and can support other protest movements held at the site. As Danielle Endres and Samantha Senda-Cook have noted, "Rhetorical performances of place in protest are a rich intersection of bodies, material aspects, past meanings, present performances, and future possibilities."[41] The rich rhetorical history of Freedom Corner and the civic actions that took place there ensure that it will continue to engender rhetorical performances of place in protest for the local and national community. For example, since the memorial was built in 2002, other social protests and movements have used the Freedom Corner for their demonstrations. In 2009, G-20 protests and marches were held at Freedom Corner. In 2011, the Occupy movement held rallies at the memorial, as well. What is unique about these demonstrations is that most of the participants were non–African American and their messages centered on global issues. As such, Freedom Corner was transformed from a place "demarcating" Black and white zones to a place that embraced more diverse social movements. Through these activities, Freedom Corner has become "a symbolic meeting place for people who had nothing to do with the civil rights movement . . . but who have issues with the establishment," as did the residents of the Hill District.[42] This rhetorical transformation of Freedom Corner to serve wider communities speaks directly to Maulana Karenga's notion that African American rhetoric provides a "mutual benefit to humanity."[43]

The memorial's construction, design, and images transformed Freedom Corner from a site of protest into a memorial of past protests and a meaningful space for future protests. In 2008, community and civic leaders gathered at Freedom Corner to sign an agreement to build a multipurpose community center and a grocery store in the Hill District.[44] Because of its large spatial design, the memorial was able to host the event. In addition, because of Freedom Corner's history, it was a highly symbolic site for the signing of the "Community Benefits Agreement" between residents of the Hill District and city officials. It was a long, hard-fought victory for the neighborhood and the organizations involved to see increased development planned for the community. Per the caption on the Freedom Corner memorial, African Americans used the corner of Crawford and Center Avenues to establish "African Americans as a visible part of the landscape, with a sense of place and identity that reaches beyond a single location into the social fabric of America and beyond."

The Hill of the Past Informs and Shapes the Present

Critical memory of the destruction of the Lower Hill continues to animate the arguments of community leaders about future urban projects proposed for the Hill District. In 2011, the civic arena, built over the bulldozed remains of the Lower Hill, was scheduled to be demolished. However, members of Preservation Pittsburgh and "Reuse the Igloo," who were *not* members of the Hill District, fought to save the structure. Their argument for saving the building, with its retractable roof and as the home of the Pittsburgh Penguins hockey team, rested primarily on claims that the building was "a historic landmark," "a wonder of Pittsburgh," and "an engineering marvel."[45] Incredulously, one supporter of the arena tried to use the injustice of urban renewal as a way to save the building, writing in an op-ed:

> If you talk to those who grew up on the Lower Hill, you realize quickly what a great injustice was imposed by the process of urban renewal. The concept of community involvement in determining the future was a foreign concept for the most part in the 1950s and early '60s. The Civic Arena is a tough building to love because of what it symbolizes to most who grew up on the Hill: the destruction of a vibrant multi-cultural community. The proposed demolition of the arena is a classic example of getting ahead of ourselves and following the same non-participatory process that got us into trouble in the first place.[46]

This non-Black writer writes from the perspective of someone who has never lived in the Hill District but now wants to bring this space into the larger community of Pittsburgh. The writer argues that saving the arena would be a greater good for the larger region. A similar argument for "progress" was made in the 1950s to build the arena.

However, the critical memory of the Lower Hill served as a "place of invention" to refute any attempts to save the building that had caused so much harm. Sala Udin, a resident of the Hill District and a former resident of the Lower Hill, urged the Pittsburgh city council to reject any attempts to save the building. As he said during the proceedings: "The demolition of my home along with 8,000 others in the 1950s and 1960s began a mul-tigenerational wound. The redevelopment can begin a healing process to preserve the people, and I hope that once this arena is demolished we can depend on this entire preservation community to support the development of the people with the same vigor that you now support of the preservation of a building."[47] Udin drew from critical memory of urban renewal in the Hill District to offer a counterstory to people who were attempting to disremem-ber the past in order to save the arena.

All of these places and events demonstrate how African American resi-dents in Pittsburgh used critical memory as resistance to urban renewal. The Freedom Corner served both symbolically and materially in a struggle for power over neighborhood development with the city government. Freedom Corner also continues to unite the community, asking us to rethink how the connections between place, protest, and critical memory affect public discourse. While the past actions of African Americans in Pittsburgh were able to affect urban renewal public discourse by modifying city plans, current residents have also been able to use critical memory of urban renewal—sym-bolically and materially—to strengthen unity in the surrounding commu-nity. As each rhetorical performance at Freedom Corner builds on the goals of the African American community, we see how the community's civic identity—informed by place past and present—continues to serve African American residents in establishing political and rhetorical agency against urban renewal projects.

Critical Memory in St. Paul

Rondo was one of about twenty-five hundred neighborhoods that were displaced between 1949 and 1973 across the United States, of which the overwhelming majority were African American. After the I-43 highway was built in 1968 in St. Paul, Rondo Avenue was renamed Concordia Avenue. Bringing awareness to what happened to the communities destroyed by the highway after urban renewal is one mission of the organizations that formed in response. On July 4, 1982, twenty-six years after highway construction had begun, former and current residents of Rondo met at People's Park to discuss a plan to celebrate Rondo.[48] They met every week at the Martin Luther King Center to plan an ambitious four-day series of summer events, including a parade and celebration to commemorate the neighborhood with the theme "I remember Rondo." These events were the product of the friendship between Floyd Smaller, who grew up on St. Anthony Avenue in Rondo, and Marvin Anderson, whose father had co-owned and lost the Rangh Apartments. According to Anderson, Smaller provided "validation and support for my idea, without which I would not have pursued Rondo Days. His friendship and having my back lies at the foundation of all we have wrought in Rondo since 1982."[49] Both wanted to "recapture the good old days" of Rondo with a celebration "incorporating many cultural elements reflecting what we experienced as youths growing up in Rondo."[50] In their joint oral history interview, they described the "unsatisfied emotion" of residents and what happened to Rondo. Anderson said, "What the Rondo celebration did was to tap [into] reservoirs of emotion and disappointment over the way the community was destroyed and use that energy to build the celebration."[51] The event and subsequent events were also meant to heal and unify after the "amputation of our community."[52] The creators of the event would later incorporate and become Rondo Avenue, Inc. (RAI).

The first celebration was held July 1–3, 1983. The pamphlet created to publicize the event speaks to the agency of critical memory: "The Remember RONDO commemoration is significant and collective. It speaks to unifying the total community and its harlequin residents, past and present—Blacks,

Whites, Hispanics, Native-Americans, Protestants, Catholics and Jews—who nurtured the soil and influenced the fruit. Come back to Rondo as we go forward. We invite your participation, membership, presence at the events, memories of the past, and joining in the fun. There's something for everyone."[53] Critical memory of Rondo as both healing and unifying is realized in the events of the celebration.

One event of the celebration included a creative writing contest, which added to the historical discourse surrounding Rondo within the St. Paul African American community. There were three categories for the contest. Senior citizens sixty-two and over were asked to respond to the writing prompt "What the Rondo Community Meant to Me"; those eighteen to sixty-two were asked to write about "What Growing up in the Rondo Community Meant (Means) to Me"; and those under eighteen were asked to write about "What the Remember Rondo Celebration Means to Me."[54] The finalists of each category presented their essays or had them read at one of the planned events. Each essay category allowed a participant to draw from either their lived experience in Rondo or the history of the community, all of which would help bolster the memory of the community from the residents' perspective. Reading these essays publicly would also contribute to the critical memory of Rondo. Other cultural productions included a history booklet and photo album, poetry contests, and a dramatic play, "Remember Rondo," written by Alex Pate and performed by community actors.

The Rondo Days celebration exemplifies Baker's idea that critical memory's work "is the collective maintenance of a record that draws into relationship significant instants of time past and the uprooted homelessness of now."[55] The celebrations served as time for Black joy in remembering what Rondo used to be, as well as time for Black sorrow in dwelling over what was lost, what happened, and how it happened.[56] Both feelings, although competing, can function to bring the people together. An editorial in the local Black newspaper noted that the event was meant to "unify the total community."[57] According to Smaller and Anderson, the initial celebration was an overwhelming success and "the old community that was separated by the freeway was brought back together."[58] Subsequent celebrations were held and would later become one of the African American festivals in Minnesota.

The success of the early celebrations also brought St. Paul media coverage and the telling and retelling of the history of Rondo. The RAI lobbied and succeeded in 1983 to have then mayor George Latimer sign a proclamation for "Remember Rondo Days" in St. Paul. However, despite the proclamation, the city endorsed a competing event, "The Taste of Minnesota," which was held during the same Fourth of July weekend.[59] The refrain of "Remember Rondo" would repeat itself in subsequent celebrations, media interviews, educational speeches, and the activism of the RAI.

The changing political values in St. Paul, particularly those advocated by African American residents, brought the community's critical memory of Rondo increasingly into the sphere of urban planning and embodied discursively in the efforts of the RAI. However, when in 2006 conversations began about building a light-rail project five blocks north of the I-43 highway in St. Paul, African Americans would have to continue enacting rhetorical citizenship to prevent another planned urban development project for the Rondo community. The relationship at work in St. Paul's political dialogue retained inequality in planning city "progress," at least to a certain degree. The shape of this relationship, as invented by the RAI and St. Paul residents, maintained some of the antagonism of the past; Black residents were again being asked to sacrifice for St. Paul's progress.

Critical memory of Rondo was deployed in opposition to the plan to build the light-rail. The NAACP, along with Rondo residents and business, rallied against the proposal in order to defend their neighborhood. According to reports, "[Community residents] allege the Metropolitan Council failed to fully analyze the project's effects on poor people and minorities."[60] African Americans in Rondo easily made the connection between the interstate highway construction project and the light-rail line planned for University Avenue. The effects on the community would be very similar to those of the highway. As before, Rondo residents, business owners, and the NAACP joined together to oppose the proposal. Together, they filed a lawsuit against local project planners and the Federal Transit Administration.[61] Also joining the lawsuit was Pilgrim Baptist Church, which had served as the central meeting location for the fight against highway construction in the 1950s. Another connection to the historical resistance tradition in Rondo was Nathaniel Khaliq. Now serving as president of the St. Paul NAACP in their fight against the light-rail, Khaliq as a little boy had watched his grandfather Reverend Davis being dragged out of his Rondo home as he fought against the interstate.

Although the residents could not stop the light-rail's expansion, they were able to ensure the light-rail would serve their community and the rest of the city. In the original plan for the light-rail, the train would have passed through Rondo without any stops. However, community activists successfully fought to gain some concessions for the community, including three stops on the line to better serve residents. Their activism also influenced the Federal Transit Administration to change its "cost effectiveness index," which "preferred shorter travel times and longer distances between stops,"[62] to a model that incorporated a civil rights perspective to fully serve marginalized communities. In this example, the critical memory of Rondo as suffering from midcentury transportation plans served to galvanize and unite the community against the city's twenty-first-century mass transportation plans.

Rondo Plaza: A Material Resource for Critical Memory

The continued efforts of the RAI and their "Remember Rondo" mantra would eventually reach a significant milestone. In 2015, several city and state officials and dozens of others gathered at the corner of Concordia Avenue (formerly Rondo Avenue) and Fisk Street in St. Paul with plans to transform a vacant lot into Rondo Plaza. "Today we acknowledge the sins of our past," said Chris Coleman, mayor of St. Paul. "We regret the stain of racism that allowed so callous a decision as the one that led to family being dragged from their homes creating a diaspora of the African-American community in the City of Saint Paul."[63] Charles Zelle, Minnesota commissioner of transportation, added: "An era when the Minnesota Highway Department built an interstate through the heart of the Rondo Community. We would never, we could never, build that kind of atrocity today."[64] Black St. Paul residents' critical memory of Rondo's destruction, lost relationships, and lost businesses altered the public memory of "progress" through highway construction and eventually succeeded in the community receiving an apology from state and local leaders. This milestone was just one accomplishment of agency and critical memory.

Marvin Anderson, Floyd Smaller, the Rondo Avenue, Inc., and activist Nathaniel Khaliq wanted to capture the history of Rondo in a commemorative plaza. This idea first formed when a two-story commercial building at the corner of Concordia and Fisk burned down.[65] The building, the "last vestige" of the heyday of Rondo, was a community and cultural landmark and had "functioned over the decades as a restaurant, coffee shop, dance parlor, and VFW hall."[66] Anderson organized and gave a wake for the building, with friends and residents in attendance. The stories and memories told that day sparked the group to do something more.

Similar to the Hill District's Freedom Corner, the RAI wanted to visually capture the language of resistance, loss, and struggle of African Americans in St. Paul. The RAI sought and received a $250,000 community development block grant, as well as funding from several foundations, to create a memorial plaza in the vacant lot at 820 Concordia Avenue. For the design of the plaza, they turned to Nathan Johnson and James Garrett Jr., African American architects with ties to the community. According to Johnson, the plaza was to be a memorial, but "it had to be playful, too."[67] Upon completion, Anderson remarked, "Our commemorative plaza is the nation's first plaza constructed to commemorate a community that was destroyed by urban renewal and freeway construction."[68] The plaza provides a brick path for visitors to walk and read the panels telling the story of Rondo. There are also benches for visitors to sit and reflect on what happened to the community residents.

The Rondo Plaza includes a display and images of the homes, businesses, and community spaces lost to the highway. The panels tell the stories of families, where they lived, what their childhoods were like, and what they lost (fig. 14). In one of the panels, Nate Galloway provides a narrative of the home he grew up in at 755 Rondo Avenue. He references the community's resistance to unfair home appraisals and how they watched the highway trench continue "to carve its way through the neighborhood, forcing families to leave."[69] Both visually and discursively, this panel makes present the critical memory of Rondo.

The plaza also includes images of the immigrants who now call Rondo home, making both the plaza and the community a welcoming place for other

Fig. 14. Views of Rondo Plaza, St. Paul. Photo: author

marginalized peoples. It situates Rondo's critical memory of resisting highway construction as a feature to be remembered in discussions involving immigration and inclusivity. Rondo welcomes others because the community elders know what it is like to not be welcomed in other parts of the community.

Speaking at the dedication of Rondo Plaza in July 2018, Gail Smaller noted that "the commemorative park is not a memorial. We are not here today because we're at a funeral. The spirit of Rondo is still alive in our elders, in [the current] generation and in the young people."[70] But, for some, this site contains "sacred" displays that bear witness to what occurred and the people involved. In their discussion of national parks, Michael Halloran and Gregory Clark explain that there are a "range of sites at which objects are held up to public view by rhetorics that transform seemingly mundane things into the sacred objects of a 'religion' whose purpose is to unite us as a 'congregation' of citizens—in short, a civic religion."[71] Similarly, for a community that developed and built their own historical site, Rondo Plaza has become a sacred place for the community and serves to unite its citizens.

The plaza functions as a material resource for critical memory and serves what Gallagher and LaWare describe as an "evocation of fundamental issues regarding the city in both its social and material manifestations."[72] This evocation of what was lost with the city's decision to target Rondo for the highway project is important to prevent any future loss of the neighbor or planning without community consent. The plaza also serves as a " cultural projection, providing the rhetorical means, the materiality, through which social groups seek to further their own interests and assert some control over public space."[73] But for Anderson and the RAI, the plaza was just the first step for a much larger project that sought to reconnect the northern and southern halves of the neighborhood.

The Land Bridge as "Reparations" and Healing

The founding members of the RAI and the Rondo Plaza later created the nonprofit ReConnect Rondo. This organization has plans to construct a "community land bridge" that will connect the parts of Rondo split by the I-94 highway, thus "recreat[ing] the land that was lost during the highway's construction."[74] The proposed land bridge will "stretch for several blocks over the interstate and could house everything from a large park and a performing arts center to commercial space alongside multi- and single-family housing."[75] The organization is arguing for a $500 million investment with the hope of attracting new residents to the community, increasing permanent jobs, and generating approximately $4 million annually.[76] One of their goals is for the project to serve as a model for and a symbol of reconciliation.[77]

The argument for this project rests, at least in large part, on what Rondo lost when the highway cut through it and the ramifications of these losses. For instance, a fact sheet developed by ReConnect Rondo lists Rondo's economic and social losses under the heading "Wrong Is Wrong" as follows:

Loss of 700 homes ($35M intergenerational loss)
$35M = 4,800 college degrees at U of M (1980)
Loss of 61% of Rondo residents
Loss of 48% of Rondo homeowners
$157.5M home equity value loss
Inadequate compensation[78]

This undiluted assessment of what the community lost from the actions of the state and local governments highlights that whatever benefits the Twin Cities gained from I-94 came at a great economic and social cost for the residents of Rondo. ReConnect Rondo's land bridge is a restorative justice project for the community—a way to "restore wealth and control for African Americans and the Rondo community," "revitalize, protect and promote Rondo as a thriving, heritage-rich neighborhood," and help "reverse racial disparity gaps in Minnesota."[79] The creation of the plaza and the future African American cultural enterprise district is a way "to make it up to those who have lost so much."[80]

Through these symbolic and material efforts, ReConnect Rondo offers a counternarrative that challenges the past master narrative of urban renewal, particularly that "progress" and the inhabitants of racialized spaces are inimical. As chapter 2 makes clear, the questions of racialized spaces and progress that dominated political and social debate over urban planning in the mid-twentieth-century fused landscape, a proxy for the health of the city, against the African American body. But ReConnect Rondo counters this narrative, proposing instead that for St. Paul and the state to become healthy again, they must accept and support this well-researched project. The critical memory of the Rondo neighborhood refuses to let the public ignore how racial disparity continues to hurt Minnesota. By empowering African Americans, the ReConnect Rondo project seeks to help heal injustices of not only the past but also the present.

Situating the past alongside the present in this way is a powerful rhetorical strategy of critical memory and placekeeping, especially considering the current national response to the murder of George Floyd, which took place just ten miles from Rondo in Minneapolis. ReConnect Rondo makes use of this strategy in a press release announcing their testifying the land bridge in the Minnesota legislature. The press release states, "The persistent effort by St. Paul's black community to 'cap' and reconnect the community torn apart by the construction of I-94, is being seen in a whole new light in the post–George Floyd era."[81] The organization makes continued reference to the harm caused by highway construction as an appeal for investment in an economic plan to revitalize the community. Critical memory of Rondo being "torn apart" serves as a rhetorical strategy for both economic gain and community healing. This strategy is another example of an alternate form of engagement that Black people employ to make change, which the framework of Black Rhetorical Citizenship makes visible.

From one perspective, Rondo residents' placekeeping of historical Rondo—their ongoing restorative and protective care of the neighborhood—exemplifies critical memory as enacting agency at its most explicit. Rondo Residents first formed a grassroots organization to keep historical and cultural Rondo alive. The celebrations had a unifying effect on the community and transformed these activities from cultural community celebrations into material spaces and government advocacy. From another perspective, however, the critical memory of Rondo created space for arguments that could meet the demands of ongoing government policies such as the light-rail project. Thus, the community's critical memory of geographical Rondo served as a continual place of invention, empowering the community as active agents in preserving the neighborhood's present and serving its future. These actions counter the narratives embedded in public memory—specifically, that highway construction was a positive thing for St. Paul and that all of its citizens agreed with the city's urban renewal decisions. Instead, the critical memory of Rondo's residents highlights how the highway created an "unnecessary scar" through the African American community and hindered its growth. And no longer would African American communities become the place for least resistance for urban planning projects.

Critical Memory in Milwaukee

Public memory of the Black Freedom Movement and civil rights struggle in Milwaukee centers around the 1967 open housing marches, highlighted by the participation of Father Groppi and, to a lesser degree, the fight against desegregation in schools led by Lloyd Barbee (as described in chapter 3). The late surge of African Americans from the Great Migration may have limited the organized resistance to urban renewal in Milwaukee because a smaller community was engaging in civil rights battles on numerous fronts with fewer resources (as compared to Pittsburgh, for example).

However, the community's response to urban renewal and highway construction was a catalyzing spark in the machine built to fight for "full citizenship" in Milwaukee, which included open housing. The African American community in Milwaukee had suffered tremendously from both urban renewal projects and highway construction, which caused significant housing shortages that were further compounded by the lack of open housing policies. Although the highway improved the living conditions for some African Americans who were lucky enough to find new housing, forced relocation meant the end of Bronzeville. Accordingly, African Americans increased their concentration in the "Inner-Northside of Milwaukee,"[82] which included the neighborhoods surrounding Bronzeville—Hillside, Halyard Park, and Lindsay Heights.[83]

With their increasing numbers in the late 1960s and early '70s, African Americans used civic action within government institutions to address the wrongs committed to their community by urban renewal policies and projects. Although the increased Black population that migrated to Milwaukee in later years meant a lesser personal connection to historical Bronzeville, many still understood its historical effects in the context of the Civil Rights Movement. Thus, even after urban renewal's immediate destructive impact on Bronzeville, many Black Milwaukee residents still enacted agency with allies in the city government. Residents regularly critiqued the city's lack of dialogue for public planning, expressed concern over city segregation, and offered new policies designed to provide more community input to urban redevelopment.

The critical memory of Bronzeville frequently focuses on a narrative of economic loss for African Americans in Milwaukee. This narrative highlights how the Black community was constantly under assault by federal policies and local practices that hindered their economic and geographic mobility. This critical memory speaks directly to Milwaukee's present. To date, Milwaukee is consistently ranked as the nation's most racially segregated city,[84] the second poorest city,[85] the worst city in America for Black Americans,[86] and the worst place to raise Black children in the country.[87] On the heels of the fiftieth anniversary of Milwaukee's historic open housing marches, renewed attention to ongoing residential segregation highlights how little has changed since the late 1960s.[88] Matthew Desmond's devastating account of the racialized crisis of eviction in Milwaukee has further compelled policymakers, nonprofit organizations, and community groups to consider the legacy of twentieth-century housing practices in contemporary racial inequality.[89]

This milieu of racism, disenfranchisement, and discrimination, along with the cultural traditions of the community, is constitutive of the critical memory of Bronzeville. Thus, this critical memory has been used to argue for more economic development, increased affordable housing, and the development of cultural institutions.

The Bronzeville Plaques

The memory of Bronzeville seems to have served as a bright star for the African American residents of Milwaukee. Several memoirs and books have been written by former Bronzeville residents detailing how the community was lost when displaced by the highway.[90] These accounts are a celebratory look back at the "heyday" of Bronzeville and its many economic institutions, likening it to Harlem. But they are also a lament to the community that was lost.

This spirit of celebration and lament was central to the "Community Sensitive Design" project, which sought to refurbish the Walnut Street bridge in decorative wrought iron fences and colorful West African Adinkra symbols and to place bronze plaques telling the story of historical Bronzeville. The plaques on the Walnut Street bridge, for example, overlook I-43 and were placed by the Department of Transportation to commemorate the removal of Bronzeville when the highway was constructed. The plaques and their origins are a material representation of the critical memory of Bronzeville.[91] The community artists involved in designing the plaques were George McCormick, a woodcarving and metalwork artist[92]; Tejumla Ologboni, a storyteller, folklorist, and oral historian[93]; and Muneer Bahauddeen, a sculptor.[94] These artists were assembled to work on this project by Clayborn Benson, the founder and executive director of the Wisconsin Black Historical Society.[95] Incorporating African American artists from the local Milwaukee community ensured the story of Bronzeville would be told from the community's perspective.

When standing on the bridge near one of the plaques (fig. 15), you can hear the whizzing of cars driving on I-43 below you. The bridge itself is wearing with age. The plaques, too, are slowly degrading, and motorists are unlikely

Fig. 15. Walnut Street Bridge, Milwaukee. Photo: author

to notice them when driving by in their vehicles. While nondescript in their appearance, the plaques tell the story of those who lived and worked there before the highway, and of what was lost after the highway was built. The plaques and their location attempt to capture the urban practices of racialized spaces within an urban environment. They serve as material markers of community pride and economic accomplishments within a hostile environment. As Richard Marble notes on the rhetorical nature of commemorative plaques, "The past persists in spaces, in words, and in the intersection of the two."[96] Bronzeville's past is invoked in both the location of plaques and the language inscribed on them.

The four bronze plaques are placed at the corners of the bridge. The "meaning of the symbols" plaque shows the African and African American symbols depicted in the artwork and their meanings. The "pioneers and pathfinders of Bronzeville" plaque lists six names and their accomplishments for the community—Felmers Chaney, Ardie Halyard, William Kelly, J. Howard Offutt, Bernice C. Lindsay, and Joe Harris. The business district plaque lists more than fifty businesses, with their addresses, that were present prior to the building of the highway. The "BRONZEVILLE MILWAUKEE" plaque (fig. 16) tells the story as to what happened to Bronzeville.

Fig. 16. "BRONZEVILLE MILWAUKEE" plaque on the Walnut St. Bridge. Photo: author.

Written on the second line of the "BRONZEVILLE MILWAUKEE" plaque is "The Walnut Street Community." The writing on the plaque is small, and the text is long with its seven paragraphs. Designed to look like a scroll, it includes a Black man and a Black woman on either side, appearing to hold up the scroll, which is much larger than them (see the bottom of fig. 16). The first section of the scroll describes the housing hardships African Americans faced in the 1960s before the Fair Housing Act. The first sentence of this section reads: "In most cities across the nation, African Americans were denied access to the newer and more affluent parts of those cites, Milwaukee was no exception." Here the writing situates the experiences of African Americans in Bronzeville within the national struggle within the Black Freedom Movement.

Although the first section of the plaque highlights the hardships faced by the Bronzeville community, the second section portrays the residents as agents in creating a better life for themselves despite discriminatory practices. It describes Black Milwaukee as "responding to this segregation by putting their energy into developing their own community, transforming this 'ghetto' or 'inner city' into a lively and exciting business, social and entertainment district," which became known as Bronzeville. This section highlights the critical memory of Bronzeville and foreshadows how this memory will be used in the present and moving forward.

The next two paragraphs of the "BRONZEVILLE MILWAUKEE" plaque describe life in Bronzeville, how residents were proud of their accomplishments, and how they "welcomed everyone to come to this neighborhood." Despite the racial geographic boundaries invoked by the rest of the city, Bronzeville was welcoming to all groups of people. This emphasis is important to the community's legacy because it exposes the unfair treatment in restricting African American housing mobility in the rest of Milwaukee.

The final paragraph tells of the end of Bronzeville. Urban renewal projects and highways "removed these homes and businesses." This section of the narrative makes it clear that the Bronzeville community was destroyed by outside forces. Because it was written by members of the Milwaukee Black community, it ensures that the public memory of the highway is influenced by the critical memory of Bronzeville.

Through critical memory, the plaque bears witness to what Bronzeville was and what was lost when it was bulldozed to build a highway. The plaque bears witness to the events of the past, and it also highlights the welcoming nature of African American communities. They were discriminated against, but they did not discriminate, which suggests a model for all communities. The plaque also highlights and romanticizes the vibrant nightlife of Bronzeville and the celebrities that played there. Duke Ellington is specifically mentioned on the plaque. The materialist rhetoric of the bridge and plaques works alongside community groups such as the Walnut Street Social Club, an organization formed by former residents, to maintain the memory of Bronzeville.[97] The Bronzeville plaque underlies the critical memory of urban renewal and aids the cause of remembrance and restoration. Its creation, an act of Black Rhetorical Citizenship, allowed the artists to connect the site with a destructive, powerful past and distribute agency within the community to work toward a more promising future.

Bronzeville Redevelopment Plans

A notable feature of African Americans' resistance to urban renewal in Milwaukee was that community leaders were seemingly rooted in government partnerships. Because of Vel Phillips, Black Milwaukee residents had government representation much earlier than Pittsburgh and St. Paul. The Walnut Street Improvement Committee developed city partnerships to increase housing for the community, and these relationships grew through various federal and state projects. Consequently, a mixture of private organizations and government offices have drawn from the critical memory of urban renewal's legacy in Milwaukee—a narrative of economic loss—which has led to a renewed focus on economic development.

The Bronzeville Cultural and Entertainment District is a City of Milwaukee redevelopment initiative inspired by Milwaukee's original Bronzeville, and it is striving to revitalize the area of Milwaukee where African American culture has been a mainstay. The Bronzeville Redevelopment Plan seeks to create economic development in a predominantly African American neighborhood in a way that recaptures the enthusiasm and attractiveness of the original Bronzeville District. In 2005, Milwaukee's Department of City Development created the Bronzeville Market Analysis and District Plan with the help of "interviews with key stakeholders for this project as well as from a public meeting with neighborhood residents, employers, City representatives and staff, and other interested parties."[98] The report acknowledges the strength of critically remembering Bronzeville's past: "Over the past few decades, the Bronzeville neighborhood has declined due to changing demographics of the City and region, the interstate construction, and economic cycles. However, for many African-Americans in Milwaukee, the spirit and memory of Bronzeville remain strong, which was quite evident during the fieldwork undertaken for this study. Today, there is growing interest in redeveloping the neighborhood as a special destination and business, entertainment and cultural center for those who want to partake and participate in the Bronzeville spirit and new business venues on North Avenue."[99] In a time with increased political power by African Americans (Milwaukee is 38 percent African American), residents are imagining the rebirth of Brownsville, restoring it to its historic economic glory. Critical memory of Bronzeville supports this narrative of rebirth. And, importantly, urban planning in the community has grown from residents' partnerships with city, county, and state governments rather than from adversarial relationships. This restorative vision of Bronzeville and its economic potential also served to ignite community pride and unification, and situate critical memory of Bronzeville as a source of support for the new development in the area.

Critical memory is also deployed rhetorically in the community's "Bronzeville Week," an annual event that showcases Black businesses and includes a parade. As a unifying event for the community, Bronzeville Week reminds the city what was lost and asserts that urban planning will not happen again without full community involvement. This week of activities celebrates Bronzeville as an "economic and social hub of its time."[100] First held in 2011 at the approval of the Milwaukee Common Council, the event was spearheaded by council member Milele Coggs, who has family history in the Bronzeville neighborhood. Bronzeville Week is held to showcase the Bronzeville District and reclaim what was lost by urban renewal.[101]

Milwaukee's vibrant active African American community is committed to remembering Bronzeville not only through activities like Bronzeville Week but also by actively working with the city government on issues concerning their community. The community's continued activism and critical memory of urban renewal in Bronzeville, alongside government partnerships within the African American community, led in part to the County of Milwaukee creating the Office on African American Affairs in 2016. The office targets the large concentration of poverty in the Milwaukee north side, with the goal to "initiate a long-term effort to improve the condition of Milwaukee's African American community" and with a mission to "serve an integral role in recognizing and resolving the County's racial inequities for the benefit of all its citizenry and for the region to achieve its full potential."[102] When the office was created, one council person noted that "Milwaukee's racial inequities have existed for as long as Milwaukee has had a measurable African American population." He additionally highlighted that "[Milwaukee's north side] wraps around an unacceptable concentration of poverty . . . [which] will not surprise anyone since the city's African-American poverty rate of 38% is among the worst for U.S. cities."[103] While every American metropolitan area struggles with income inequality, concentrated poverty, unequal incarceration rates, disparate health outcomes, and poor overall quality of life for African Americans, Milwaukee is unique in the comprehensive issues— including hyper segregation and loss of manufacturing jobs—faced by its African American population.

Critical memory in Milwaukee serves to help revitalize the Black community in Milwaukee through economic projects. It continues to hold government officials, some of whom are also members of the African American community, accountable for their decisions. Critical memory also helps organize people during the Bronzeville Week celebration and remind them of Milwaukee's rich African American legacy of culture, arts, and history, all of which continue to unify the community.

The Implications of Critical Memory in the Urban North

Critical memory is an important rhetorical resource for African American communities, particularly those devastated by a mixture of urban renewal and highway projects. During the 1950s and '60s, these urban renewal practices relied on a rhetoric of racial boundaries, creating a housing crisis in the urban North that King eventually recognized was just as important as the segregation problems in the South.

The policies that separated and isolated African Americans regardless of economic class still affect America today. Ta-Nehisi Coates, in his June 2014 *Atlantic Monthly* article, "The Case for Reparations," has rekindled the heated debate over reparations with an examination of the effects of bad housing policies and restrictive covenants. These and other events, according to Coates, prevented Black citizens from building wealth over decades and were all supported, sanctioned, and legalized by local, state, and federal governments. As Coates describes: "Two hundred fifty years of slavery. Ninety years of Jim Crow. Sixty years of separate but equal. Thirty-five years of racist housing policy. Until we reckon with our compounding moral debts, America will never be whole."[104] The highly segregated Northern metropolitan areas maintained restrictive housing policies alongside other segregationist efforts when planning urban development, essentially excluding Black communities from enacting full citizenship. From this deep well of the critical memory of urban renewal, the tide against eminent domain turned in 2006 when then president George Bush signed an executive order preventing federal agencies from seizing private property for "commercial development except for public projects such as hospitals or roads."[105] However, this ruling does not affect eminent domain decisions at the state and local levels.

Critical memory of urban renewal has also been realized in other social movements. Recently, Black Lives Matter (BLM) activists protested police brutality by blocking highways in cities, including St. Paul, Milwaukee, Chicago, and Atlanta. It is not surprising that the highway BLM protesters chose to block in St. Paul was created through a former urban renewal project that destroyed the economic center of the African American community in the 1960s. It is also no surprise that Black protest events often begin at the Freedom Corner in Pittsburgh. Likewise, major protests over the treatment of African Americans by police officers in summer 2016 took place in a Milwaukee neighborhood affected by urban renewal in the 1960s. Critical memory of these spaces is a rhetorical tactic of resistance and protest rooted in the African American fight against Northern urban renewal in the 1950s and 1960s, ensuring that the relevance of these events is still understood today.

Finally, the material sites that memorialize lost neighborhoods and communities extend our understanding of memory and rhetorics of place as a central component of Black Rhetorical Citizenship. The tensions between African Americans' notion of citizenship and the arguments over place and space are often at the center of African American rhetorical history and the fight for full citizenship rights. The memory of lost places still animates the local politics of race in place-specific ways and impacts the civic engagement practices of the African American community. The material sites of critical memory serve as a reminder to the community to remain vigilant and civically engaged. But, more important, the material sites and critical memories are connected to BRC's focus on rhetorical agency. Understanding how the memory of places act rhetorically to support arguments may enhance our understanding of how rhetorical actors enhance or distribute agency within social movements such as the Black Freedom Movement.

CONCLUSION: BLACK RHETORICAL CITIZENSHIP AND RESISTANCE

DOUB: I was just talking to Clifford next door. He say the man is gonna board his place up next month.

BECKER: Yeah, I know. The man from the city was by here two weeks ago, too. They're gonna tear it all down, this whole block.

DOUB: The man was by here and you ain't told nobody! What he say?

BECKER: They're gonna board the place up first of next month.

DOUB: Why in the hell didn't you tell somebody!

BECKER: I'm telling you now.

—August Wilson, excerpt from *Jitney*, Act 1 Scene 2

In 1978, the young poet and playwright August Wilson moved from Pittsburgh, where he had founded the Black Horizon Theater, to St. Paul, Minnesota.[1] It was in St. Paul that Wilson wrote his first play, *Jitney*. The play centers on an alternative cab service run by African Americans in Pittsburgh's Hill District. Set in the 1970s, its ensemble cast struggles with the everyday life of being Black in the urban North and their reliance on money earned in the underground economy. The jitney station is threatened by urban redevelopment and will be "boarded up" in two weeks. In Act 2, Scene 2, the jitney drivers meet to discuss how to address the city's plans for boarding up their station, tearing down the block for rebuilding, and jeopardizing their livelihood. Becker, the owner of the jitney station, urges the group to stand together, resist the city's authority, and fight for the place that they all call home:

I say we stay here. We already here. The people know we here. We been here for eighteen years . . . and I don't see no reason to move. City or no city. I look around and all I see is boarded-up buildings. Some of them been boarded up for more than ten years. If they want to build some houses that's when they can tear it down. When they ready to build the houses. They board this place up the first of the month and let it sit boarded-up for the next fifteen . . . twenty years.[2]

The group begins to organize and plan how to bring other members of the community together to lay the groundwork for collective action to save their neighborhood. Although this scene is brief, it reflects the rhetorics of place, deliberation, and civic action that often circulated in and about African American communities. The scene of organizing and planning sheds light on the experiences of the marginalized communities suffering from an urban renewal master narrative that often constructs negative perceptions of places and the people who live there in an attempt to rewrite their community narratives.

Although Wilson imagined this conversation on resistance, his lived experience of resisting urban renewal in Pittsburgh, as described in chapter 1, likely informed his writing of the play. Certainly, he had also heard the stories, narratives, and laments of what happened to Rondo and the community's loss of place with the construction of the highway in St. Paul. Although the play was set in Pittsburgh, it could have been set in any Black neighborhood in the urban North, including Milwaukee and the Twin Cities.

Just as Wilson's play gave presence to the experiences of Black communities during urban renewal, Struggle for the City has attempted to illuminate how African Americans used "full citizenship" to assess their rights as equal citizens of this country. In pursuing this goal of full citizenship, they were putting into action the goals of a democracy in a country claiming, hypocritically, that it had already been doing so. In short, African American communities were enacting Black Rhetorical Citizenship (BRC).

By attempting to uncover the community's action, instead of focusing on what was done to them, we can better understand Black agency in the context of citizenship, the community's struggle for social and economic justice, and the importance of places lost during urban renewal. We also see how government policies reinforce the unifying actions taken against urban renewal. Centering the unifying actions that Black citizens took against urban renewal also helps us draw larger conclusions about the nature of rhetorical agency,

American culture and democracy, and the meaning of citizenship itself. This rhetorical history also offers insight into the present and future of African Americans' response to urban planning in the United States.

Urban Renewal, Practices of Citizenship, and Black Agency

The three communities examined here—Hill District, Rondo, and Bronzeville—reveal that rhetorical citizenship and civic engagement within the Black Freedom Movement are emergent phenomena. Each community had different circumstances, situations, and exigencies of urban renewal, leading to different ways of deliberating and organizing, forms of arguments, and desires and wishes vis-à-vis the urban renewal projects within their cities. The strategies used by residents in the Lower Hill, Rondo, and Bronzeville reflected their community histories and, to a lesser extent, their geographies. The Black community in Pittsburgh was the largest of the three and had more resources to execute different tactics of resistance. The smaller Black community in Milwaukee was primarily isolated in the north-central part of the city. Recruiting allies both within and outside the community was important to the goals of their movement. The Black community in St. Paul sought to open housing as a central part of their fight against the highway. While we see similarities and overlap in their responses to the threats, each community and community group decided on a course of action that they felt would help them accomplish their goals and resist the master narrative of urban renewal.

Arguments by local government to implement urban renewal policies were rooted in federal deliberations over the Housing Acts of 1949 and 1954 and seeped into local governments' arguments for specific urban renewal policies and projects. From these sources, as the chapters of this book have illustrated, the master narrative of urban renewal was repeated by federal, state, and local government officials in local newspaper editorials, public hearings, and other outlets. This repetition portrayed urban renewal as not only necessary for the health of the city but an inevitable occurrence. The master narrative consisted of disease metaphors ("blight") and euphemisms ("Renaissance"), which increased its persuasive power. Within this narrative, African American communities were situated as obstacles to progress. A measured rehabilitation of specific dilapidated buildings would have been a true source of progress for the city. One effect of this master narrative was that it also persuaded many influential African Americans to first endorse the urban renewal plans, which delayed community efforts to resist these plans.

Since urban centers in the urban North suffered from legal and sometimes violent segregation practices, the fight over housing and resistance to urban renewal were central to the growing Black Freedom Movement in the Northern cities. Despite tensions between the Civil Rights Movement and the strengthening Black Power Movement over resistance methods in urban centers, housing conditions affected all African Americans, as did the threat of urban renewal projects taking away homes without suitable replacements. The rhetorical strategies of resistance employed by African Americans in these communities were necessary in the sense that, while enacted differently, they helped the communities remain unified in their resistance to urban renewal.

In Pittsburgh, the rhetorical strategies of place were used by the Citizens Committee for Hill District Renewal and African American residents to resist urban renewal and unify the community. By enacting these strategies, including (1) counternarratives, (2) visual rhetoric of place, and (3) the rhetorical construction of "Freedom Corner," the African American community not only affected urban renewal public discourse by modifying city plans but also strengthened unity in the surrounding community. These rhetorical strategies of place allowed residents to claim agency in a variety of ways that included designing architectural models and naming and claiming a street corner in their neighborhood, Freedom Corner, as a site for community gatherings and deliberations. Each rhetorical performance held at Freedom Corner built on the goals of unity and resistance and further established African American residents' political and rhetorical agency as citizens resisting city construction projects. Conceptually, Freedom Corner and the map of the larger community asks us to rethink how place and resistance affect public discourse, especially when these places are simultaneously restricted and threatened.

In St. Paul, the community was unified in arguing for fair assessment of their properties and open housing laws. They relied heavily on traditional features of African American leadership—a preacher and business owner led the Rondo–St. Anthony Improvement Association—to argue on their behalf against city and state plans. The leaders enacted a rhetorical strategy of placemaking that simultaneously prioritized the dignity and humanity of Rondo residents and the value and the worth of the Rondo neighborhood in order for it to be saved.

In response to the laws, racist housing covenants, and redlining, African Americans in St. Paul employed placemaking as a rhetorical strategy of place, which functions as an act of citizenship. This rhetorical strategy of place was employed, in part, due to the size of the community in St. Paul, which was much smaller than the Black population in Pittsburgh. Leaders argued vigorously to reroute the highway and receive higher property appraisals. They also sought to disrupt the borders of racialized spaces through open housing laws, which would enable Black residents to live anywhere in the city. These enactments of rhetorical agency, which included civic education, protests, and community organizing against highway construction, drew from Rondo residents' sense of autonomy, civic rights, and oral traditions to argue for their community. Within a BRC framework, these tactics of resistance, which may initially appear unimportant, not only become more visible but also increase in magnitude. Placemaking as rhetorical agency strengthened the bonds within the community and provided a continued source to inspire civic action.

While place functioned differently for Milwaukee residents than it did for those in Pittsburgh and St. Paul, it had a similar effect of unifying the community, distributing agency, and producing more active citizens. In Milwaukee, unification of community was centered on the belief that citizens needed to be educated in the policies of urban renewal and housing, as well as in the most effective ways to make arguments in public hearings. Through the initiative of the Urban League and Northside Community Inventory Committee, the leadership seminars in Milwaukee served as a site for rhetorical education for residents. Residents resisted urban renewal policies in part by building relationships with local organizations, including universities, to increase their ethos and provide residents with training from subject matter experts. The educational setting of the leadership seminars provided a secure and contemplative space for residents to learn about issues that directly affected their community. The creation of such spaces was among the rhetorical strategies of resistance to urban renewal and other housing policies that unified African American communities. These strategies of resistance also highlight how citizenship and leadership are linked within the African American rhetorical context. Rhetorical education, as a strategy of resistance for African Americans, distributes leadership and agency across the community, creating more informed, unified, and rhetoric-savvy citizens.

All three case studies reveal the connection of citizenship, leadership, and agency within the African American rhetorical context. Rhetorical agency was enacted to improve the residents' chances of influencing housing policies and to ensure residents would have greater standing in their cities. Whether their attempts to modify policy were successful or not, these respective acts of citizenship are worth examining because they reveal the organizing skills and strategies of the communities. In other words, people can be agentive even when they don't accomplish certain goals or achieve specific outcomes. The citizens of the Hill District, Bronzeville, and Rondo may not have been able to halt the destruction of their neighborhoods, which might suggest they were unable enact rhetorical agency. However, when we interpret rhetorical agency through the lens of BRC, we see that place-based rhetorical agency has significance beyond the immediate outcomes and consequences of the situations that produce it. The communities' rhetorical tactics and strategies of resistance—their rhetorical agency—remains ongoing through the critical memories of these neighborhoods, created and kept alive by past, present, and future citizens.

An examination of these case studies highlights the *circulation* of agency within a community, as opposed to the agency of an individual, demonstrating how African American residents in Pittsburgh, St. Paul, and Milwaukee enacted *citizenship* when they were threatened by urban renewal policies. And despite the homes and businesses that were destroyed and the highways that were built, these communities' fights against urban renewal and housing policies had positive effects. Organizational skills developed through civic engagement may help explain the high rate of voting in the African American community as compared to other racial demographics. In addition, other marginalized groups, such as the Young Lords in Chicago and the Women's Movement, have modeled similar strategies from the Black Freedom Movement.[3] Thus, analyzing rhetorical agency in situations where groups and movements did not achieve their primary goal can provide insights into tactics that proved successful in other aspects of the Black Freedom Movement—aspects and events that merit continued attention and study. And, importantly, this examination will continue to uncover the names of individuals at the grassroots level who were also important to the movement but have remained otherwise unknown.

A Black Rhetorical Citizenship Framework

Employing the dual lenses of rhetorical citizenship and African American rhetoric to track African American residents' responses to urban renewal and public housing policies requires combining the diverse set of analytical tools offered by both rhetorical history and a rhetorical citizenship approach, including tools from rhetoric, narrative, and discourse. As Kathleen Turner posits, because writing a deep and rich rhetorical history from the "bottom up" contributes knowledge to both rhetoric and history, it requires the "construction of a kind of methodological jigsaw."[4] When the subject matter is the rhetorical history of the Black Freedom Movement, I maintain that we must also take a BRC approach, which incorporates the theories of African American rhetoric and, importantly, uncovers how the agency of Black Americans in their freedom struggle is intimately tied to space and place.

For example, the BRC framework focuses on the agency of the residents involved and their rhetorical, cultural, and spatial histories, whereas a top-down approach (government figures and institutions) focuses only on the highway and the actions of the city government. By centering the people at the heart of the struggle, the BRC framework uncovers the rhetorical actions and agency of Davis and the Rondo Neighborhood Association in St. Paul—civic education, protests, strategic allyship, and community organizing, all of which demonstrate *rhetorical* resistance to highway construction.

Additionally, by shifting the analytic focus from national leaders to local leaders and participants, the BRC framework helps to uncover the unsung work of so many African American *women* who were often the driving force of the movement. When we use this bottom-up approach to studying the Black Freedom Movement, African American women's leading and organizing at the local level, as James Collins has argued, can no longer be neglected in the civil rights historiography.[5] Rhetoric scholars should employ BRC to help uncover women's role in the ongoing Black Freedom Movement.

Struggle for the City has also shown how rhetorics of place are a central part of African American rhetoric and were especially vital in the circulation of urban renewal arguments within the Black Freedom Movement. By focusing on urban renewal as a *rhetorical* event, these case studies complicate Maulana Karenga's assertions that African American rhetoric is a rhetoric of "communal deliberation" because it leaves out the places in which those actions occur and the meaning of those places to the community.[6] Yet place for African Americans, both locally and nationally in the United States, has always had to be navigated and claimed by them for their use, and the urban renewal era was no exception. Complacency amid this time of significant urban change would have had a disastrous result. Urban renewal projects were just one of many fights that the African American community had to undertake. However, urban renewal in the North in many ways was a connector between other civil rights battles, like school desegregation, fair housing, and fair labor practices for construction jobs. The critical usage of rhetorics of place created "standing"—a place-based connection to citizenship—and provided different avenues for residents' arguments to be addressed by city officials. It is my hope that this book's analysis of urban renewal discourse will contribute to both African American rhetorical history and African American rhetoric by demonstrating the connection between rhetorics of place and citizenship and adding place to conversations of resistance rhetoric within the Black Freedom Movement.

I hope this book has also made clear that additional rhetorical histories of the Black Freedom Movement in the North are needed to enable a more robust understanding of how rhetoric, particularly rhetorics of place, shapes historical events. Because rhetoricians can simultaneously provide new perspectives on rhetorical theory and contribute new knowledge to historical events, these rhetorical histories have the potential to provide new perspectives on civic engagement rhetorics and expand our knowledge of political organizing. These studies should also consider how methodological choice can shape analytic insight, especially when investigating the citizenship practices of marginalized communities. The Black Rhetorical Citizenship framework I developed in this study blends rhetorical, narrative, and discursive analytic methods under the theoretical framework of rhetorical citizenship. By rooting African American rhetorical theory of community, resistance, and place in the Black Freedom Struggle, the BRC framework enables us to contribute new insights to broader studies of African American rhetoric and rhetorical theory.

Pedagogy and the Public Work of Rhetoric

This project's focus on citizenship can inform our pedagogy, especially when we are teaching first-generation college students, single parents, or laid-off workers. These are the voices that often get overlooked as subjects in rhetorical studies, particularly those related to social movements. But, more important, they are the audience for this project. These students can be leaders without being Martin Luther King Jr. or Barbara Jordan. When we teach basic rhetorical theory and argumentation in our first-year writing and speech classes, we should point to examples in the Black Freedom Movement where ordinary people made a difference. As a project of rhetorical history, this book may help instructors strike a balance between the academic and civic purposes of writing and speaking, allowing students to see a community of citizens who, through individual and collective actions, used distinctive discursive activities to make a difference in their lives. Students should be encouraged to write and speak outside the classroom in civic settings. What we see in the actions of the African American residents of Milwaukee, Pittsburgh, and St. Paul is what we hope our students would do when faced with a similar type of rhetorical situation.

This project provides ways in which rhetoricians can engage not only in the "public work of rhetoric," as espoused by John M. Ackerman and David J. Coogan in their edited collection of the same name, but also as scholars of understudied movements both historical and current. Ackerman and Coogan and seventeen other rhetoric scholars argue that civic engagement is a rhetorical act through which "citizen-scholars" can pursue democratic ideals in diverse civic communities "on a negotiated search for the common good."[7] This public work of rhetoric can be accomplished by learning the "material and discursive histories of communities," bringing their rhetorical expertise, and jointly defining the terms for social change.[8]

To illustrate, many of the same neighborhoods that were under assault by urban renewal are now being threatened with gentrification, what I call the sequel to urban renewal. Low-income African American and Latino/a populations are being displaced by private developers and corporate interests. These events require analysis—using our discipline's varied methodological tools—of the strategies of resistance residents are employing against gentrification, which will provide a better understanding of the rhetorical situations these communities face. In addition to studying these movements, rhetoricians and their students can assist these communities by helping those interested in learning effective strategies of public discourse.

The Future of Rhetorical Studies and the Black Freedom Movement

In "The Future of African American Rhetoric," Molefi Asante asserts that the future of African American rhetoric hinged on the assertion of "ethical leadership" and "seeing ourselves as agents in the world rather than objects or victims."[9] As Ronald Heifetz reminds us, leadership should be viewed as open to anyone and not just to those with authority. This idea of leadership blurs leading and following, granting these roles fluidity and mobility rather than fixing them in a social or institutional structure.[10] In other words, leadership is a form of intercommunal reciprocity that can be employed by individuals regardless of their position in an organization, and leaders should encourage "leadership" by those not in leadership positions. Leadership does not mean that an authority figure makes all the decisions, but that leadership can exist within each individual citizen. Essentially, leadership as intercommunal reciprocity transforms "the activity of a citizen from any walk of life mobilizing people" for action in adverse situations.[11] This book examines African Americans as rhetorical agents in an adverse rhetorical situation. Full citizenship did not always apply to African Americans because they were not always recognized as citizens or treated as citizens. Future examinations of the Black Freedom Movement must incorporate or acknowledge African American rhetorical history and traditions. To do so means we can no longer rely solely on the archives of large institutions. Black newspapers, Black church archives, and oral histories from those involved (and not just the traditional higher profile leaders) must also be examined to provide a fuller context of the rhetorical history.

In this project, I explained how the language of urban renewal can shape our understanding of the Black Freedom Movement. Debates continue in civil rights scholarship over the relationship between the traditional Civil Rights Movement and the Black Power Movement, as do conversations over the importance of the "classical" Civil Rights Movement. The debate over what has become known as the "long movement thesis" is a necessary one. In short, this debate centers on whether there is a single continuous struggle for Black freedom that includes the Labor Movement of the 1930s, the Civil Rights Movement (1954–65), and the Black Power Movements of the late 1960s and early 1970s, or whether each is a separate and distinct social movement.[12] The tensions between the two different perspectives on the chronological approaches to examining the Black Freedom Struggle are resulting in new and exciting historical literature of the movement(s).

We are beginning to see a shift toward examining the Civil Rights Movement and the Black Power Movement through a globalization lens. Scholars are showing how the movement(s) in the United States influenced other social movements around the world. In addition to reinforcing the idea that scholars are influenced by the times in which we are writing, this new scholarship indicates that the civil rights legacy of African Americans still contains stories that have not yet been heard and, thus, have potential to create new rhetorical understanding. Moving forward, I offer several ways of further examining the rhetorical history of urban renewal that may provide new pathways to understand the Black Freedom Movement.

For one, future rhetorical scholarship on public policy decisions should consider how rhetorical agency manifests away from a single rhetor. Instead of focusing primarily on top-down approaches to agency, such as presidential speeches, we can gain insight by examining the extent to which ordinary citizens enact agency and rhetorical leadership and the different ways in which their rhetorical actions are consequential. In addition to the roles that mass media play in policy decisions, an examination of other institutions, such as schools and churches, may help broaden our understanding of political truths. I also suggest that when analyzing how public policies operate, rhetorical critics must first examine how master narratives are established and perpetuated. This sort of examination may prove useful to community organizers in creating "community knowledge," as well as to composition scholars who teach community writing.

Examining African American lives in urban centers and how such places act rhetorically may provide insight for scholars examining other locations within the Black Freedom Struggle. The Black Lives Matter (BLM) movement, which was founded by three African American women after the Trayvon Martin shooting in 2013, has held numerous demonstrations and made their presence known on many college campuses. According to the BLM website, "Black Lives Matter is an ideological and political intervention in a world where Black lives are systematically and intentionally targeted for demise."[13] In 2016, Black Lives Matter activists protested police brutality by blocking highways in cities such as St. Paul, Chicago, and Atlanta. BLM protesters in St. Paul chose to block a highway that, as a product of an urban renewal project, destroyed the economic center of the African American community in the 1960s. Milwaukee was also recently the site of civic unrest; in summer 2016, a neighborhood affected by urban renewal held major protests over the treatment of African Americans by police officers. The roots of these strategies of resistance and protest in the urban North can be found, in part, in the African American fight against urban renewal during the 1950s and 1960s. These protests also demonstrate the crucial role that acts of rhetorical citizenship have played and continue to play in the African American struggle for "full citizenship."

Yet rhetoric scholars must do more than just "examine" historical moments because the Black Freedom Movement continues, as reflected in BLM and the fight to keep the gains from the Civil Rights Movement. To support current freedom movements, scholars must use "rhetoric's generative or inventive power and less of its critical/analytical power"[14] to help current community organizations. Efforts could include helping to retain and

maintain community organizing materials as an archive or providing rhetorical education if requested by the community, similar to the leadership
seminars in Milwaukee. Participation in local social justice movements is the
present and the future of rhetorical studies.

Final Words

The convergence of structural, racial, and economic inequalities stacked
the deck against the Hill District, Bronzeville, and Rondo residents, yet residents fought against urban renewal anyway. To be an African American in
the United States often means that your belonging is questioned and your
communities are targeted. For many, the solution is to be civically engaged.[15]
The experiences of the people who lived in these communities remind of
this American truism. African Americans have had to struggle to find places
to live and fight against being forced from the places that urban renewal projects and interstate highways sought to destroy. These projects, built under
"the myth of consensus,"[16] were not meant to enhance the lives of African
Americans who lived in these spaces. Instead, the space for Black faces was
being transformed into white space.[17] What were previously undesirable
areas became highly desirable, but only to reinforce racialized borders and
geographies. Black people, who were already devalued as citizens, also had
their properties and businesses devalued and seized at values far less than
what they were worth to their owners.

Yet African American communities, many of whom still believed in the
American ideals of democracies and justice, refused to let the projects and
these seizures go unchallenged. Collectively, these targeted communities
had the same narrative. Collectively, we can imagine them saying:

> We're just trying to make a place for ourselves in this world. We've got
> to belong somewhere.
>
> Our ancestors were brought to this country against their will. Folks
> are living the Deep South because of Jim Crow, because of persecution.
> We come here because of this idealization of life in the North. There
> are jobs, and you can vote. Now, we're being forced to move again—
> another forced migration.
>
> We're being told where we can and cannot go. At some point, you're
> going to have to deal with us. You can try to keep us on the north side.
> You can try to keep us in the Hill District or in Rondo.

But, at some point, you're going to have to deal with us. You're taking this land to build highways or whatever. But we're here; we're going
to be here.

We're not going anywhere.

This imagined statement of Black grassroots and community groups highlights a crucial piece of the Black urban experience and challenges a still predominant viewpoint that the Black urban population took only few actions to
influence their surroundings in the 1950s urban North. And now these same
communities are facing the sequel to urban renewal—gentrification. A more
recent billboard placed in Pittsburgh that responded to the threat of gentrification and was every bit as powerful and demanding as the Freedom Corner billboard was forcibly taken down because it offended the landlord. The
billboard projected a phrase filled with the critical memory of urban renewal
while enacting Black Rhetorical Citizenship in response to gentrification. In
bold, capitalized, white letters atop a black background, the billboard simply
stated, "There are black people in the future."[18]

NOTES

PROLOGUE

1. James Grossman, in *Land of Hope*, highlights migrants' "perceptions of their place" in their newly adopted Midwestern city and uncovers their perceptions of structural forces in both the places they left and the places they arrived, the experience of movement, and the racial attitudes they encountered.

2. See Geenen, *Milwaukee's Bronzeville*; Cavett, *Voices of Rondo*.

INTRODUCTION

1. Yuen, "Green Line."

2. In this book, I use the terms Black and African American interchangeably.

3. See Handley, "Line Drawn."

4. Triece, *Urban Renewal*, xv.

5. See, for example, P. D. Jones, *Selma of the North*.

6. Given the overlap in movements, I prefer to use the term Black Freedom Movement in my study because the fight over urban renewal (especially in smaller cities) brought the traditional organizations of the Black Freedom Struggle, such as the NAACP, alongside the budding Black Power / self-help organizations. Although this study does not include the more militant organizations of the movement, it does focus on organizations that leaned on the self-help philosophy of the Black Power Movement, as well as on cities that often get overlooked in traditional civil rights scholarship.

7. P. Levine, "All That Matters."

8. According to Wilkerson in *The Warmth of Other Suns*, there were three "streams" that fed the Great Migration: North, Midwest, and West. African Americans from Alabama, Arkansas, and Mississippi fed the Midwestern stream, which included Pittsburgh, Milwaukee, and St. Paul.

9. The Civil Rights Movement cannot be separated from the Black Power Movement because people in cities with smaller African American populations were involved in both movements. Many African Americans from the North participated in Freedom Rides and voting registration drives in places like Alabama and Mississippi. Some returned home and later became involved with the Black Power Movement. The fight over urban renewal brought the traditional organizations of the Black Freedom Struggle, such as the NAACP, alongside the budding Black Power organizations. Given this overlap of movements, I use the term Black Freedom Movement, which incorporates both the Civil Rights Movement and the Black Power Movement.

10. See M. Brooks, *Voice That Could Stir an Army*; J. H. Miller, "Empowering Communities"; and Schneider, "Sea Island."

11. Scholars have questioned whether the Black Power Movement constituted a separate movement or a continuation of the original Civil Rights Movement. Urban historians Matthew Countryman and Patrick D. Jones examined the civil rights struggle of African

Americans in Philadelphia and Milwaukee during the twentieth century. Countryman argues that the goals of the Black Power and Civil Rights movements were intertwined, but the Black Power activists helped to organize the movement in a manner that was more community oriented than the movements of the Southern Christian Leadership Conference. He concludes that the greatest achievement of the Black Power Movement was its critique of America's failure to provide "full citizenship" as promised. Jones highlights the growing conflict between the NAACP and the Black Power philosophy in Milwaukee during the African American community's fight for an open housing law and the clashes between the NAACP Youth Commandos and working-class whites in the surrounding neighborhoods. In each examination, we see the tensions of class struggle, strategy building, and ideology disputes within the Civil Rights Movement.

12. Flanagan, "Housing Act of 1954," 267–68.

13. Eisenhower, "Statement by the President."

14. Gotham, "City Without Slums," 287.

15. Pritchett, *Robert Clifton Weaver*, 7–8.

16. Pritchett, *Robert Clifton Weaver*, 7–8.

17. Lindemann-Nelson, *Damaged Identities*, 6.

18. Perry, *More Beautiful*, 43.

19. A phrase first used by John Winthrop in a 1630 sermon, "Model of Christian Charity," which appears in numerous literature anthologies, including *American Literature*. The phrase has been used by many political figures, including former president Ronald Reagan.

20. Aristotle, *On Rhetoric*, 200, 220.

21. Aristotle, *On Rhetoric*, 218.

22. Perelman and Olbrechts-Tyteca, *New Rhetoric*, 398–99.

23. Lakoff and Johnson, *Metaphors*, 4.

24. Fairclough, *Discourse*, 194.

25. Commer, "Perelman's Dissociation," 3–4.

26. Lakoff and Johnson, *Metaphors*, 28–30.

27. Berger, "How Embedded Knowledge Structures," 269.

28. Berger, "How Embedded Knowledge Structures," 269.

29. Herscher, "Urbanism of Racial Capitalism," 59. Herscher traces how blight migrated from agriculture to the urban context and later became a "technical term for the urban condition."

30. Breger, "Concept and Causes," 370.

31. "Housing Act of 1954," 244; emphasis added.

32. *Merriam-Webster*, s.v. "renew," accessed April 19, 2017, https://www.merriam-webster.com/dictionary/renew.

33. Johnstone, *Discourse Analysis*, 59.

34. Cohn, "Sex and Death," 690.

35. Burke, *Rhetoric of Motives*, 26.

36. "Housing Act of 1949," Pub. L. 81–171.

37. "Housing Act of 1954," 878.

38. Burke quoted in Crable, *Ralph Ellison and Kenneth Burke*, 165.

39. Asen, "Discourse Theory," 191.

40. See S. Logan, *We Are Coming*.

41. Asen, "Discourse Theory," 195.

42. Karenga, "Nommo, Kawaida."

43. See Gilyard and Banks, *On African-American Rhetoric*.

44. Kock and Villadsen, *Rhetorical Citizenship and Public Deliberation*, 5.

45. See, for example, Kock and Villadsen, *Rhetorical Citizenship and Public Deliberation*, 5, and Kock and Villadsen, *Contemporary Rhetorical Citizenship*.

46. Kock and Villadsen, *Rhetorical Citizenship and Public Deliberation*, 1.
47. See also Maddux, *Practicing Citizenship*.
48. Kock and Villadsen, *Contemporary Rhetorical Citizenship*, 10.
49. Kock and Villadsen, *Contemporary Rhetorical Citizenship*, 10.
50. Keith and Cossart, "Search for 'Real' Democracy," 46.
51. Baxter and Jack, "Qualitative Case Study Methodology," 544.
52. Johansson, "On Case Study Methodology," 2.
53. K. Wilson, "Interpreting the Discursive Field," xvi.
54. For more on race, ethnicity, and legal citizenship, see Ong et al., "Cultural Citizenship."
55. D. Gordon, *Black Identity*, 23.
56. Klein, "Spectacular Citizenships," 102.
57. Rai, *Democracy's Lot*, 6.
58. Danielle Allen believes the interaction between rhetoric and citizenship can provide a road map to better race relations in the United States. On the other hand, Karma Chavez argues that the framework of citizenship does little to question and transform its reliance on colonialism and modern nation-state building.
59. Chavez prefers the term "world making practices" to replace the ideas of citizenship for marginalized groups.
60. Fehrenbacher, *Dred Scott Case*, 187.
61. R. Logan, *What the Negro Wants*, 14.
62. Forbes, "Every Man Fights," 157.
63. See Foreman et al., *Colored Conventions Movement*.
64. Karenga, "Nommo, Kawaida," 3.
65. Murch, *Living for the City*, 147.
66. See Rothstein, *Color of Law*.
67. Neely and Samura, "Social Geographies," 1936.
68. Nunley, "From the Harbor," 223.
69. Berlin, "Making of African America," 15.
70. Berlin, "Making of African America," 19.
71. Endres and Senda-Cook, "Location Matters," 257.

CHAPTER 1

1. Quoted in Lustig, "Home."
2. Glasco, "Next Page."
3. Glasco, "Next Page."
4. Differences arose along class and especially among those who immigrated from the segregated South to Northern cities for more economic and civic opportunities.
5. Kock and Villadsen, "Contemporary Rhetorical Citizenship," 13.
6. Von Hoffman, "Study in Contradictions."
7. "Housing Act of 1949," Pub. L. 81–171.
8. Von Hoffman, "Study in Contradictions," 299.
9. Truman, "Statement by the President."
10. "Housing Act of 1949," Pub. L. 81–171.
11. In 1972, the name of the National Association of Real Estate Boards was changed to the National Association of REALTORS® (NAR). The acronym NAREB is now used by the National Association of Real Estate Brokers, Inc., which is an equal opportunity and civil rights advocacy organization for African American real estate professionals, consumers, and communities in America that was founded in Tampa, Florida, in 1947.

12. C. Gordon, *Mapping Decline*, 197.

13. Gotham, "City Without Slums," 296.

14. Gotham, "City Without Slums," 76.

15. Von Hoffman, "Enter the Housing Industry," 13.

16. Gotham, "City Without Slums," 287.

17. Hirsch, *Making the Second Ghetto*, 271.

18. Gotham, "City Without Slums," 287.

19. Pritchett, *Robert Clifton Weaver*, 3.

20. Niemuth, "Urban Renewal," 11.

21. Niemuth, "Urban Renewal," 11.

22. "Housing Act of 1949," Pub. L. 81–171; "Housing Act of 1954," Pub. L. 83–560.

23. Martin Anderson, *Federal Bulldozer*, 2.

24. Fullilove, *Root Shock*, 171.

25. "City of the Future."

26. "City of the Future."

27. Some businesses located in the Hill District include Crawford Grille No. 1, Proctor's Hair Shop, Stanley's Tavern, and the Washington Playground, where the Homestead Grays of the Negro Leagues played.

28. Trotter and Day, *Race and Renaissance*, 15.

29. Trotter and Day, *Race and Renaissance*, 15.

30. "Allegheny Conference on Community Development (Pittsburgh, Pa.), Records, 1920–1993," n.d., MSS 285, Library and Archives Division, Senator John Heinz History Center.

31. Love, "Giant Center."

32. "Cultural Center."

33. Herscher, "Urbanism of Racial Capitalism," 60.

34. Herscher, "Urbanism of Racial Capitalism," 59–60.

35. Herscher, "Urbanism of Racial Capitalism," 59–60.

36. "Allegheny Conference."

37. "City Council Expected."

38. See Sontag, *Illness as Metaphor*; Hauser and Schwarz, "War on Prevention"; Flusberg et al., "War Metaphors."

39. "Fight on Blight."

40. "Redeveloping Lower Hill."

41. "Operation Fix-Up."

42. "Cultural Center."

43. "Cultural Center," par. 6.

44. "City Council."

45. Herscher, "Urbanism of Racial Capitalism," 62.

46. "Lower Hill Officially."

47. *Merriam-Webster*, s.v. "Renaissance," accessed April 19, 2017, https://www.merriam-webster.com/dictionary/Renaissance.

48. *Merriam-Webster*, s.v. "Renaissance."

49. "Hill District."

50. "City Council Expected."

51. "Redeveloping Lower Hill."

52. "Fine, but Where."

53. "City Council Expected."

54. "Fine, but Where."

55. "Redevelopment to Erase Blight."

56. P. L. Jones, "Hill Housing Future."

57. Trotter, *Pittsburgh and the Urban League*, 125.

58. "5th Ave. High Student."

59. "Challenge."

60. Lubove, *Twentieth-Century Pittsburgh*.

61. Robick, "Blight."

62. Grant, "Obituary."

63. Glasco, "Next Page."

64. "Hill Committee Sets First Public Meeting."

65. Karenga, "Nommo, Kawaida," 3.

66. Pittsburgh residents also use rhetorics of place as a form of critical memory, which I discuss in chapter 4.

67. Asen, "Discourse Theory," 199.

68. Keen, "Theory of Narrative Empathy," 216. A counternarrative must have the ability to persuade or resonate with its readers. Narrative theorist Suzanne Keen describes how two features of narratives—"character identification" and "narrative situation"—help readers develop empathy for the characters and/or the narrator of a narrative.

69. Perelman and Olbrechts-Tyteca, *New Rhetoric*, 116.

70. Perelman and Olbrechts-Tyteca, *New Rhetoric*, 119.

71. Karon, "Presence in 'The New Rhetoric,'" 97.

72. Lindemann-Nelson, *Damaged Identities*, 7.

73. Lindemann-Nelson, *Damaged Identities*, 6.

74. See S. Logan, *We Are Coming*.

75. Nunley, *Keepin' It Hushed*.

76. Bal, *Narratology*, 18.

77. Clark, "Down Memory Lane," par. 1–2 (emphasis added).

78. Clark, "Down Memory Lane," par 8.

79. Clark, "Down Memory Lane," par 10.

80. Clark, "Down Memory Lane," par 10.

81. "Wylie Avenue."

82. Perelman and Olbrechts-Tyteca, *New Rhetoric*.

83. Labov and Waletzky, "Narrative Analysis," 21.

84. In narrative theory, these events are called the fabula, which "is a series of logically and chronologically related events that are caused or experienced by actors." Bal, *Narratology*, 5.

85. Labov and Waletzky, "Narrative Analysis," 35.

86. "Wylie Avenue."

87. Chatman, "Characters and Narrators," 196. According to Chatman, the way in which a story is told—and by whom—may affect how the reader perceives the characters in the narrative. Chatman describes "filter" as the narrator's retelling of "a story neutrally or from or through one or another character's consciousness."

88. Davis, "'Pgh. Story' Moves."

89. Davis, "'Pgh. Story' Moves."

90. Davis, "'Pgh. Story' Moves."

91. Chatman, "Characters and Narrators," 197.

92. Garland, "'Help Us!'"

93. K. Wilson, "Interpreting the Discursive Field," 301.

94. HACLab Pittsburgh.

95. Koger, "Citizens Unveil Plan."

96. Koger, "Citizens Unveil Plan."

97. Koger, "Citizens Unveil Plan."

98. Koger, "Citizens Unveil Plan."

99. See Samahy, Grimley, and Kubo, *Imagining the Modern*. Hill District residents were members of the design team. The maps were created under the direction of residents and not drawn to scale. The more important the area or building was to the community, the larger it appeared on the map.

100. The CCHDR believed in the concept of "self-renewal." This concept is discussed in relation to urban renewal in the next chapter.

101. Robick, "Blight," 99.

102. Endres and Senda-Cook, "Location Matters," 258.

103. Endres and Senda-Cook, "Location Matters," 258.

104. See https://www.freedomcorner.org.

105. Vanguri, *Rhetorics of Names*, 1.

106. Ralph Proctor Jr., "Oral History of the Lower Hill," personal interview, November 19, 2012.

107. Moody, "Freedom Corner Memorial."

108. "Line Drawn."

109. Proctor, "Oral History."

110. Morrow, "Freedom Corner Opens."

111. Dieterich-Ward, *Beyond Rust*, 178.

112. "Black Monday Set in Pittsburgh."

113. "City Fathers."

114. Johnstone, *Discourse Analysis*, 233.

115. A. Smith, *Rhetoric of Black Revolution*, 1.

116. "Line Drawn."

117. Tuan, *Space and Place*, 6.

118. Quoted in Glasco, "Next Page."

119. Edelman, *Constructing the Political Spectacle*, 12.

120. Martin Anderson, *Federal Bulldozer*, 20.

CHAPTER 2

1. Urban Land Institute, *Advisory Services Panel Report*.

2. Altshuler, *City Planning Process*.

3. RSIA is an acronym I created for this book.

4. Altshuler, *City Planning Process*, 60.

5. "St. Paul Man."

6. Hunter et al., "Black Placemaking," 32.

7. Hunter et al., "Black Placemaking," 34.

8. Mountford, "On Gender and Rhetorical Space," 42.

9. See Van Dusen and Holley, *Detroit's Birwood Wall*.

10. Fleming, *City of Rhetoric*.

11. Neely and Samura, "Social Geographies."

12. Taylor and Holm, *African Americans*, 6.

13. Taylor and Holm, *African Americans*, 11.

14. Taylor and Holm, *African Americans*, 35.

15. Nathaniel Abdul Khaliq, Rondo Oral History Project, audio recording, July 9, 2004, Minnesota Historical Society, OH 110.17; Urban Land Institute, *Advisory Services Panel Report*.

16. Johnson, "African Americans."

17. Mohl, "Interstates," 12.

18. Mohl, "Interstates," 12.

19. Rondo Avenue, Inc. (Saint Paul, Minn.), "Rondo Avenue, Inc. Records," Box 1, Minnesota Historical Society, http://www2.mnhs.org/library/findaids/01118.xml.

20. Rogers, "Citizens Organize."

21. Condit, "Functions of Epideictic," 289.

22. Pritchett, *Robert Clifton Weaver*, 153.

23. McGraw, "Urban Renewal," 45.

24. McGraw, "Urban Renewal," 47.

25. "Housing Act of 1954."

26. Mills, *Cutting Along*, 3–4.

27. Howard-Pitney, *Afro-American Jeremiad*.

28. "Religious Life and Social Organization in Rondo," Remembering Rondo | A History Harvest, https://omeka.macalester.edu/rondo/exhibits/show/eat--pray--jam--culture-in-old/religious-life-and-social-orga.

29. See https://www.pilgrimbaptistchurch.org/history.

30. "Twin City Church News."

31. Marable, *Black Leadership*, xiii.

32. Marable, *Black Leadership*, xiii.

33. Altshuler, *City Planning Process*, 62.

34. "St. Paul Leaders Walk Out."

35. "Timothy Howard's Service."

36. Fleming, *City of Rhetoric*, 196.

37. Urban Land Institute, *Advisory Services Panel Report*, 12.

38. Deskins and Bettinger, "Geographical Identities," 57.

39. Nunley, "From the Harbor," 225.

40. One newspaper serviced St. Paul and the other Minneapolis, but they were both from the same publisher and would often have the same content.

41. Sen, "Placemaking."

42. Pierce, Martin, and Murphy, "Relational Place-Making," 54.

43. Altshuler, *City Planning Process*, 60.

44. Rogers, "Citizens Organize."

45. Rogers, "Citizens Organize."

46. Altshuler, *City Planning Process*, 61.

47. Rogers, "Citizens Organize."

48. Cavanaugh, "Politics and Freeways."

49. Altshuler, *City Planning Process*, 62.

50. "Pioneering St. Paul Leader."

51. Cavanaugh, "Politics and Freeways."

52. Altshuler, *City Planning Process*, 43.

53. Reicher, "St. Paul City Planner."

54. Altshuler, *City Planning Process*, 43.

55. Altshuler, *City Planning Process*, 43.

56. "Area Represented," 1.

57. "Area Represented," 1.

58. Cavanaugh, "Politics and Freeways."

59. Reicher, "St. Paul City Planner."

60. "Sunday's Saint Paul," 4.

61. Rogers, "Citizens Organize."

62. White, *How Far the Promised Land?*, 130.

63. Delegard and Petersen, "Mapping Prejudice."

64. Freund, *Colored Property*.

65. Freund, *Colored Property*; Gotham, "City Without Slums"; Gonda, *Unjust Deeds*.

66. Gotham, "City Without Slums."
67. Gotham, "City Without Slums."
68. Gonda, *Unjust Deeds.*
69. Kaul, "With Covenants."
70. Delegard and Petersen, "Mapping Prejudice."
71. Mountford, "On Gender and Rhetorical Spaces," 50.
72. "Union Gospel Mission Records," May 1962, Box 4, Minnesota Historical Society, http://www2.mnhs.org/library/findaids/00040.xml.
73. "Union Gospel Mission Records."
74. "Union Gospel Mission Records."
75. Altshuler, *City Planning Process,* 63.
76. Marvin Roger Anderson, Rondo Oral History Project, audio recording, November 3, 2004, Minnesota Historical Society, OH 110.3.
77. Marvin Anderson, Rondo Oral History Project, 17.
78. "Advert for Rangh Court," *Remembering Rondo | A History Harvest,* n.d., https://omeka.macalester.edu/rondo/items/show/62.
79. "Howard Urges Families," 1.
80. "Howard Urges Families," 1.
81. Handley, "'Line Drawn'"; Handley et al., "Unearthing Deep Roots."
82. White, *How Far the Promised Land?,* 129–30.
83. Marvin Anderson, Rondo Oral History Project, 21.
84. Marvin Anderson, Rondo Oral History Project, 21.
85. Altshuler, *City Planning Process,* 65.
86. Altshuler, *City Planning Process,* 65.
87. Altshuler, *City Planning Process,* 66.
88. Altshuler, *City Planning Process,* 66.
89. "Timothy Howard's Service."
90. Altshuler, *City Planning Process,* 68.
91. Sen, "Placemaking."
92. Yusef Mgeni, Rondo Oral History Project, audio recording, April 26, 2004, Minnesota Historical Society, OH 110.21.
93. Brown, *Black Skyscraper,* 27.
94. "Rondo–St. Anthony Area."
95. I engage here with Robert Topinka's notion of resistance within rhetorical spaces. Topinka, "Resisting the Fixity."
96. Wilkerson, *Warmth of Other Suns.*
97. Khaliq, Rondo Oral History Project.
98. Khaliq, Rondo Oral History Project.
99. Khaliq, Rondo Oral History Project.
100. "Pastor Threatens Cops."
101. D. Gordon, *Black Identity,* 22.
102. Topinka, "Resisting the Fixity."
103. Endres and Senda-Cook, "Location Matters."
104. Fullilove, *Root Shock.*
105. Jordan, "America Must Remove," 1.
106. Fleming, *City of Rhetoric.*

CHAPTER 3

1. Niemuth, "Urban Renewal," 12.
2. Barbera, "Improvised World," 106–14.

3. "Hillside Property Purchase."

4. Bernard D. Toliver, "Milwaukee NAACP Housing Committee," November 1957, Box 3, Folder 11, University of Wisconsin–Milwaukee Libraries Archives Department.

5. Toliver, "Milwaukee NAACP Housing Committee."

6. Niemuth, "Urban Renewal," 7.

7. The term "cultural reciprocity" was suggested to me by Christian O. Lundberg during a discussion about this project at the 2016 RSA Network Forum in Atlanta, Georgia.

8. Miner, *Lessons from the Heartland*, section 2.

9. K. Smith, "From Socialism to Racism."

10. K. Smith, "From Socialism to Racism," 71.

11. Miner, *Lessons from the Heartland*, section 2.

12. P. D. Jones, *Selma of the North*, 29.

13. K. Smith, "From Socialism to Racism," 86.

14. K. Smith, "From Socialism to Racism," 86.

15. K. Smith, "From Socialism to Racism," 73; Niemuth, "Urban Renewal," 37.

16. K. Smith, "From Socialism to Racism."

17. K. Smith, "From Socialism to Racism."

18. Maier, "Mayor Looks," 31.

19. Milwaukee CRP Application, quoted in Honer, "Unworkable Program," 26.

20. Honer, "Unworkable Program," 27.

21. K. Smith, "From Socialism to Racism," 71–95.

22. Records of Mayor Henry W. Maier Administration, Milwaukee, Wisconsin, 1957–1989 (Milwaukee Series 44), Box 188, Folder 7, University of Wisconsin–Milwaukee Libraries, Archives Department, May 8, 2016, http://digital.library.wisc.edu/1711.dl/wiarchives.uw-whs-milw0044.

23. "Film to Show Renewal." The movie was filmed by *Life* magazine and created to show how blight can affect transportation, schools, parking, and other urban related issues. The event was hosted by the Citizens Urban Renewal Committee and the Vocational School.

24. "Milwaukee Urban Renewal Program."

25. Records of Mayor Henry W. Maier.

26. Records of Mayor Henry W. Maier.

27. "Democrats Open County."

28. Records of Mayor Henry W. Maier.

29. "Hillside Property Purchase."

30. "Hillside Property Purchase."

31. Niemuth, "Urban Renewal," 12.

32. "Editorial."

33. "Editorial."

34. Gonda, *Unjust Deeds*, 21.

35. Trotter, *Black Milwaukee*, 70.

36. Trotter, *Black Milwaukee*, 70.

37. Trotter, *Black Milwaukee*, 71.

38. Quinn, "Racially Restrictive Covenants."

39. Sandler, "Hyler Overcame Racism."

40. Cassidy, "Integration Pioneer," 1.

41. Gonda, *Unjust Deeds*; Freund, *Colored Property*.

42. Anne Bonds, Derek Handley, Reggie Jackson, and Lawrence Hoffman, "Mapping Racism and Resistance in Milwaukee County," Morris Fromkin Memorial Lecture, University of Wisconsin–Milwaukee, November 4, 2021.

43. K. Smith, "From Socialism to Racism," 93.

44. Lucinda Gordon, "Leadership Training Classes," October 1964, Box 15, Folder 37, University of Wisconsin–Milwaukee Libraries Archives Department.

45. K. Smith, "From Socialism to Racism," 91.

46. K. Smith, "From Socialism to Racism," 92.

47. Metcalfe, "Commanding a Movement," 6.

48. "Vel Phillips Papers," 1946–2009, Box 1 and Box 65, University of Wisconsin–Milwaukee Libraries Archives Department, http://digital.library.wisc.edu/1711.dl /wiarchives.uw-whs-mil00231. In her draft for this speech, all the words were capitalized. I made the decision to write them in sentence format for this book.

49. "Vel Phillips Papers." In Phillips's draft of the speech, she typed the word "Colored" but lined it out and wrote "Negro." She did this for all the uses of the word "Colored."

50. "Vel Phillips Papers."

51. "March on Milwaukee—Civil Rights History Project," Libraries Digital Collection, University of Wisconsin–Milwaukee Libraries, https://uwm.edu/marchonmilwaukee/.

52. Term coined by CNN commentator Van Jones and quoted in Blake, "This Is What."

53. "March on Milwaukee: More Than One Struggle," Oral History Collection Recorded Interviews, n.d. Series 1, Box 1, Folder 8, Marquette University, Department of Special Collections and University Archives, https://www.marquette.edu/library /archives/Mss/MOM/MOM-series1.php. Said in a recorded interview with Mary C. Arms.

54. Metcalfe, "Commanding a Movement," 5.

55. "March on Milwaukee: More Than."

56. L. Gordon, "Leadership Training Classes."

57. "Words of the Week," 30.

58. "Words of the Week," 30.

59. "Words of the Week," 30.

60. Milwaukee Urban League, Press Release, 1964, Box 15, Folder 31, Correspondence and Memoranda, 1963–1966, University of Wisconsin–Milwaukee Libraries Archives Department.

61. Milwaukee Urban League, Press Release.

62. University of Wisconsin Extension (UWEX) Annual Report 1964–1965, Box 4, Folder 50, University of Wisconsin Extension Center for Community Economic Development Records, 1965–1992, University of Wisconsin–Milwaukee Libraries, Archives Department. May 8, 2016.

63. A. Clarke Hagensick, Faculty Staff Biographical File, box 11, folder Hagensick, A. Clarke, (1983), University of Wisconsin.

64. UWEX Annual Report.

65. Niemuth, "Urban Renewal," 14.

66. Asante, "Future of African American Rhetoric," 291.

67. Staudacher's course is rooted in the tradition of the discussion movement as described by William Keith in Democracy as Discussion.

68. Joseph M. Staudacher, "Effective Speaking in Group Situations," Marquette University–Milwaukee School of Speech, Wisconsin Historical Society Library Archives Department.

69. Staudacher, "Effective Speaking in Group Situations."

70. Enoch, Refiguring Rhetorical Education, 8–9.

71. Milwaukee Urban League.

72. Milwaukee Urban League.

73. L. Gordon, "Leadership Training Classes."

74. L. Gordon, "Leadership Training Classes."

75. Milwaukee Urban League.

76. UWEX Annual Report.

77. Milwaukee Urban League.

78. UWEX Annual Report.

79. Sara Ettenheim, Faculty Staff Biographical Files, box 11, folder Ettenheim, Sara (Mrs. George), University of Wisconsin–Milwaukee Libraries Archives Department.

80. Sara Ettenheim, Faculty Staff Biographical Files, box 11, folder Ettenheim, Sara (Mrs. George), University of Wisconsin–Milwaukee Libraries Archives Department. Years later, Ettenheim would discover that the Milwaukee Police Department's "Special Assignment Squad" kept a file of her activities dating back to when she began her work with the seminars in 1964.

81. Niemuth, "Urban Renewal," 11.

82. Warren Bloomberg, Biographical Files, box 11, University of Wisconsin–Milwaukee Libraries Archives Department.

83. UWEX Annual Report.

84. UWEX Annual Report.

85. Milwaukee Urban League.

86. P. D. Jones, "Black Empowerment," 142.

87. "WAICO," 1.

88. P. D. Jones, "Black Empowerment."

89. Higgins and Brush, "Personal Experience Narrative," 694.

90. See Geisler, "How Ought We," 2. Cheryl Geisler defines rhetorical agency as the ability of rhetors to act and be heard while adapting to shifting circumstances.

91. Campbell, "Agency," 1. Campbell has noted that "'agency' is polysemic and ambiguous, a term that can refer to invention, strategies, authorship, institutional power, identity, subjectivity, practices, and subject positions, among others."

92. Hauser, *Vernacular Voices*.

93. Cooper, "Rhetorical Agency," 421.

94. Berrnet quoted in Cooper, "Rhetorical Agency," 421.

95. Cooper, "Rhetorical Agency," 421.

96. Leff, "Tradition and Agency," 136.

97. Considering recent scholarship about the politics of gender and sexuality that were also shaping parts of the Black Freedom Movement, we should also keep in mind those who might have been or felt excluded from these spaces.

98. Lundberg and Gunn, "'Ouija Board,'" 96–98.

99. Riordan, "Grassroots and Community Activism," 47.

100. *Charlotte Russell Partridge and Miriam Frink Papers 1862–1980*, Box 65, Folder 22, University of Wisconsin–Milwaukee Archives.

101. "WAICO Fights for Residential."

102. Riordan, "Grassroots and Community Activism."

103. "WAICO Fights for Residential."

104. Riordan, "Grassroots and Community Activism."

105. "WAICO," 1.

106. Ture and Hamilton, *Black Power*, 44.

107. Riordan, "Grassroots and Community Activism."

108. Riordan, "Grassroots and Community Activism."

109. Riordan, "Grassroots and Community Activism."

110. Trotter, *Black Milwaukee*.

111. Marable, *Black Leadership*.

112. A. Smith, *Rhetoric of Black Revolution*. Smith is now known as Molefi Asante.

113. Olson, "What Is Rhetorical Leadership?"

114. Ture and Hamilton, *Black Power*.

115. Kelley, *Power of Followership*, 27. Kelley argues that a follower must have a "courageous conscience" because there will be times when a leader will ask them to do unethical things.

116. Kelley, *Power of Followership*, 27.

117. Payne, *I've Got the Light*, 84.

118. Alkebulan, "Spiritual Essence," 37.

119. Alkebulan, "Spiritual Essence," 68. Charles Payne refers to this style of leadership as a "philosophy of collective leadership."

120. Alkebulan, "Spiritual Essence," 75.

121. J. H. Miller, "Empowering Communities," 157.

122. Schneider, "Freedom Schooling," 54.

123. Heifetz, *Leadership Without Easy Answers*, 128.

124. Schneider, "Freedom Schooling," 53.

125. Schneider, "Freedom Schooling," 64.

126. Higgins and Brush, "Personal Experience Narrative," 695.

127. Higgins and Brush, "Personal Experience Narrative," 694–95.

128. Squires, "Rethinking the Black Public Sphere."

129. Higgins and Brush, "Personal Experience Narrative," 695.

130. I discuss hush harbor rhetoric in more detail in chapter 2.

131. Higgins and Brush, "Personal Experience Narrative," 695.

132. J. H. Miller, "Empowering Communities," 51.

133. University of Wisconsin Extension Center for Community Economic Development Records, 1965–1992, University of Wisconsin–Milwaukee Libraries Archives Department, http://digital.library.wisc.edu/1711.dl/wiarchives.uw-mil-uwmaco154.

CHAPTER 4

1. Pearce, "When Martin Luther King Jr."

2. "1966 Ware Lecture."

3. "Civil Rights Act of 1968."

4. Teaford, *Rough Road to Renaissance*, 310.

5. Belcher, "Miami's Colored over Segregation," 209.

6. Tuan, *Space and Place*, 8.

7. Baker, "Critical Memory."

8. Baker, "Critical Memory," 3.

9. Baker, "Critical Memory," 31.

10. Baker, "Critical Memory," 3.

11. Vanderhaagen, *Children's Biographies*, 11. Chapter 2 of this book provides an excellent historiography of memory in rhetorical and historical studies.

12. Vanderhaagen, *Children's Biographies*, 6.

13. Duquette Smith and Bergman, "You Were on Indian Land," 160–88.

14. Triece, *Urban Renewal*, 47. Triece uses the term "*conscious remembering* to describe how residents recollected the role of capitalist processes and systemic racism in Detroit's history, in essence, forcing the past onto the present and rejecting 'whiteness' rhetorical silence' (Crenshaw 1997) perpetuated through dominant accounts of public memory."

15. Dagbovie, *Reclaiming the Black Past*, vi.

16. Dagbovie, *Reclaiming the Black Past*, ix.

17. Vanderhaagen, *Children's Biographies*, 34.

18. Vanderhaagen, *Children's Biographies*, 11.

19. Mando, "Constructing the Vicarious Experience."

20. Glaude, *Democracy in Black*, 46.

21. Baker, "Critical Memory," 31.

22. Fullilove, *Root Shock*, 11.

23. Lyon, "Introduction," xix.

24. Bedoya, "Spatial Justice," 1.

25. Rai, *Democracy's Lot*, 34.

26. Rai, *Democracy's Lot*, 34.

27. Gallagher and LaWare, "Sparring with Public Memory," 89.

28. Lubove, *Twentieth-Century Pittsburgh*. For an image of the Hill District Citizen Development Corporation's brick-and-mortar headquarters circa 1972–1975, see https://collection.carnegieart.org/objects/1df747ae-d978-427a-8c44-e9e6a4a3dd38.

29. "About the Hill CDC," Hill Community Development Corp, n.d., https://www.hilldistrict.org/about.

30. "About the Hill CDC."

31. "Lessons of Freedom Corner," 15.

32. Barnes, "Civil Rights Monument," C–1.

33. Barnes, "Civil Rights Monument," C–1.

34. "Lessons of Freedom Corner," 17.

35. "Lessons of Freedom Corner," 17.

36. Proctor, "Oral History of the Lower Hill."

37. "Lessons of Freedom Corner," 17.

38. "Lessons of Freedom Corner," 17.

39. "Lessons of Freedom Corner," 15.

40. "Lessons of Freedom Corner," 17.

41. Endres and Senda-Cook, "Location Matters," 261.

42. Proctor, "Oral History of the Lower Hill."

43. Karenga, "Nommo, Kawaida," 4.

44. "URA Approves Signing."

45. Majors, "Many Ask Council."

46. Pfaffmann, "Forum."

47. Majors, "Many Ask Council."

48. Floyd George Smaller Jr. and Marvin Roger Anderson, Rondo Oral History Project, audio recording, February 13, 2004, Minnesota Historical Society, OH 110.28.

49. Marvin R. Anderson, "Rondo Review," email, May 9, 2023.

50. Smaller and Anderson, Rondo Oral History Project.

51. Smaller and Anderson, Rondo Oral History Project.

52. Smaller and Anderson, Rondo Oral History Project.

53. Smaller and Anderson, Rondo Oral History Project.

54. Rondo Avenue, Inc., "Rondo Avenue, Inc. Records."

55. Baker, "Critical Memory," 3.

56. Corrigan, *Black Feelings*.

57. Rondo Avenue, Inc., "Rondo Avenue, Inc. Records."

58. Smaller and Anderson, Rondo Oral History Project.

59. Smaller and Anderson, Rondo Oral History Project.

60. Yuen, "Central Corridor."

61. Yuen, "Central Corridor."

62. Yuen, "Green Line."

63. Costantini and KARE, "Rondo Neighborhood Gets Apologies."

64. Costantini and KARE, "Rondo Neighborhood Gets Apologies."

65. Hoekstra, "Rondo Commemorative Plaza."

66. Hoekstra, "Rondo Commemorative Plaza."

67. Hoekstra, "Rondo Commemorative Plaza."

68. Robinson, "Commemorative Plaza Revives."

69. Rondo Avenue, Inc., *Story of 755 Rondo*, July 2018, Rondo Commemorative Plaza, St. Paul, MN. Viewed July 26, 2019.

70. "Dedication of Rondo Plaza."

71. Halloran and Clark, "National Park Landscapes," 148.

72. Gallagher and LaWare, "Sparring with Public Memory," 88.

73. Gallagher and LaWare, "Sparring with Public Memory," 88.

74. Janzer, "St. Paul's ReConnect Rondo."

75. Janzer, "St. Paul's ReConnect Rondo."

76. "ReConnect Rondo Fact Sheet," https://reconnectrondo.com/wp-content /uploads/2021/08/ReConnect-Rondo-Fact-Sheet-1.pdf.

77. "ReConnect Rondo Fact Sheet."

78. "ReConnect Rondo Fact Sheet." These losses are based on the organization's "Rondo Past Prosperity Study."

79. "ReConnect Rondo Fact Sheet."

80. "ReConnect Rondo Fact Sheet."

81. "Rondo Effort for a Land Bridge over I-94 Being Heard at MN Legislature Tuesday, Seen as a Restorative Move Broadly Embraced in the Post-George Floyd Era," ReConnect Rondo, press release, January 29, 2021, https://reconnectrondo.com/wp -content/uploads/2021/03/ReConnect-Rondo-Legislative-Hearing-PR-1.29.21.pdf.

82. House, "Relocation of Families Displaced," 75.

83. S. Jones, *Voices of Milwaukee Bronzeville*. It was the Hillside urban renewal project that dealt the first blow leading to the demise of Bronzeville.

84. Florida, "U.S. Cities."

85. Kennedy, "America's 11 Poorest Cities."

86. J. Miller, "Save Milwaukee"; Mock, "Milwaukee Is the Worst Place."

87. "Race for Results: Building a Path to Opportunity for All Children," The Annie E. Casey Foundation, March 30, 2014, https://www.aecf.org/resources/race-for-results.

88. Bonds, "Race and Ethnicity"; M. Levine, "State of Black Milwaukee."

89. Desmond, *Evicted*.

90. See S. Jones, *Voices of Milwaukee Bronzeville*; Geenen, *Milwaukee's Bronzeville*; and Black, Harpole, and Di Frances, *Bronzeville*.

91. There are four plaques, each with the same writing and design, placed on four corners of the bridge next to the sidewalk.

92. Wisconsin Folks, "George McCormick's Main Page," http://wisconsinfolks.org /mccormick1.htm.

93. Raton, "Tejumaloa Ologboni."

94. "Muneer Bahauddeen," Picturing Milwaukee: Washington Park, http://acts housing.weebly.com/muneer-bahauddeen.html.

95. Hockerman, "Artwork Will Add Local Flavor."

96. Marback, "Tale of Two Plaques," 257.

97. Reuben Harpole Jr., "Oral History Interview," interview by Jack Doughtery, June 6, 1995, video, UWM Manuscript Collection 217, Box 7, Audio 30, University of Wisconsin–Milwaukee Libraries Archives Department, https://collections.lib.uwm.edu/digital /collection/march/id/1632/.

98. City of Milwaukee Department of City Development, "Bronzeville Market Analysis and District Plan."

99. City of Milwaukee Department of City Development, "Bronzeville Market Analysis and District Plan," 1.

100. City of Milwaukee, "About Bronzeville," https://city.milwaukee.gov/Bronzeville /About.

101. City of Milwaukee, "About Bronzeville."

102. Milwaukee County, "Milwaukee County Office of Equity," https://county .milwaukee.gov/EN/Office-of-Equity.

103. Behm, "Easing Racial Disparities."

104. Coates, "Case for Reparations."

105. Associated Press, "Bush Limits Eminent-Domain Seizures." However, Debbie Becher argues that the government took action to get rid of the federal use of eminent domain as the result of a white plaintiff saving their home. Becher, "Race as a Set of Symbolic Resources."

CONCLUSION

1. S. Smith, "August Wilson's St. Paul Roots."

2. A. Wilson, *Jitney*.

3. See Hinojosa, *Apostles of Change*; Randolph, *Florynce "Flo" Kennedy*.

4. Turner, *Doing Rhetorical History*, 12.

5. See Collins, "Taking the Lead." Collins situates the organizing efforts of Dorothy Williams of Pittsburgh youth in the early 1960s as being important to the larger African American struggle for civil rights.

6. Karenga, "Nommo, Kawaida," 3.

7. Ackerman and Coogan, *Public Work*, 2.

8. Ackerman and Coogan, *Public Work*, 2.

9. Asante, "Future of African American Rhetoric," 291.

10. The Urban League's leadership seminars followed three of Heifetz's leadership principles: (1) keeping the focus on the issue of urban renewal, (2) giving "work back to the people," and (3) protecting "voices of leadership without authority." Asante, "Future of African American Rhetoric," 128.

11. Heifetz, *Leadership Without Easy Answers*, 20.

12. Cha-Jua and Lang, "'Long Movement,'" 265.

13. "Herstory," *Black Lives Matter*, n.d., https://blacklivesmatter.com/herstory/.

14. Handley et al., "Unearthing Deep Roots," 137.

15. Cathy Cohen's work on Black youth and political alienation suggests many African Americans are engaged, but not with civics, and more interested in revolution than participation.

16. Avila quoted in *Driving While Black*.

17. See Finney, *Black Faces, White Spaces*.

18. *Pittsburgh Post-Gazette*, "'There Are Black People.'"

BIBLIOGRAPHY

Abbott, H. Porter. *The Cambridge Introduction to Narrative*. 2nd ed. Cambridge: Cambridge University Press, 2008.

Ackerman, John M., and David J. Coogan. *The Public Work of Rhetoric: Citizen-Scholars and Civic Engagement*. Columbia: University of South Carolina Press, 2010.

Alkebulan, Adisa A. "The Spiritual Essence of African American Rhetoric." In *Understanding African American Rhetoric: Classical Origins to Contemporary Innovations*, edited by Ronald L. Jackson II and Elaine B. Richardson, 23–40. New York: Routledge, 2014.

Allen, Danielle. *Talking to Strangers: Anxieties of Citizenship Since* Brown v. Board of Education. Chicago: University of Chicago Press, 2009.

Altshuler, Alan A. *The City Planning Process: A Political Analysis*. Ithaca: Cornell University Press, 1965.

Anderson, Martin. *The Federal Bulldozer: A Critical Analysis of Urban Renewal, 1949–1962*. Cambridge: MIT Press, 1964.

"Area Represented at Senate Hearings on Freeway Routes." *St. Paul Recorder*, March 8, 1957, 1. https://www.mnhs.org/newspapers/lccn/sn83016804/1957-03-08/ed-1/seq-1.

Aristotle. *On Rhetoric: A Theory of Civic Discourse*. Translated by George A. Kennedy. 2nd ed. Oxford: Oxford University Press, 2007.

Asante, Molefi Kete. "The Future of African American Rhetoric." In *Understanding African American Rhetoric: Classical Origins of Contemporary Innovations*, edited by Ronald L. Jackson II and Elaine B. Richardson, 285–91. New York: Routledge, 2003.

Asen, Robert. "A Discourse Theory of Citizenship." *Quarterly Journal of Speech* 90, no. 2 (May 2004): 189–211.

Associated Press. "Bush Limits Eminent-Domain Seizures." *Washington Post*, June 24, 2006. http://www.washingtonpost.com/wp-dyn/content/article/2006/06/23/AR2006062301722.html.

Baker, Houston A., Jr. "Critical Memory and the Black Public Sphere." *Public Culture* 7, no. 1 (January 1994): 3–33. https://doi.org/10.1215/08992363-7-1-3.

Bal, Mieke. *Narratology: Introduction to the Theory of Narrative*. 2nd ed. Toronto: University of Toronto Press, 1997.

Baldwin, James. "The American Dream and the American Negro." *New York Times*, March 7, 1965. https://archive.nytimes.com/www.nytimes.com/books/98/03/29/specials/baldwin-dream.html.

Barbera, Benjamin. "An Improvised World: Jazz and Community in Milwaukee, 1950–1970." University of Wisconsin–Milwaukee. UWM Digital Commons, 2012.

Barnes, Tom. "Civil Rights Monument to Open Sunday." *Pittsburgh Post-Gazette*, March 5, 2002, section C.

Barton, Craig Evan, ed. *Sites of Memory: Perspectives on Architecture and Race*. New York: Princeton Architectural Press, 2001.

Baxter, Pamela, and Susan Jack. "Qualitative Case Study Methodology: Study Design and Implementation for Novice Researchers." *Qualitative Report* 13, no. 4 (December 2008): 544–59.

Becher, Debbie. "Race as a Set of Symbolic Resources." In *Race and Real Estate*, edited by Adrienne Brown and Valerie Smith, 125–44. Oxford: Oxford University Press, 2015.

Bedoya, Roberto. "Spatial Justice: Rasquachification, Race and the City." *Creative Time Reports*, September 15, 2014. https://creativetime.org/reports/2014/09/15/spatial -justice-rasquachification-race-and-the-city/.

Behm, Don. "Easing Racial Disparities Tops Chris Abele's 2nd Term Agenda." *Milwaukee Journal Sentinel*, April 29, 2016. https://www.jsonline.com/story/news/local /milwaukee/2016/04/30/easing-racial-disparities-tops-chris-abeles-2nd-term -agenda/84964306/.

Belcher, Nathaniel. "Miami's Colored over Segregation." In *Sites of Memory: Perspectives on Architecture and Race*, edited by Craig E. Barton. New York: Princeton Architectural Press, 2001.

Berger, Linda L. "How Embedded Knowledge Structures Affect Judicial Decision Making: A Rhetorical Analysis of Metaphor, Narrative, and Imagination in Child Custody Disputes." *Southern California Interdisciplinary Law Journal* 18, no. 259 (2009): 259–308. https://ssrn.com/abstract=1231584.

Berlin, Ira. *The Making of African America: The Four Great Migrations*. Repr. ed. New York: Penguin, 2010.

Black, Ivory Abena, Reuben Harpole, and Sally Di Frances. *Bronzeville, a Milwaukee Lifestyle*. Milwaukee: Publishers Group, 2006.

"Black Monday Set in Pittsburgh." *News and Courier*, September 15, 1969.

Blake, John. "This Is What 'Whitelash' Looks Like." *CNN*, November 11, 2016. https:// www.cnn.com/2016/11/11/us/obama-trump-white-backlash/index.html.

Bonds, Anne. "Race and Ethnicity: Property, Race, and the Carceral State." *Progress in Human Geography* 43, no. 3 (June 2019): 574–83. https://doi.org/10.1177 /0309132517751297.

Breger, G. E. "The Concept and Causes of Urban Blight." *Land Economics* 43, no. 4 (November 1967): 369–76. https://doi.org/10.2307/3145542.

Brooks, Kyle. "Between Nostalgia and Critical Memory." *Political Theology Network*, April 4, 2018. https://politicaltheology.com/between-nostalgia-and-critical-memory/.

Brooks, Maegan Parker. *A Voice That Could Stir an Army: Fannie Lou Hamer and the Rhetoric of the Black Freedom Movement*. Repr. ed. Jackson: University Press of Mississippi, 2016.

Brown, Adrienne. *The Black Skyscraper: Architecture and the Perception of Race*. Baltimore: Johns Hopkins University Press, 2017.

Burke, Kenneth. *A Rhetoric of Motives*. Berkeley: University of California Press, 1969.

Campbell, Karlyn Kohrs. "Agency: Promiscuous and Protean." *Communication and Critical/Cultural Studies* 2, no. 1 (March 2005): 1–19. https://doi.org/10.1080 /1479142042000332134.

Cassidy, George. "Integration Pioneer Faced Obstacles." *Journal Sentinel* (Milwaukee), December 27, 1987, 1.

Cavanaugh, Patricia. "Politics and Freeways: Building the Twin Cities Interstate System." Report, University of Minnesota: Center for Urban and Regional Affairs, October 2006. http://conservancy.umn.edu/handle/11299/2082.

Cavett, Kate. *Voices of Rondo: Oral Histories of Saint Paul's Historic Black Community*. Reissue ed. Minneapolis: University of Minnesota Press, 2017.

Cha-Jua, Sundiata Keita, and Clarence Lang. "The 'Long Movement' as Vampire: Temporal and Spatial Fallacies in Recent Black Freedom Studies." *Journal of African American History* 92, no. 2 (2007): 265–88. https://doi.org/10.2307/20064183.

"Challenge." *Pittsburgh Courier*, city ed., October 21, 1950, 1. https://www.proquest.com /docview/202245100.

Chatman, Seymour. "Characters and Narrators: Filter, Center, Slant, and Interest-Focus." *Poetics Today* 7, no. 2 (January 1986): 189–204. https://doi.org/10.2307/1772758.

Chavez, Karma R. *Queer Migration Politics: Activist Rhetoric and Coalitional Possibilities*. Urbana: University of Illinois Press, 2013.

"City Council Expected to Put Its Approval on Lower Hill Project." *Pittsburgh Press*, July 6, 1955. http://news.google.com/newspapers?id=ibwbAAAAIBAJ&sjid =4koEAAAAIBAJ&pg=7352,1277599.

"City Fathers 'Twisted Truth' on Scott Demand." *Pittsburgh Courier*, July 24 1965, 1. https://www.proquest.com/docview/202486400.

City of Milwaukee Department of City Development. "Bronzeville Market Analysis and District Plan." Milwaukee: City of Milwaukee Department of City Development, 2005. http://www.city.milwaukee.gov/MarketAnalysis.pdf.

"City of the Future—All Within a City of Today." *Pittsburgh Post-Gazette*, October 30, 1947.

"Civil Rights Act of 1968 [Public Law 90–284, 82 Stat. 73]." GovInfo. https://www .govinfo.gov/content/pkg/COMPS-343/pdf/COMPS-343.pdf.

Clark, John L. "Down Memory Lane: Mrs. Burwell Recalls Days of Lower Hill." *Pittsburgh Courier*, city ed., February 24, 1962. http://www.proquest.com/hnppittsburghcourier/docview/202435455.

Coates, Ta-Nehisi. "The Case for Reparations." *Atlantic*, May 22, 2014. https://www.theatlantic.com/magazine/archive/2014/06/the-case-for-reparations/361631/.

Cohn, Carol. "Sex and Death in the Rational World of Defense Intellectuals." *Signs* 12, no. 4 (1987): 687–718.

Collins, James. "Taking the Lead: Dorothy Williams, NAACP Youth Councils, and Civil Rights Protests in Pittsburgh, 1961–1964." *Journal of African American History* 88, no. 2 (April 2003): 126–37. https://doi.org/10.2307/3559061.

Commer, Carolyn. "Perelman's Dissociation and Metaphor: Working Together to Structure and Re-Structure Reality." Unpublished essay, Carnegie Mellon University, 2010.

Condit, Celeste Michelle. "The Functions of Epideictic: The Boston Massacre Orations as Exemplar." *Communication Quarterly* 33, no. 4 (September 1985): 284–98. https://doi.org/10.1080/01463378509369608.

Cooper, Marilyn M. "Rhetorical Agency as Emergent and Enacted." *College Composition and Communication* 62, no. 3 (February 2011): 420–49.

Corrigan, Lisa M. *Black Feelings: Race and Affect in the Long Sixties*. Jackson: University Press of Mississippi, 2020.

Costantini, Allen, and KARE. "Rondo Neighborhood Gets Apologies for I-94." KARE 11, July 17, 2015. https://www.kare11.com/article/news/local/rondo-neighborhood -gets-apologies-for-i-94/89-105454642.

Crable, Bryan. *Ralph Ellison and Kenneth Burke: At the Roots of the Racial Divide*. Charlottesville: University of Virginia Press, 2011.

"Cultural Center to Lift Face of Lower Hill." *Pittsburgh Press*, December 12, 1953. http:// news.google.com/newspapers?nid=1144&dat=19531212&id=1F4bAAAAIBAJ& sjid=pooEAAAAIBAJ&pg=6812,3884043.

Dagbovie, Pero G. *Reclaiming the Black Past: The Use and Misuse of African American History in the 21st Century*. London: Verso, 2018.

Davis, Julius. "'Pgh. Story' Moves Reader to Tears: Your Comments on Supplement 'Pittsburgh Story' Moves Nostalgic Reader to Tears, Recalls Boyhood Days in Old Hill." *Pittsburgh Courier*, city ed., March 10, 1962. http://www.proquest.com /hnppittsburghcourier/docview/202477834.

"Dedication of Rondo Plaza—July 2018." St. Paul Neighborhood Network, July 14, 2018. Video, 1:12:48. https://youtu.be/hyntCzNyhBY.

Delegard, Kirsten, and Penny Petersen. "Moses and Mary Burkes Make a Home Near Lake Harriet." Mapping Prejudice, University of Minnesota Libraries. https://mappingprejudice.umn.edu/moses-and-mary-burkes-make-home-near-lake-harriet.

"Democrats Open County, City Campaigns." *Pittsburgh Post Gazette*, September 26, 1953. http://news.google.com/newspapers?id=QoYNAAAAIBAJ&sjid=120DAAAAIBAJ&pg=1282,800366.

Deskins, Donald R., Jr. and Christopher Bettinger. "Black and White Spaces in Selected Metropolitan Areas." In *Geographical Identities of Ethnic America: Race, Space, and Place*, edited by Kate A. Berry and Martha L. Henderson, 38–63 Reno: University of Nevada Press, 2001.

Desmond, Matthew. *Evicted: Poverty and Profit in the American City*. New York: Crown, 2016.

Dieterich-Ward, Allen. *Beyond Rust: Metropolitan Pittsburgh and the Fate of Industrial America*. Philadelphia: University of Pennsylvania Press, 2015.

Driving While Black: Race, Space and Mobility in America. PBS, 2020. Video. https://www.pbs.org/video/driving-while-black-race-space-and-mobility-in-america-achvfr/.

Duquette Smith, Cynthia, and Teresa Bergman. "You Were on Indian Land: Alcatraz Island as Recalcitrant Memory Space." In *Places of Public Memory: The Rhetoric of Museums and Memorials*, edited by Greg Dickinson, Carole Blair, and Brian L. Ott, 160–88. Tuscaloosa: University Alabama Press, 2010.

Edelman, Murray J. *Constructing the Political Spectacle*. Chicago: University of Chicago Press, 1988.

"Editorial." *Milwaukee Defender*, no. 14 (February 28, 1957): 2.

Eisenhower, Dwight. "Statement by the President upon Signing the Housing Act of 1954." *American Presidency Project*, August 2, 1954. Online by Gerhard Peters and John T. Woolley. http://www.presidency.ucsb.edu/node/232403.

Endres, Danielle, and Samantha Senda-Cook. "Location Matters: The Rhetoric of Place in Protest." *Quarterly Journal of Speech* 97, no. 3 (August 2011): 257–82. https://doi.org/10.1080/00335630.2011.585167.

Enoch, Jessica. *Refiguring Rhetorical Education: Women Teaching African American, Native American, and Chicano/a Students, 1865–1911*. Carbondale: Southern Illinois University Press, 2008.

Fairclough, Norman. *Discourse and Social Change*. New ed. Cambridge: Polity Press, 1993.

Fehrenbacher, Don E. *The Dred Scott Case: Its Significance in American Law and Politics*. Oxford: Oxford University Press, 2001.

"5th Ave. High Student Wins Prize in Duquesne Univ. Essay Contest: 'What Pittsburgh's Redevelopment Program Means to an Eleventh-Grade Student.'" *Pittsburgh Courier*, city ed., January 16, 1954, A7. https://www.proquest.com/docview/202289711.

"The Fight on Blight." *Pittsburgh Press*, October 18, 1953. http://news.google.com/newspapers?id=yUAqAAAAIBAJ&sjid=mooEAAAAIBAJ&pg=6362,513228.

"Film to Show Renewal in Other Cities." *Milwaukee Sentinel*, March 28, 1957, 3.

"Fine, but Where'll We Get the Money?" *Pittsburgh Press*, March 1, 1953. http://news.google.com/newspapers?id=sXwbAAAAIBAJ&sjid=kk0E%20AAAAIBAJ&pg=6413,146848.

Finney, Carolyn. *Black Faces, White Spaces: Reimagining the Relationship of African Americans to the Great Outdoors*. Chapel Hill: University of North Carolina Press, 2014.

Flanagan, Richard M. "The Housing Act of 1954: The Sea Change in National Urban Policy." *Urban Affairs Review* 33, no. 2 (November 1997): 265–86. https://doi.org /10.1177/107808749703300207.

Fleming, David. *City of Rhetoric: Revitalizing the Public Sphere in Metropolitan America.* Albany: SUNY Press, 2008.

Florida, Richard. "The U.S. Cities Where the Poor Are Most Segregated from Everyone Else." *Bloomberg City Lab*, March 24, 2014. https://www.bloomberg.com/news /articles/2014-03-24/the-u-s-cities-where-the-poor-are-most-segregated-from -everyone-else.

Flusberg, Stephen J., Teenie Matlock, and Paul H. Thibodeau. "War Metaphors in Public Discourse." *Metaphor and Symbol* 33, no. 1 (2018): 1–18. https://doi.org/10.1080 /10926488.2018.1407992.

Forbes, Ella. "Every Man Fights for His Freedom: The Rhetoric of African American Resistance in the Mid-Nineteenth Century." In *Understanding African American Rhetoric*, edited by Ronald L. Jackson II and Elaine B. Richardson, 155–70. New York: Routledge, 2003.

Foreman, P. Gabrielle, Jim Casey, and Sarah Lynn Patterson, eds. *The Colored Conventions Movement: Black Organizing in the Nineteenth Century.* Chapel Hill: University of North Carolina Press, 2021.

Freund, David M. P. *Colored Property: State Policy and White Racial Politics in Suburban America.* Chicago: University of Chicago Press, 2010.

Fullilove, Mindy. *Root Shock: How Tearing Up City Neighborhoods Hurts America, and What We Can Do About It.* New York: Ballantine, 2004.

Gallagher, Victoria J., and Margaret R. LaWare. "Sparring with Public Memory: The Rhetorical Embodiment of Race, Power, and Conflict in the Monument to Joe Louis." In *Places of Public Memory: The Rhetoric of Museums and Memorials*, edited by Greg Dickinson, Carole Blair, and Brian L. Ott, 68–87. Rhetoric, Culture, and Social Critique. Tuscaloosa: University of Alabama Press, 2010.

Garland, Phyl. "'Help Us!' Urban Renewal 'DP's' Plead." *Pittsburgh Courier*, city ed., November 25, 1961. http://www.proquest.com/hnppittsburghcourier/docview /202415525.

Geenen, Paul H. *Milwaukee's Bronzeville, 1900–1950.* Charleston: Arcadia, 2006.

Geisler, Cheryl. "How Ought We to Understand the Concept of Rhetorical Agency? Report from the ARS." *Rhetoric Society Quarterly* 34, no. 3 (July 2004): 9–17.

Gilyard, Keith, and Adam Banks. *On African-American Rhetoric.* New York: Routledge, 2018.

Glasco, Laurence. "The Next Page: That Arena on the Hill." *Pittsburgh Post-Gazette*, June 5, 2010. http://www.post-gazette.com/stories/opinion/perspectives/the-next -page-that-arena-on-the-hill-253978/.

Glaude, Eddie S., Jr. *Democracy in Black: How Race Still Enslaves the American Soul.* Repr. ed. New York: Crown, 2017.

Gonda, Jeffrey D. *Unjust Deeds: The Restrictive Covenant Cases and the Making of the Civil Rights Movement.* Chapel Hill: University of North Carolina Press, 2019.

Gordon, Colin. *Mapping Decline: St. Louis and the Fate of the American City.* Philadelphia: University of Pennsylvania Press, 2009.

Gordon, Dexter B. *Black Identity: Rhetoric, Ideology, and Nineteenth-Century Black Nationalism.* Carbondale: Southern Illinois University Press, 2006.

Gotham, Kevin Fox. "A City Without Slums: Urban Renewal, Public Housing, and Downtown Revitalization in Kansas City, Missouri." *American Journal of Economics and Sociology* 60, no. 1 (January 2001): 285–316. https://doi.org/10.1111/1536 -7150.00064.

Grant, Tim. "Obituary: Robert R. Lavelle / Founder of Hill District's Dwelling House Savings and Loan." *Pittsburgh Post-Gazette*, July 6, 2010. https://www.post-gazette .com/news/obituaries/2010/07/06/Obituary-Robert-R-Lavelle-Founder-of-Hill -District-s-Dwelling-House-Savings-Loan/stories/201007060168.

Grossman, James R. *Land of Hope: Chicago, Black Southerners, and the Great Migration.* Chicago: University of Chicago Press, 1991.

Hallen, Phil. "Phil Hallen: Pittsburgh's Freedom Corner Revisited." *Pittsburgh Post-Gazette*, July 23, 2020. https://www.post-gazette.com/opinion/Op-Ed/2020 /07/23/Phil-Hallen-Pittsburgh-Freedom-Corner-revisited-Civil-Rights/stories /202007230029.

Halloran, S. Michael, and Gregory Clark. "National Park Landscapes and the Rhetorical Display of Civic Religion." In *Rhetorics of Display*, edited by Lawrence J. Prelli, 141–56. Columbia: University of South Carolina Press, 2006.

Handley, Derek G. "'The Line Drawn': Freedom Corner and Rhetorics of Place in Pittsburgh, 1960s–2000s." *Rhetoric Review* 38, no. 2 (April 2019): 173–89. https://doi .org/10.1080/07350198.2019.1582239.

Handley, Derek G., Victoria Gallagher, Danielle DeVasto, Mridula Mascarenhas, and Rhana A. Gittens. "Unearthing Deep Roots: Tapping Rhetoric's Generative Power to Improve Community and Urban Development Projects." *Review of Communication* 20, no. 2 (April 2020): 135–43. https://doi.org/10.1080/15358593.2020 .1737194.

Harrel, Willie J., Jr. *Origins of the African American Jeremiad: The Rhetorical Strategies of Social Protest and Activism, 1760–1861.* Jefferson, NC: McFarland, 2011.

Hauser, David J., and Norbert Schwarz. "The War on Prevention: Bellicose Cancer Metaphors Hurt (Some) Prevention Intentions." *Personality and Social Psychology Bulletin* 41, no. 1 (January 2015): 66–77. https://doi.org/10.1177/0146167214557006.

Hauser, Gerard A. *Vernacular Voices: The Rhetoric of Publics and Public Spheres.* Columbia: University of South Carolina Press, 1999.

Heifetz, Ronald A. *Leadership Without Easy Answers.* Cambridge: Harvard University Press, 1994.

Herscher, Andrew. "The Urbanism of Racial Capitalism." *Comparative Studies of South Asia, Africa and the Middle East* 40, no. 1 (May 2020): 57–65. https://doi.org/10 .1215/1089201X-8186049.

Higgins, Lorraine D., and Lisa D. Brush. "Personal Experience Narrative and Public Debate: Writing the Wrongs of Welfare." *College Composition and Communication* 57, no. 4 (June 2006): 694–729. https://doi.org/10.2307/20456913.

"Hill Committee Sets First Public Meeting." *Pittsburgh Courier*, March 30, 1963, 3.

"The Hill District." *Pittsburgh Post-Gazette*, March 28, 1951. http://news.google.com /newspapers?id=TwMiAAAAIBAJ&sjid=cE0EAAAAIBAJ&pg=2796,4956153.

"Hillside Property Purchase to Begin: Little Opposition Noted." *Milwaukee Defender*, May 29, 1957.

Hinojosa, Felipe. *Apostles of Change: Latino Radical Politics, Church Occupations, and the Fight to Save the Barrio.* Austin: University of Texas Press, 2021.

Hirsch, Arnold. *Making the Second Ghetto: Race and Housing in Chicago, 1940–1960.* Chicago: University of Chicago Press, 2021.

Hockerman, Elizabeth. "Artwork Will Add Local Flavor to Marquette Interchange." *BizTimes—Milwaukee Business News*, May 14, 2004. https://biztimes.com/artwork -will-add-local-flavor-to-marquette-interchange/.

Hoekstra, Joel. "Rondo Commemorative Plaza." *Architecture MN*, October 22, 2018. https://www.aia-mn.org/rondo-commemorative-plaza/.

Honer, Matthew J. "The Unworkable Program: Urban Renewal in Kilbourntown-3 and Midtown, Milwaukee." Master's thesis, University of Wisconsin–Eau Claire, 2015.

House, Patricia A. "Relocation of Families Displaced by Expressway Development: Milwaukee Case Study." *Land Economics* 46, no. 1 (February 1970): 75–78. https://doi .org/10.2307/3145426.

"Housing Act of 1949." https://www.govinfo.gov/content/pkg/COMPS-10349/pdf /COMPS-10349.pdf.

"Housing Act of 1954: Hearings Before the Committee on Banking and Currency." US Government Printing Office, 1954.

Howard-Pitney, David. *The Afro-American Jeremiad: Appeals for Justice in America.* Philadelphia: Temple University Press, 1993.

"Howard Urges Families Affected by Freeway Against Hurried Action." *St. Paul Recorder,* August 3, 1956, 1. https://www.mnhs.org/newspapers/lccn/sn83016804/1956 -08-03/ed-1/seq-1.

Hunter, Marcus Anthony, Mary Pattillo, Zandria F. Robinson, and Keeanga-Yamahtta Taylor. "Black Placemaking: Celebration, Play, and Poetry." *Theory, Culture and Society* 33, nos. 7–8 (December 2016): 31–56. https://doi.org/10.1177/0263276416635259.

Jacobs, Jane. *The Death and Life of Great American Cities.* New York: Vintage, 1992.

Janzer, Cinnamon. "St. Paul's ReConnect Rondo Is Working to Right Past Highway Development Wrongs." *Next City,* June 23, 2021. https://nextcity.org/urbanist-news /st-pauls-reconnect-rondo-working-to-right-past-highway-development-wrongs.

Johansson, Rolf. "On Case Study Methodology." *Open House International* 32 (September 2007): 48–54. https://doi.org/10.1108/OHI-03-2007-B0006.

Johnson, Roberta Ann. "African Americans and Homelessness: Moving Through History." *Journal of Black Studies* 40, no. 4 (March 2008): 583–605.

Johnstone, Barbara. *Discourse Analysis.* Introducing Linguistics 3. Malden, MA: Blackwell, 2002.

Jones, Patrick D. "Black Empowerment in Milwaukee." In *Neighborhood Rebels: Black Power at the Local Level,* edited by Peniel E. Joseph, 45–65. New York: Palgrave Macmillan, 2010.

———. *The Selma of the North: Civil Rights Insurgency in Milwaukee.* Cambridge: Harvard University Press, 2009.

Jones, Patrick L. "Hill Housing Future, What Will It Mean?" *Pittsburgh Courier,* city ed., May 6, 1950, 31. https://www.proquest.com/docview/202237973.

Jones, Sandra E. *Voices of Milwaukee Bronzeville.* Charleston, SC: The History Press, 2021.

Jordan, Mildred T. "America Must Remove Cancer of Segregation Rev. King Tells Pastors." *St. Paul Recorder,* January 25, 1957. https://newspapers.mnhs.org/jsp/viewer .jsp?doc_id=mnhi0031/1DFC6C5F/59030601.

Karenga, Maulana. "Nommo, Kawaida, and Communicative Practice: Bringing Good into the World." In *Understanding African American Rhetoric: Classical Origins to Contemporary Innovations,* edited by Ronald L. Jackson II and Elaine B. Richardson, 3–22. New York: Routledge, 2003.

Karon, Louise A. "Presence in 'The New Rhetoric.'" *Philosophy and Rhetoric* 9, no. 2 (April 1976): 96–111. https://doi.org/10.2307/40236972.

Kaul, Greta. "With Covenants, Racism Was Written into Minneapolis Housing: The Scars Are Still Visible." *MinnPost,* February 22, 2019. https://www.minnpost.com /metro/2019/02/with-covenants-racism-was-written-into-minneapolis-housing -the-scars-are-still-visible/.

Keen, Suzanne. "A Theory of Narrative Empathy." *Narrative* 14, no. 3 (October 2006): 207–36.

Keith, William M. *Democracy as Discussion: Civic Education and the American Forum Movement.* Lanham, MD: Lexington Books, 2007.

Keith, William, and Paula Cossart. "The Search for 'Real' Democracy and Public Deliberation in France and the United States, 1870–1940." In *Rhetorical Citizenship and*

    Public Deliberation, edited by Christian Kock and Lisa S. Villadsen, 46–60. University Park: Pennsylvania State University Press, 2012.

Kelley, Robert E. *The Power of Followership*. New York: Doubleday Business, 1992.

Kennedy, Bruce. "America's 11 Poorest Cities." *CBS News*, February 18, 2015. https://www.cbsnews.com/media/americas-11-poorest-cities/.

Klein, Emily. "Spectacular Citizenships: Staging Latina Resistance Through Urban Performances of Pain." *Frontiers: A Journal of Women Studies* 32, no. 1 (2011): 102–24. https://doi.org/10.5250/fronjwomestud.32.1.0102.

Kock, Christian, and Lisa S. Villadsen, eds. *Contemporary Rhetorical Citizenship*. Leiden: Leiden University Press, 2015.

———. *Rhetorical Citizenship and Public Deliberation*. University Park: Pennsylvania State University Press, 2012.

Koger, Ralph E. "Citizens Unveil Plan for Solvent Folks to Renew, Remain in Hill." *Pittsburgh Courier*, January 16, 1965, 1. https://www.proquest.com/docview/202454779.

Labov, William, and Joshua Waletzky. "Narrative Analysis: Oral Versions of Personal Experience." *Journal of Narrative and Life History* 7, nos. 1–4 (1997): 3–38.

Lakoff, George, and Mark Johnson. *Metaphors We Live By*. 2nd ed. Chicago: University of Chicago Press, 2003.

Leff, Michael. "Tradition and Agency in Humanistic Rhetoric." *Philosophy and Rhetoric* 36, no. 2 (2003): 135–47.

"The Lessons of Freedom Corner: A Learning Guide." *Freedom Corner Committee*, 2001.

Levine, Marc V. "The State of Black Milwaukee in National Perspective: Racial Inequality in the Nation's 50 Largest Metropolitan Areas. In 65 Charts and Tables." *Center for Economic Development Publications* 56 (2020). https://dc.uwm.edu/ced_pubs/56.

Levine, Peter. "All That Matters Is Equanimity, Community, and Truth." *Peter Levine: A Blog for Civic Renewal* (blog), September 17, 2012. https://peterlevine.ws/?p=9724.

Lindemann-Nelson, Hilde. *Damaged Identities, Narrative Repair*. Ithaca: Cornell University Press, 2001.

"The Line Drawn, a Place to Stand." *Pittsburgh Post-Gazette*, April 5, 1998, B-1.

Logan, Rayford Whittingham. *What the Negro Wants*. Notre Dame: University of Notre Dame Press, 1944.

Logan, Shirley Wilson. *We Are Coming: The Persuasive Discourse of Nineteenth-Century Black Women*. Carbondale: Southern Illinois University Press, 1999.

Love, Gilbert. "Giant Center for Sports, Conventions Proposed for Pittsburgh of Tomorrow." *Pittsburgh Press*, October 30, 1947, http://news.google.com/newspapers?id=mS8bAAAAIBAJ&sjid=GkoEAAAAIBAJ&pg=5107,5813760.

"Lower Hill Officially 'Blighted.'" *Pittsburgh Press*, September 19, 1950, http://news.google.com/newspapers?id=x3gbAAAAIBAJ&sjid=ZUoEAAAAIBAJ&pg=4334,1342955.

Lubove, Roy. *Government, Business, and Environmental Change*. Vol. 1 of *Twentieth-Century Pittsburgh*. New York: John Wiley and Sons, 1969.

———. *The Post-Steel Era*. Vol. 2 of *Twentieth-Century Pittsburgh*. Pittsburgh: University of Pittsburgh Press, 1995.

Lundberg, Christian, and Joshua Gunn. "'Ouija Board, Are There Any Communications?' Agency, Ontotheology, and the Death of the Humanist Subject, or, Continuing the ARS Conversation." *Rhetoric Society Quarterly* 35, no. 4 (September 2005): 83–105. https://doi.org/10.1080/02773940509391323.

Lustig, Jessica. "Home: An Interview with John Edgar Wideman." *African American Review* 26, no. 3 (Autumn 1992): 453–57. https://doi.org/10.2307/3041917.

Lyon, Cherstin M. "Introduction." In *Citizenship and Place: Case Studies on the Borders of Citizenship*, edited by Cherstin M. Lyon and Allison F. Goebel, ix–xx. Lanham, MD: Rowman & Littlefield, 2018.

Maddux, Kristy. *Practicing Citizenship: Women's Rhetoric at the 1893 Chicago World's Fair.* University Park: Penn State University Press, 2019. Maier, Henry W. "A Mayor Looks at Urban Renewal." *Challenge* 14, no. 4 (March 1966): 30–43. https://doi.org /10.1080/05775132.1966.11469854.

Majors, Dan. "Many Ask Council to Preserve Civic Arena." *Pittsburgh Post-Gazette*, May 24, 2011. https://www.post-gazette.com/local/city/2011/05/24/Many-ask-council -to-preserve-Civic-Arena/stories/201105240141.

Mando, Justin. "Constructing the Vicarious Experience of Proximity in a Marcellus Shale Public Hearing." *Environmental Communication* 10, no. 3 (May 2016): 352–64. https://doi.org/10.1080/17524032.2015.1133438.

———. *Fracking and the Rhetoric of Place: How We Argue from Where We Stand.* Lanham, MD: Lexington Books, 2021.

Marable, Manning. *Black Leadership.* New York: Columbia University Press, 2013.

Marback, Richard. "A Tale of Two Plaques: Rhetoric in Cape Town." *Rhetoric Review* 23, no. 3 (July 2004): 253–68. https://doi.org/10.1207/s15327981rr2303_4.

McGraw, B. T. "Urban Renewal in the Interest of All the People." *Phylon Quarterly* 19, no. 1 (1958): 45–55. https://doi.org/10.2307/273003.

Metcalfe, Erica. "Commanding a Movement: The Youth Council Commandos' Quest for Quality Housing." *Wisconsin Magazine of History* 98, no. 2 (2014): 2–15.

Miller, Jay. "Save Milwaukee from 'Worst City for Blacks' Ranking." *Milwaukee Journal Sentinel*, November 3, 2015. http://www.jsonline.com/blogs/purple-wisconsin /339936551.html.

Miller, Joshua H. "Empowering Communities: Ella Baker's Decentralized Leadership Style and Conversational Eloquence." *Southern Communication Journal* 81, no. 3 (May 2016): 156–67. https://doi.org/10.1080/1041794X.2016.1149613.

Mills, Quincy T. *Cutting Along the Color Line: Black Barbers and Barber Shops in America.* Philadelphia: University of Pennsylvania Press, 2013.

"Milwaukee Urban Renewal Program Moving Along in Fine Style." *Milwaukee Journal*, June 26, 1956, 1. NewsBank: Milwaukee Journal Sentinel Historical Newspapers.

Miner, Barbara. *Lessons from the Heartland: A Turbulent Half-Century of Public Education in an Iconic American City.* New York: The New Press, 2013.

Mock, Brentin. "Milwaukee Is the Worst Place for African Americans Because of County Sheriff David Clarke." *Bloomberg*, October 30, 2015, https://www.bloomberg.com /news/articles/2015-10-30/milwaukee-is-the-worst-place-for-african-americans -because-of-county-sheriff-david-clarke.

Mohl, Raymond A. "The Interstates and the Cities: Highways, Housing, and the Freeway Revolt." Poverty and Race Research Action Council, January 1, 2002. https://www .prrac.org/the-interstates-and-the-cities-highways-housing-and-the-freeway-revolt/.

Moody, Chuck, and Staff Writer. "Freedom Corner Memorial Recalls Civil Rights Struggle." *Pittsburgh Catholic*, April 27, 2001.

Morrow, Christian. "Freedom Corner Opens to Public." *New Pittsburgh Courier*, March 30, 2002. https://www.proquest.com/docview/201808521.

Mountford, Roxanne. "On Gender and Rhetorical Space." *Rhetoric Society Quarterly* 31, no. 1 (January 2001): 41–71. https://doi.org/10.1080/02773940109391194.

Murch, Donna Jean. *Living for the City: Migration, Education, and the Rise of the Black Panther Party in Oakland, California.* Chapel Hill: University of North Carolina Press, 2010.

Neely, Brooke, and Michelle Samura. "Social Geographies of Race: Connecting Race and Space." *Ethnic and Racial Studies* 34, no. 11 (2011): 1933–52. https://doi.org/10 .1080/01419870.2011.559262.

Nelson, Diana. "The Lower Hill Before the Arena: A Rambunctious, Crowded, Loud Place with 'Everything You Needed.'" *Pittsburgh Post-Gazette*, April 17, 2011.

http://www.post-gazette.com/local/city/2011/04/17/The-Lower-Hill-before-the
-arena-A-rambunctious-crowded-loud-place-with-everything-you-needed/stories
ᴉ01104170282.

Nelson, ᵒm. "Pioneering St. Paul Leader, Bill Wilson, Dies." *MPR News*, December 30,
20. . https://www.mprnews.org/story/2019/12/30/pioneering-st-paul-leader-bill
-wils ᴉ-dies.

Niemuth, Ni. ᵗ. "Urban Renewal and the Development of Milwaukee's African American Con. ᴉunity: 1960–1980." Master's thesis, University of Wisconsin–Milwaukee, 2014. ᴉttp://dc.uwm.edu/cgi/viewcontent.cgi?article=1421&context=etd.

"1966 Ware Lectᵘ. ᵖ: Don't Sleep Through the Revolution, by Dr. Martin Luther King,
Jr." UUA.org, ᴉnuary 17, 2ᴑ13. https://www.uua.org/ga/past/1966/ware.

Nunley, Vorris L. "Frᵗ ᴉ the Harbor to Da Academic Hood: Hush Harbors and an African American ᴉ ᵉtorical Tradition." In *African American Rhetoric(s): Interdisciplinary Perspectᵢ ᵗ, edited by Elaine B. Richardson and Ronald L. Jackson II,
221–41. Carbondale. ᴉouthern Illinois University Press, 2007.

———. *Keepin' It Hushed: ᴉ ᵉ Barbershop and African American Hush Harbor Rhetoric*.
Detroit: Wayne State Uᴗ iversity Press, 2011.

Olson, Kathryn M. "What Is Rh ᵗorical Leadership? My Perspective Statement." University of Wisconsin–Milwauᴗ ᵗe, revised September 2011. https://uwm.edu/rhetorical
-leadership/wp-content/upᴉ ᴉds/sites/322/2016/02/whatisrl.pdf.

Ong, Aihwa, Virginia R. Domingᵘᴗ ᵗ, Jonathan Friedman, Nina Glick Schiller, Verena
Stolcke, David Y. H. Wu, and . ᴉu Ying. "Cultural Citizenship as Subject-Making:
Immigrants Negotiate Racial aᴉᴊ Cultural Boundaries in the United States [and
Comments and Reply]." *Current Anthropology* 37, no. 5 (December 1996): 737–62.

"Operation Fix-Up." *Pittsburgh Press*, April 27, 1952. http://news.google.com/newspapers
?id=EZAcAAAAIBAJ&sjid=4I4EAAAAIBAJ&pg=2982,4999176.

"Pastor Threatens Cops." *St. Paul Dispatch*, September 28, 1956.

Payne, Charles M. *I've Got the Light of Freedom: The Organizing Tradition and the Mississippi Freedom Struggle*. Berkeley: University of California Press, 1995.

Pearce, Matt. "When Martin Luther King Jr. Took His Fight into the North, and Saw a
New Level of Hatred." *Los Angeles Times*, January 18, 2016. http://www.latimes
.com/nation/la-na-mlk-chicago-20160118-story.html.

Perelman, Chaïm, and Lucie Olbrechts-Tyteca. *The New Rhetoric*. New ed. Notre Dame:
University of Notre Dame Press, 1991.

Perry, Imani. *More Beautiful and More Terrible: The Embrace and Transcendence of Racial
Inequality in the United States*. New York: New York University Press, 2011.

Pfaffmann, Rob. "Forum: The Civic Arena Is a Treasure." *Pittsburgh Post-Gazette*, June 6,
2002.

Pierce, Joseph, Deborah G. Martin, and James T. Murphy. "Relational Place-Making: The
Networked Politics of Place." *Transactions of the Institute of British Geographers*
36, no. 1 (January 2011): 54–70. https://doi.org/10.1111/j.1475-5661.2010.00411.x.

Pittsburgh Post-Gazette. "'There Are Black People in the Future'—Tale of a Billboard."
April 6, 2018. https://www.post-gazette.com/local/city/2018/04/06/There-Are
-Black-People-in-the-Futire-billboard-Eve-Picker-Jon-Rubin-Alisha-Wormsley
/stories/201804060115.

Pritchett, Wendell E. *Robert Clifton Weaver and the American City: The Life and Times of
an Urban Reformer*. Chicago: University of Chicago Press, 2008.

Quinn, Lois. "Racially Restrictive Covenants: The Making of All-White Suburbs in Milwaukee County." *ETI Publications* 178 (1979): 1–18. https://dc.uwm.edu/eti_pubs
/178/.

Rai, Candice. *Democracy's Lot: Rhetoric, Publics, and the Places of Invention*. Tuscaloosa:
University of Alabama Press, 2016.

Randolph, Sherie M. *Florynce "Flo" Kennedy: The Life of a Black Feminist Radical*. Chapel Hill: University of North Carolina Press, 2015.

Raton, Taki S. "Tejumaloa Ologboni—An Iconic Glow of Cultural Genius." *Milwaukee Courier*, February 26, 2011. https://milwaukeecourieronline.com/index.php/2011/02/26/tejumaloa-ologboni-an-iconic-glow-of-cultural-genius/.

"Redeveloping Lower Hill." *Pittsburgh Post-Gazette*, March 27, 1951. http://news.google.com/newspapers?id=weYMAAAAIBAJ&sjid=020DAAAAIBAJ&pg=2711,6038906.

"Redevelopment to Erase Blight in Hill District." *Pittsburgh Courier*, city ed., September 23, 1950. http://www.proquest.com/hnppittsburghcourier/docview/202250657.

Reicher, Matt. "St. Paul City Planner George Herrold and His Proposed 'Northern Route' for Interstate 94 | Matt Reicher." *NewsBreak Original*, July 18, 2022. https://original.newsbreak.com/@ron-dansley-1587459/2897858516230-george-herrold-and-his-proposed-northern-route-for-interstate-94.

Riordan, Madeline Mary. "Grassroots and Community Activism Within Milwaukee's Black Community: A Response to Central City Renewal and Revitalization Efforts in the Walnut Street Area, 1960s to 1980s." Master's thesis, University of Wisconsin–Milwaukee, 2016. https://dc.uwm.edu/cgi/viewcontent.cgi?article=2251&context=etd.

Robick, Brian David. "Blight: The Development of a Contested Concept." PhD diss., Carnegie Mellon University, 2011.https://www.proquest.com/docview/864740266.

Robinson, Erin. "Commemorative Plaza Revives the Spirit of Rondo." *Minnesota Spokesman Recorder*, July 18, 2018. https://spokesman-recorder.com/2018/07/18/commemorative-plaza-revives-the-spirit-of-rondo/.

Rogers, Charles. "Citizens Organize to Face Problem of St. Paul Freeway; Cite Purposes." *St. Paul Recorder*, May 25, 1965. https://www.mnhs.org/newspapers/lccn/sn83016804/1956-05-25/ed-1.

"Rondo–St. Anthony Area Gets Progress Report on Freeway Program." *St. Paul Recorder*, June 28, 1957. https://newspapers.mnhs.org/jsp/viewer.jsp?doc_id=mnhi0031/1DFC6C5F/57062801.

Rothstein, Richard. *The Color of Law: A Forgotten History of How Our Government Segregated America*. Repr. ed. New York: Liveright, 2018.

Samahy, Rami el, Chris Grimley, and Michael Kubo. *Imagining the Modern: Architecture and Urbanism of the Pittsburgh Renaissance*. New York: The Monacelli Press, 2019.

Sandler, Larry. "Hyler Overcame Racism to Build His House in Tosa." *Milwaukee Journal Sentinel*, January 1, 2005.

Schneider, Stephen. "Freedom Schooling: Stokely Carmichael and Critical Rhetorical Education." *College Composition and Communication* 58, no. 1 (2006): 46–69.

———. "The Sea Island Citizenship Schools: Literacy, Community Organization, and the Civil Rights Movement." *College English* 70, no. 2 (2007): 144–67. https://doi.org/10.2307/25472258.

Sen, Arijit. "Placemaking." *Encyclopedia of Milwaukee*, n.d. https://emke.uwm.edu/entry/placemaking/.

Smith, Arthur L. *Rhetoric of Black Revolution*. 2nd ed. Boston: Allyn and Bacon, 1970.

Smith, Kevin D. "From Socialism to Racism: The Politics of Class and Identity in Postwar Milwaukee." *Michigan Historical Review* 29, no. 1 (2003): 71–95. https://doi.org/10.2307/20174004.

Smith, Scott W. "August Wilson's St. Paul Roots." *Screenwriting from Iowa* (blog), October 9, 2010. https://screenwritingfromiowa.wordpress.com/2010/10/09/august-wilsons-st-pau-rootsl/.

Sontag, Susan. *Illness as Metaphor and AIDS and Its Metaphors*. New York: Picador, 2001.

Squires, Catherine R. "Rethinking the Black Public Sphere: An Alternative Vocabulary for Multiple Public Spheres." *Communication Theory* 12, no. 4 (2002): 446–68. https://doi.org/10.1111/j.1468-2885.2002.tb00278.x.

"St. Paul Leaders Walk Out on Milton Rosen." *St. Paul Recorder*, March 8, 1957. https://newspapers.mnhs.org/jsp/viewer.jsp?doc_id=mnhi0031/1DFIOV5F/57030801.

"St. Paul Man Is Honored by Negro Laymen's Group." *Minneapolis Star*, August 27, 1959.

Sugrue, Thomas J. *Sweet Land of Liberty: The Forgotten Struggle for Civil Rights in the North*. New York: Random House, 2009.

"Sunday's Saint Paul NAACP Meet Devoted to Housing Problems." *St. Paul Recorder*, April 11, 1958. https://newspapers.mnhs.org/jsp/viewer.jsp?doc_id=mnhi0031/1DFC6C5F/58041101.

Taylor, David V., and Bill Holm. *African Americans in Minnesota*. St. Paul: Minnesota Historical Society Press, 2002.

Teaford, Jon C. *The Rough Road to Renaissance: Urban Revitalization in America, 1940–1985*. Baltimore: Johns Hopkins University Press, 1990.

"Timothy Howard's Service to Community Praised at Testimonial and Reception." *St. Paul Recorder*, March 6, 1959. https://newspapers.mnhs.org/jsp/viewer.jsp?doc_id=mnhi0031/1DFC6C5F/59030601.

Topinka, Robert J. "Resisting the Fixity of Suburban Space: The Walker as Rhetorician." *Rhetoric Society Quarterly* 42, no. 1 (2012): 65–84. https://doi.org/10.1080/02773945.2011.622342.

Triece, Mary E. *Urban Renewal and Resistance: Race, Space, and the City in the Late Twentieth to the Early Twenty-First Century*. Lanham, MD: Lexington Books, 2016.

Trotter, Joe William, Jr. *Black Milwaukee: The Making of an Industrial Proletariat, 1915–45*. Urbana: University of Illinois Press, 1985.

———. *Pittsburgh and the Urban League Movement: A Century of Social Service and Activism*. Lexington: University Press of Kentucky, 2020.

Trotter, Joe W., and Jared N. Day. *Race and Renaissance: African Americans in Pittsburgh Since World War II*. Pittsburgh: University of Pittsburgh Press, 2010.

Truman, Harry S. "Statement by the President upon Signing the Housing Act of 1949." *The American Presidency Project*, July 15, 1949. Online by Gerhard Peters and John T. Woolley. https://www.presidency.ucsb.edu/node/229714.

Tuan, Yi-fu. *Space and Place: The Perspective of Experience*. Minneapolis: University of Minnesota Press, 2002.

Ture, Kwame, and Charles V. Hamilton. *Black Power: The Politics of Liberation*. New York: Vintage, 1992.

Turner, Kathleen J. *Doing Rhetorical History: Concepts and Cases*. Tuscaloosa: University of Alabama Press, 1998.

"Twin City Church News." *St. Paul Recorder*, February 17, 1956. https://newspapers.mnhs.org/jsp/viewer.jsp?doc_id=mnhi0031/1DFC6C5F/56021701.

"URA Approves Signing of CBA for Hill District." *WDUQ News*, July 10, 2008.

Urban Land Institute. *A ULI Advisory Services Panel Report—Saint Paul, Minnesota*. Washington, DC: Urban Land Institute, 2018. https://americas.uli.org/wp-content/uploads/ULI-Documents/ULI_StPaul_Rondo_FINAL.pdf.

Vanderhaagen, Sara C. *Children's Biographies of African American Women: Rhetoric, Public Memory, and Agency*. Columbia: University of South Carolina Press, 2018.

Van Dusen, Gerald C., and Jim Holley. *Detroit's Birwood Wall: Hatred and Healing in the West Eight Mile Community*. Charleston: The History Press, 2019.

Vanguri, Star Medzerian. *Rhetorics of Names and Naming*. New York: Routledge, 2016.

Von Hoffman, Alexander. "Enter the Housing Industry, Stage Right: A Working Paper on the History of Housing Policy." Joint Center for Housing Studies, Harvard

University, 2008. https://jchs.harvard.edu/sites/default/files/media/imp/w08-1 _von_hoffman.pdf.

———. "A Study in Contradictions: The Origins and Legacy of the Housing Act of 1949." *Housing Policy Debate* 11, no. 2 (2000): 299–326.

"WAICO." *Milwaukee Star*, January 27, 1968.

"WAICO Fights for Residential Improvements." *Milwaukee Star*, November 11, 1967.

White, Walter Francis. *How Far the Promised Land?* New York: Viking, 1955.

Wilkerson, Isabel. *The Warmth of Other Suns: The Epic Story of America's Great Migration.* Repr. ed. New York: Vintage, 2011.

Wilson, August. *Jitney.* Repr. ed. Woodstock, NY: The Overlook Press, 2003.

Wilson, Kirt H. "Interpreting the Discursive Field of the Montgomery Bus Boycott: Martin Luther King Jr.'s Holt Street Address." *Rhetoric and Public Affairs* 8, no. 2 (2005): 299–326. https://doi.org/10.1353/rap.2005.0081.

Winthrop, John. "A Model of Christian Charity." In *American Literature*, edited by William E. Cain, 1:68–83. New York: Penguin Academics, 2004.

"Words of the Week." *Jet*, May 10, 1962.

"Wylie Avenue: The Street Which Began at a Church and Ended at a Jail." *Pittsburgh Courier*, city ed., February 24, 1962. http://www.proquest.com/hnppittsburghcourier /docview/202443341.

Yuen, Laura. "Central Corridor: In the Shadow of Rondo." *Minnesota Public Radio News*, April 29, 2010. https://www.mprnews.org/story/2010/04/20/centcorridor3-rondo.

———. "Green Line Overcomes Community Objections." *Minnesota Public Radio News*, June 12, 2014. https://www.mprnews.org/story/2014/06/11/green-line-overcomes -community-objections.

INDEX

Page numbers in italics refer to figures.

RHETORIC AND **DEMOCRATIC** DELIBERATION

Other books in the series:

RHETORICAND**DEMOCRATIC**DELIBERATION